The Conflict of the Ages

Part III

They Deliberately Forgot: the Flood and the Ice Age

Student Edition

Michael J. and Mary C. Findley

The Conflict of the Ages
Part Three Student Edition
They Deliberately Forgot:
The Flood And The Ice Age

by

Michael J. and Mary C. Findley

copyright by Michael J. and Mary C. Findley 2012

Published by Findley Family Video

The Conflict of the Ages Part Three Student Edition
They Deliberately Forgot: The Flood And The Ice Age

by Michael J. and Mary C. Findley

copyright 2013 Findley Family Video Publications

Any images not sourced in the text are from Public Domain sources or the authors' personal collection.

No part of this publication may be reproduced in whole or in part, or stored in any retrieval system, or transmitted in any form by any means, electronic, mechanical, photocopying, recording, or otherwise, without permission of the publisher. Exception is made for short excerpts used in reviews.

"Speaking the truth in love."

Scripture references are as follows: The Bible: The King James Version, public domain. The New International Version, from the HOLY BIBLE, NEW INTERNATIONAL VERSION Registered. NIV Registered. Copyright 1973, 1978, 1984 by International Bible Society. Used by permission of Zondervan. All rights reserved. The New American Standard Version: Scripture quotations taken from the New American Standard Bible Registered, Copyright 1960, 1962, 1963, 1968, 1971, 1972, 1973, 1975, 1977, 1995 by The Lockman Foundation Used by permission. The Orthodox Jewish Bible fourth edition, OJB. Copyright 2002,2003,2008,2010, 2011 by Artists for Israel International. All rights reserved used by permission. Holy Bible: International Standard Version® Release 2.0. Copyright © 1996-2013 by ISV Foundation. Used by permission of Davidson Press, LLC. ALL RIGHTS RESERVED INTERNATIONALLY.

Table of Contents

End of Main Text

Other Books and Products from Findley Family Video

Note to the Reader

Quoted references in the text include a superscript number (or letter for the introductory section). Each such item in the text refers to complete source references and/or more detailed information at the end of this work. These "endnotes" take the place of footnotes. In some cases a quotation is included in a graphic. That graphic will also have a numbered reference to the complete source in the endnotes. A source frequently quoted from may only have an endnote at the point when it is first referred to, not for every time the source is referenced, unless there is additional information. Examples of this would be more than one type of discussion on the topic.

This work includes three types of material:

A. Our Own Statements, Thoughts, and Opinions

B. Quotations from the Holy Scriptures

These will appear in Italic font. If no version is listed it is the King James Translation.

C. Quotes from Other Sources.

Fragment of Jubilees from Qumran

Public Domain image

Quotes from other sources vary wildly in accuracy and reliability. An example of highly reliable material outside of the Bible is the *Book of Jubilees*. The Coptic Church regards the *Book of Jubilees* as inspired Scripture. There are twenty-one copies of the *Book of Jubilees* among the Dead Sea Scrolls. The *Book of Jubilees* is not inspired. It contains errors. Note the testimony from Epiphaneus, a bishop of Salamis (A.D. 310-403?), referenced below.

> "Epiphaneus does not introduce the material from *Jubilees* as scripture, and *Jubilees* is not among the biblical books he names in his treatise *Measures and Weights*; but the information in the *Book of Jubilees* was reliable enough for him to use in refuting a sect that attributed a different origin and nature to Seth."

> "He also reproduces *Jubilees'* connection between the twenty-two works of creation until the Sabbath and the twenty-two generations until Jacob."

With Byzantine historians, "Josephus and *Jubilees* were regularly cited together, since, in the scope and the material treated, the two works were parallel."

Source for Jubilees Authority[a]

An example at the other extreme is the *Epic of Gilgamesh*. We refer to it because at the time of this writing it is considered to be the world's oldest written document. Its only true purpose was to deify man and support the local tyrant. It is mostly erroneous, sometimes dangerous, and is difficult to read and understand. Still, the *Epic of Gilgamesh* contains some useful information. There are multiple extant versions of the *Epic of Gilgamesh* with considerable variations. While there are fragments of the *Epic of Gilgamesh* dating back to the beginning of the second millennia, maybe even the third millennia, BC, the most complete extant copy is a Babylonian version found in 7th century BC library of the Assyrian king Ashurbanipal. This is the version we use. It is also the most common version, since it is the oldest complete version.

When Noah's family left the Ark they passed on the true history of mankind to their descendants. Every culture, therefore, was originally founded on accurate information. The various historical accounts included in this work still contain some accurate information. We begin each point with the information taught by the appropriate Scripture passages. That is followed by additional evidence to support the Scriptural teachings. This additional evidence includes various records as well as archeological and geological evidence.

The *Book of Jasher* needs special explanation. One reviewer critiquing this work for publication stated that the "*Book of Jasher* is not authentic. What is being cited is an 18th century forgery". This reviewer's error concerning the *Book of Jasher*, is, sadly, widespread and accepted by many otherwise very well-educated believers. If you are concerned about this error, then please examine the article in the References, Footnotes, Expanded Study and Appendix Materials (p. 579) on the *Book of Jasher*.[b]

Many ancient Jewish sources are quoted, including Philo, Josephus, the *Sedar Olam*, the *Book of Jubilees*, *the Book of the Bee*, the *Cave of Treasures*, the first *Book of Enoch*, various Talmuds and Midrashes, in addition to the *Book of Jasher*. Many non-Jewish sources are also quoted. The Jewish books are from the Second Century AD or older. None of them are inspired by God and all contain errors. Sources quoted in these modules support positions in the Word of God. There is little value in extensive study of any of these works, but they are documented in case you wish to examine them. They are all based on older works and accurately record older Jewish traditions.

I. The Record

A. The Accuracy of the Record

"These are the generations (Hebrew *toldot* ת ו ל ד ו ת) *of Noah."* While the English word *generations* is an excellent translation, as with all translations from one language to another language, it loses some meaning in the translation. In Genesis 6:9 the word *generations* [KJV] or *records* [NASB] which is *toldot* in Hebrew, is the heading or reference for a formal legal document. To put this into modern legal terms we might say, *I attest that the following statement is completely accurate and true as written.* That statement would also have a notary stamp. Adam, Noah, and Shem's genealogies are included as part of this text by Moses. It means that all of the information that follows is an honest and factual historical record of the events. The identical formula is repeated in Genesis 5:1 *"the generations (toldot) of Adam," (KJV)*

> *"This is the Sefer Toldot Adam. In the yom that barah Elohim Adam, in the demut Elohim He made him;"* Bereshis 5:1 (Orthodox Jewish Bible); Genesis 10:1 *"the generations (toldot) of the sons of Noah" (KJV) "Now these are the toldot of the Bnei Noach"* Bereshis 10:1 (Orthodox Jewish Bible); and

Genesis 11:10 *"the generations (toldot) of Shem"* (KJV) *"These are the toldot of Shem"* (Bereshis 11:10 Orthodox Jewish Bible).[1]

Thorny bush. Photo by the authors.

This sets it apart from parables and allegories. When Gideon's son Jotham told the parable of the trees and the bramble bush in Judges 9, he also gave the interpretation, and named the men that the plants in his parable represented. Jotham clearly identified his parable as a parable. The parables of Jesus are labeled as parables. Generations (*toldot*) are not parables.

B. An Overview From the Beginning

This section also includes a very brief overview of COA1 (the origin of the universe) and COA2 (the origin of evil). brief overviews will not answer every possible question about the history of the world,. Nor is it possible to progress through history if each book re-examines the previous material in detail.

The original creation was water. For the first six days, God was working. That is, God was inputting energy and matter into the universe. The original landmass of earth was formed from water in less than one day. Light was created on the first day, the sun and stars on day four, approximately 96 hours after the original creation of light. The stars were put in place and were visible on earth soon after they coalesced. *And God set them in the firmament of the heaven to give light upon the earth* (Genesis 1:17) So by the evening of the fourth day, the sun, moon, and stars were visible from the earth. When Adam was created less than 48 hours later, he was able to look up and see the stars.

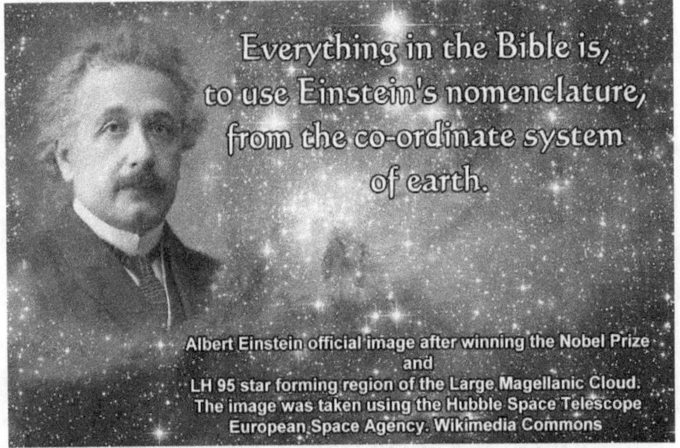

Albert Einstein official image after winning the Nobel Prize and LH 95 star forming region of the Large Magellanic Cloud. The image was taken using the Hubble Space Telescope European Space Agency. Wikimedia Commons

For that to be true, the photons or rays of light between the stars and the earth had to be put in place on the same day, Day Four. Perhaps this was instantaneous. Perhaps these light photons, or rays, were put into place in a matter of hours. One interesting theory has God creating all the stars very close to the earth and moving them into position after their creation, from the viewpoint of earth, though still on the fourth day.

A very interesting variation on this already interesting theory has the earth 6000 years old, the distant stars billions of years old, but they were all created at the same time. This points out that even though the speed of light is a constant, time is not a constant. Everything in the Bible is, to use Einstein's nomenclature, from the co-ordinate system of earth. For this hypothesis to be valid, every hour on earth equals thousands of years on distant stars.

Dr. Larry Vardiman and Dr. Russell Humphreys[2] discuss this concept in the three articles below.

> "Scriptures like Isaiah 40:22: "[God] stretches out the heavens like a [tent] curtain" (NASB), and 16 other similar verses. These verses invite us to compare the material of space to a stretchable fabric under tension, like that in a trampoline.

> And the heavens shall be rolled up like a scroll. (Isaiah 34:4, NKJV)

> The context here is the "host of heaven," which includes the stars, and "the heavens."

> When the sphere of timelessness reached zero radius and disappeared, the earth emerged, and immediately the light that had been following the sphere reached earth, even light that started billions of light years away. The stretching of the fabric of space had been occurring continuously all along the light trajectory, thus red-shifting the light wavelengths.

> On earth, it was still only the fourth day. An observer on the night side of the earth would have seen a black sky one instant, and a sky filled with stars the next. With a telescope he would also be able to see distant galaxies with suitably red-shifted spectra. From Day Four until now, about 6000 years later, an observer on earth would have been able to see stars billions of light years away.

> As Humphreys has mentioned in several publications, two Bible verses led him to the conclusion that there was a second space-stretching and time-dilation episode sometime during the year of the Genesis Flood. One of the verses is Psalm 18:9: "He bowed the heavens also, and came down: and darkness

was under his feet."

Because earth was in a timeless zone during the two space-stretching events, there is a major difference in the way clocks functioned on earth and in deep space. We aren't speaking of just a minor difference. For example, if the creation of earth occurred about 6000 years ago in earth time and the creation of objects at the edge of the universe occurred about 15 billion years ago in cosmic time, then there is a factor of about 2.5 million between the two estimates of time.[2]

After the universe, the earth, and all life on earth were created, one river originally watered the Garden of Eden. After leaving the garden, it split into four parts and watered the (entire?) earth. The only way this could be possible is for the earth's landmass to be only one continent, possibly with islands, and the Garden of Eden to be the highest watered point of land on earth. The Garden of God also had a climate where nudity was comfortable year round. The earth was watered either by a heavy mist each day or by underground streams.

> *But there went up a mist from the earth, and watered the whole face of the ground.*
> (Genesis 2:6 KJV)

> *Instead, an underground stream would rise from the earth and water the surface of the ground.* (Genesis 2:6 ISV)

At least in the Garden of Eden, there was no rain. This does not say that there was no rain anywhere on earth. We just do not know. Perhaps the Antediluvian period near the garden of Eden was just like what uniformitarians describe as the Devonian Period: slightly warmer, with lush, rich vegetation. The truth is we just do not have enough information to be certain. The climate might have been very different from today's climate. It also might have been very similar to ours.

Ezekiel tells us that before the Fall, Satan walked in *Eden, the Garden of God* which contained *the stones of fire.* These words seem to indicate that Eden had volcanic activity. Volcanic activity keeps areas of modern Yellowstone warm and comfortable throughout the bitter Wyoming, Idaho, and Montana winters. While applying existing conditions to Eden is an *assumption,* it is quite reasonable to assume similar moderating influences in the antediluvian world.

According to the genealogical record of Genesis Chapter Five, there were 1,656 years until the flood. Any disasters or catastrophes during the antediluvian period were not global. The single river which flowed through Eden then split into four rivers continuously putting silt into shallow seas. Josephus said, "the garden was watered by one river, which ran round about the whole earth..."[3] These seas were at least not as deep as the seas of today. We know this because the first forty days of the Flood added more water to the surface of our planet. We do not know if this additional water was extraterrestrial, as some creationists believe, or entirely subterranean (the fountains of the great deep). Many Creationists believe that the flood waters were entirely terrestrial; that there was no additional extraterrestrial water added to the earth during the flood. Whatever the source, more water was added to the surface of the planet.

The antediluvian world was an ideal climate for abundant life. We know this because of the abundant fossil record. Though we do not know with certainty, there could have been a landmass much larger than all the dry land today. It is likely that any depositions made during the antediluvian period were wiped out by the catastrophic flood.

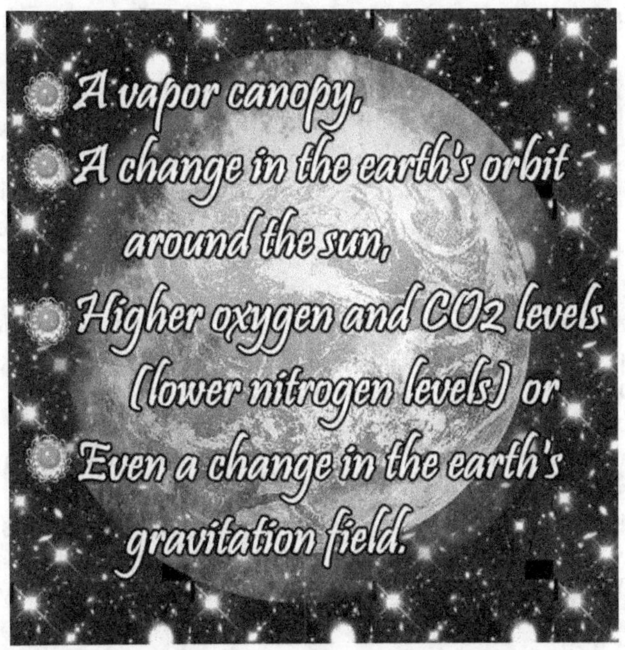

Before dismissing the change in gravity out of hand, remember that if the opening of "the sluice gates (floodgates) of heaven" meant adding water from an extraterrestrial source, then the additional water increased the earth's overall mass and the gravitational field of a planet depends on its mass. However, this change in gravity, if there was any, was likely a very small change.

The fossil record shows massive creatures, larger than any land animal today. The large size of the creatures, the number of creatures, and abundant vegetation to support these creatures, teach us that the Antediluvian climate was suited to these creatures.

Flying insects with wingspans of 75 cm (over 29.5 inches) are found entombed in amber. There are fossils of flying creatures with wingspans around 13.75 meters (about 45 feet). These are more than four times the size of the largest flying bird today. There were also 60 ton, 50 foot sauropods. While today's blue whale is twice the size of a sauropod, its mass is supported by water. The largest blue whale ever recorded was 94 feet. Blue whales average around 80 feet while weighing around 120 tons. *The Bible*, the *Book of Jasher*, the *Book of Jubilees*, Josephus, and the Sumerian Kings Lists all record much greater lifespans for men. It is likely that this increased lifespan was true for all creatures, not just men. If these creatures were like modern reptiles, they would grow as long as they lived. A longer lifespan makes growth to that size not only possible, but likely, if they continued growing their entire lives. Another possibility is that these creatures simply grew rapidly and they were fully formed adults at around thirty years old.[4]

Creatures of this size do not move about freely on land today, so conditions on earth were likely different than existing conditions. Specifics about the degree and the kinds of the changes are only theories. Some of the proposed differences between the antediluvian world and today's world are: lower gravity in the past; a water canopy protecting the earth; the earth with a different tilt to its axis (perhaps not tilted at all); some type of change in the earth's magnetic field; much lower nitrogen content in atmosphere (resulting in higher levels of oxygen and carbon dioxide); greater air pressure so that organisms could metabolize the oxygen more efficiently; greater humidity; and a much higher-quality diet.

None of these are certain. It may be that none of these were true. Some even believe the antediluvian world was far more like the existing climate. Examinations of various fossils yield conflicting data. The most reasonable conclusion is that the Antediluvian world, like today's world, had enormous variety in conditions based on location, not time. Conditions in the Sahara desert, the Himalayas, the Antarctic ice pack, the Caribbean Sea, the Amazon rain forest, the steppes of Central Asia, are all so different they could each be different worlds. We do not see the same conditions worldwide today, so there is no reason to expect to find identical conditions worldwide during the Antediluvian period.[5]

Uniformitarian evolutionists are forced by the evidence to recognize radically different conditions in the past. They simply claim that these changes took place millions of years ago. Articles about the Devonian Period always begin with their timeline mythology. All of the following statements were made by uniformitarian evolutionists. Sources are referenced in the appendix.

- "The Devonian was a relatively warm period (see p. 611)."

- "Reconstruction of tropical sea surface temperatures shows an average temperature of 86° F. CO2 levels dropped steeply throughout the Devonian period."

- "The vast seas were shallow and saw some of the largest reefs in world. It is famous for thousands of species of fishes. The warm temperatures made life on land particularly good for the plants. The plant-covered lands made a good home for ... wingless insects and spiders."

- "Near the end of the Devonian, a mass extinction event occurred."[6]

Creationists agree that there was a mass extinction event, and the Bible calls it the Flood. It simply records that there was rain for forty days and forty nights until the tops of the mountains were covered by fifteen cubits of water. It gives few details which might help us understand the geological cause. So as we examine the evidence, understand that further investigation might change our understanding of these positions.

We also must realize that every geologic period from the Cambrian through at least the Jurassic existed at the same time. Each of these made up different aspects of the Antediluvian world. The flood ended not only the Devonian Period, but most geologic periods, at the same time.

Creation Scientists today understand that the Flood included massive volcanic activity. This same kind of volcanic activity took place during the continental breakup, though at this time we do not know if the volcanic activity was the cause or simply a result. As the single continent rapidly broke apart, eventually becoming the continents we are familiar with, plate tectonics (not the slow continental drift we see today) caused multiple geysers and magma eruptions down fault lines. These repeatedly stirred the floodwaters, creating multiple new layers of sediment and moving existing layers for years. However, the rains and the rising floodwaters and the major geologic activity only lasted forty days. After the first forty days, the fountains of the great deep and the floodgates (sluice gates) of heaven stopped. The water stopped rising, stabilized then slowly began to recede.

- Most Creation Scientists believe that the physical evidence for the breakup of the large single continent seems to place the breakup during the Flood. But the *Book of Jasher* says "These are the generations of Shem; Shem begat Arpachshad and Arpachshad begat Shelach, and Shelach begat Eber and to Eber were born two children, the name of one was Peleg, for in his days the sons of men were divided, and in the latter days, the earth was divided. And the name of the second was Yoktan, meaning that in his day the lives of the sons of men were diminished and lessened." (7:19, 20)[7] This clearly says that the division of the continents took place during Peleg's lifetime, 101-340 years after the Flood.

- Josephus also says, "After this (the division of languages at the tower of Babel) they were dispersed abroad, on account of their languages, and went out by colonies every where; and each colony took possession of that land which they light upon, and unto which God led them; so that the whole continent was filled with, both the inland and the maritime countries. There were some also who passed over the sea in ships, and inhabited the islands."[8]

- The *Seder Olam* says, "It was 340 years from the Flood to the division of languages. Noah lived 10 years past the division of languages. Our father Abraham was 48 years old at the division of languages. Rabbi Yose said: Eber was such a great prophet that he called son Peleg, meaning 'earthquake,' *'for in his days was the earth divided.'* Genesis 10:25 You can't say **the division of the continents** [emphasis added] happened at Peleg's birth because..." "this verse (Genesis 10:25) must mean that the division of languages happened near the last year Peleg's life".[9] The *Seder Olam* clearly takes the "earth divided" as another way of saying "division of the continents".

Chapter Five of *Antiquities of the Jews* includes the phrases "the whole continent was filled" and "passed over the sea in ships, and inhabited the islands".[8] These, together with "the earth was divided" in the *Book of Jasher,* indicate that the ancient Jews believed the continental break-up occurred hundreds of years after the Flood.[7] The *Seder Olam* records that the continental break-up occurred nearly three hundred forty years after the Flood.[9]

Sometime after the Flood, perhaps soon after the Flood or perhaps hundreds of years later, a sudden uplift or series of uplifts put the Americas, the Alps, the Himalayas, and every other mountain range into approximately their present positions. Instead of a single uplift, perhaps there was a series of uplifts spanning hundreds or even thousands of years. Rapid erosion occurred as the Kaibab plateau rose. This rapid rise cut the beginning of the channel of the future Colorado River, which became the Grand Canyon. To keep the vertical walls from collapsing, extreme heat had to rapidly turn the newly-exposed undersea sediment to stone. This heat could have been provided by volcanic activity. In addition to the well-known volcano, Sunset Crater, northeast of Flagstaff, Arizona, "there are up to 160 volcanic cones on the plateau to the north of the Canyon rim."[10]

Perhaps the heat was generated by an exploding meteorite. It is estimated that the Tunguska projectile, which was an air blast, was three times more powerful than the Hiroshima atomic bomb blast. An air blast is far more destructive than a ground blast. *Wikipedia* lists more than forty confirmed impact crater sites with a diameter of twenty kilometers or more on earth. The smallest of these was far more powerful than the Tunguska projectile. Barringer crater, also known as Meteor Crater, is east of Flagstaff, Arizona. Based on the lack of recovered material, it seems likely that it was either the result of an air blast or broke apart before impact. Either possibility could easily have generated enough heat to turn much of the southwest to stone very rapidly.

So the catastrophic forces which caused the Flood were followed by geologic changes which continued for hundreds, perhaps thousands, of years. All of these geologic changes combined to transform the antediluvian world into the world we see today.

Judgment On The World That Was

C. Judgment On The World That Was

The Flood was not a random event. It came about because of sin.

> *And GOD saw that the wickedness of man was great in the earth, and that every imagination of the thoughts of his heart was only evil continually. And it repented the LORD that he had made man on the earth, and it grieved him at his heart. And the LORD said, I will destroy man whom I have created from the face of the earth; both man, and beast, and the creeping thing, and the fowls of the air; for it repenteth me that I have made them. (Genesis 6:5-7)*

Conflict Of The Ages Part 2; The Origin of Evil documents the origin of wickedness. Though the evidence of God's judgment on sin is all around us, people still choose wickedness today. Secular Humanists still choose to ignore all of this evidence, both written and material, and simply look at the phrase where God said *"for it repenteth (me) that (I) have made"* man. They ignore the rest of Scripture and falsely claim that God is either responsible for sin or is less than all-powerful. As Samuel told Saul, *"And also the Strength of Israel will not lie nor repent: for he is not a man, that he should repent."* (1 Samuel 15:29) When God repents, it means that our sins (in the antediluvian world, the combined sins of all humanity) have broken the heart of the God of love and that God must step in and judge our sins. It does *not* mean that God either lost control or is responsible for sin.

> *The earth also was corrupt before God, and the earth was filled with violence. And God looked upon the earth, and, behold, it was corrupt; for all flesh had corrupted his way upon the earth.* (Genesis 6:11,12)

Corruption refers to immorality, theft, and dishonesty. Violence means people fulfilled their lusts by forcefully taking what they wanted, often murdering the rightful owner.

It also means that corruption and violence were no longer restrained by what we think of as government. Corruption and violence were universal. They were not confined to certain individuals or locations.

D. The Flood Was Universal.

> *And God said unto Noah, The end of all flesh is come before me; for the earth is filled with violence through them; and, behold, I will destroy them with the earth.* (Genesis 6:13)

In this verse, God chose Noah because of Noah's righteousness.

- He decreed *the end of all flesh* and said *I will destroy them with the earth.* Those who choose to believe that the Flood was either local or nonexistent simply choose to not believe these two phrases. They are translated correctly: *The end of all flesh* and *destroy them with the earth*. All honest translations say the same thing. One example, the NASB, says: *The end of all flesh* and *I am about to destroy them with the earth*. It is the exact same meaning, almost the exact same words. If these words are interpreted as some form of allegory or parable, then language has lost its meaning. How do we communicate when words, especially the words in the Word of God, have lost all concrete meaning?

- *Ussher* said, "Before the deluge of waters upon the whole wicked world, God sent Noah..." Josephus said, "God ... determined to destroy the whole race of mankind, and to make another race that should be pure from wickedness; and cutting short their lives, and making their years not so many as they formerly lived, but one hundred and twenty only, he turned the dry land into sea; and thus were all these men destroyed." When Josephus wrote about the Flood itself he said, "the water poured down forty entire days, till it became fifteen cubits higher than the earth; which was the reason why there was no greater number preserved, [than those in the ark] since they had no place to fly to."[11]

- *Book of Jubilees* (20th Jubilee) "And the Lord said that He would destroy everything which was upon the earth, both men and cattle, and beasts, and fowls of the air, and that which moveth on the earth."[12]

- Even sources outside of the Jewish and Christian communities indicate that the Flood was universal. The Qu'ran 11:42,43 says "And Noah called out to his son, who had separated himself (apart), 'Oh my son! Embark with us and be not with the disbelievers.' The son replied. 'I will betake myself to a mountain; it will save me from the water.' Noah said: 'This day there is no saviour from the Decree of God except him on whom He has mercy.' And a wave came in between them so he (the son) drowned."[13]

- 71:26-27 "And Noah said: 'O my Lord! Leave not of the Unbelievers, a single one on earth!" [13]

- *The History of al-Tabari*, vol. 1 "The water increased wildly, and, as is assumed by the people of the Torah, rose fifteen cubits over the mountain tops. All creatures on the face of the earth, every inspirited being or tree, disappeared. No creature remained except Noah and those with him in the boat …"[14]

While the sources other than the Word of God contain errors, the statements quoted here all agree with the fact of a universal flood. At one time, around 2350 BC, everything on earth was under water except for the ark. This is a simple concept.

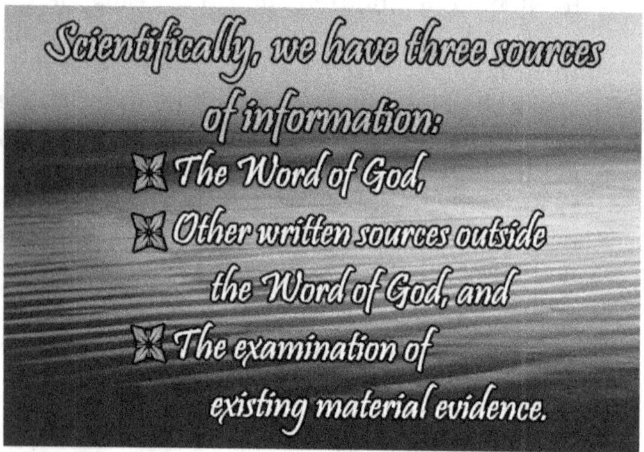

The third category includes geology and tests performed on models of the ark. We can either accept or reject the evidence. This is an examination of the evidence of the third category, which the Church has for nearly two thousand years called general revelation.

The Himalayas, the highest mountain range on earth, includes Mt. Everest. This range has a layer near the top known as the "yellow band." It contains thousands of uncrushed fossils of marine creatures known as Ammonites. Ammonites are similar in appearance to the sea organism we call a nautilus. There are only three possible ways for these fossils to be at the top of the Himalayas.

> 1) The first possibility is that they could have arrived in some completely unknown and unknowable manner.
> 2) The second possibility is that the entire earth was covered with water that covered the Himalayas in their existing position.
> 3) The third possibility is that the Himalayas were under seawater, then uplifted to their existing position in a sudden, cataclysmic event.

For the water to cover all mountain ranges in their existing positions, there would have been more than twice the total amount of water that we have now. With no evidence of that much additional water, the most reasonable and the most scientific choice is a sudden uplift of undersea sediment to form the mountains we see today after the flood deposited the strata.

A sudden uplift explains both the presence of the Ammonite fossils and volume of water now on earth. It had to be sudden because the Ammonite fossils are intact. A slow uplift would allow the yellow band to dry out in less than a century, likely less than a decade. Once the soil surrounding the Ammonite fossils dried out, the enormous pressure of the uplift would crush them to powder. The only protection the Ammonite fossils had was the plastic (moist, mud) yellow band. The mud moved with the Ammonites with enough "give" to allow the fossils to remain intact.

This also means that the deposits creating the strata which now make up the mountain chains we see today were created by the Flood, at least the early stages of the Flood. It is highly probable that these rising mountains were caused by irregular sedimentary deposits. Some areas were heavier than others, heavier by amount of material as well as type of material. The heavier areas of sedimentary deposits then pushed down on the sea floors. This additional pressure caused the sea floors to fall. In order to achieve isostatic equilibrium, lighter layers had to uplift, creating mountains. This seems to be the mechanism God used to cause the mountains to rise. Geologists call this stable result isostatic equilibrium. That is, the weight, including the water, of the entire surface of the earth is roughly in balance.

Though the Himalayas are the highest mountain range on earth, every mountain range is made up of strata of sediment. All land everywhere on earth was, at one time, under water. This is scientific, verifiable evidence. You may choose to believe that this took millions of years. That is your religious choice. But that is not a scientific choice. The most reasonable scientific choice is that isostatic equilibrium was the result of a catastrophic event.

Pseudoscience has often repeated the claim that there is not enough water on earth to cover the entire surface of the land. That *assumes* the fallacy that the mountains were in their current positions at their present elevations. However, if all the landmasses on earth today were equidistant to the earth's core, that is, a smooth sphere, then the entire earth would be covered in approximately 2.6 kilometers (1.6 miles) of water. So the liquid water we have on earth now could easily cover the highest mountains by 15 cubits if the antediluvian world had lower mountains and higher sea floors then we have today. Yes, that is an *assumption*. But it is a very reasonable *assumption* based on the evidence that marine fossils exist on the top of every high mountain chain on earth.

II. The Ark

A. The Construction of the Ark

The *Book of Jasher* says,

> "And Noah rose up, and he made the ark, in
> the place where God had commanded him,
> and Noah did as God had ordered him. In his
> five hundred and ninety-fifth year Noah
> commenced to make the ark, and he made the
> ark in five years, as the Lord had
> commanded."[15]

Just five years to build the ark certainly seems
unreasonable. Traditions record that in addition to
preaching, Noah had to grow the trees and research
and grow the food for the animals, which took 115
years. Believed worldwide, these seem to be
unsupported traditions.

Detail of 'Noah building the Ark'
by Franzosischer Meister (1675) Public Domain

"Therefore his days shall be 120 years:" (Genesis 6:3)
this means, not that human life should in future never
attain a greater age than 120 years, but that a respite of
120 years should still be granted to the human race.
This sentence, as we may gather from the context, was
made known to Noah in his 480th year, to be published
by him as *"preacher of righteousness"* (2 Peter 2:5) "to
the degenerate race."[16] [Keil and Deilitzsch]

It seems to be most reasonable to assume that Noah
worked on the ark and preparations for the flood for
the entire 120 years. Yes, Noah preached during this
time, but the greatest sermon illustration in history was
the ark itself.

> *Make thee an ark of gopher wood; rooms
> shalt thou make in the ark, and shalt pitch it
> within and without with pitch. And this is the
> fashion which thou shalt make it of: The
> length of the ark shall be three hundred
> cubits, the breadth of it fifty cubits, and the
> height of it thirty cubits. A window shalt thou
> make to the ark, and in a cubit shalt thou
> finish it above; and the door of the ark shalt*

thou set in the side thereof; with lower,
second, and third stories shalt thou make it.
(Genesis 6:14-16 KJV)

The book *Noah's Ark: A Feasibility Study* by John Woodmorappe starts with the above information, then, with reasonable assumptions comes to reasonable conclusions. *Noah's Ark: A Feasibility Study* is the best possible starting place if you are seriously interested in examining the scientific possibility of a vessel the size of the ark. The Hebrew language has words for ships and boats, none of which are used here. Our word *ark* comes from the Latin Vulgate. The Hebrew word translated *ark* is only found here and in naming the vessel Moses was placed in as a baby. The term *gopher wood* is also an unusual word. The Hebrew word translated *gopher wood* is not used anywhere else in the Bible.[17]

The ark was never intended either to navigate or to move under its own propulsion. It was only designed to float, remain upright and preserve life. Perhaps the best word for the ark is "lifeboat".[18]

The ratio Noah used to build the ark was 300L:50W:30H (30:5:3). That approximate ratio is still used on ships today, especially barges. (A feasibility study from 1994.)[19]

The study linked above is very useful. It assumes that the total volume of the ark was necessary for the number of animals on board. It then modified the ratios, keeping volume constant. The charts might difficult to understand if you are not familiar with scientific data. Based on modern hull configurations, it compares twelve different hull configurations all with same interior volume to the ark.

In 2004 Tim Lovett[20] wrote a brief article evaluating the technical aspects of this paper in relationship to information in the Word of God. *Comments on the Noah's Ark (Hong et al) paper*. Tim Lovett concluded:

> "Why is hull 9 consistently superior? It outperforms Noah's Ark in both stability and hull strength, which means that it could ride bigger waves and it would be easier to build. Considering that these are the usual objections to the construction of the Ark (couldn't handle the waves, too hard to make), it seems surprising that the ark does not appear to be optimized on these issues alone.

> The Biblical proportions are clearly adequate, Noah's Ark consistently ranks near the top in almost any weighting scheme and never below 7th place (pure seakeeping). But the extra effort required to build the longer hull seems surprising. There is certainly a lot less wood in hull 9. (In reality even more exaggerated because space is lost to the extra wood). In most cases, hull 10 is also ahead of the Biblical Ark."

> Even the optimal weighting of seakeeping (3.88), strength (3.11) and roll (0.289) cannot bring Noah's Ark out on top. From this information one would think the ark should have been a little shorter. After all, lifeboats aren't so long and skinny.[20]

> Material skipped

> Hong's seakeeping analysis assumes a

confused sea. "...the waves came from all directions with the same probability." Genesis speaks of a wind sent to dry the earth - a global scale wind without interference from landforms. A consistent wind of unlimited fetch would generate mature waves, having long wavelengths and probably all in the same direction - at least from the Ark's perspective. In such a case a longer vessel is better, provided it doesn't end up broaching (going side-on to the waves).

The proportions God chose for Noah's Ark indicate that the waves did not come equally from all directions, but had a dominant heading. The length of the ark is beyond the optimum for a confused sea, which compromises roll stability. However, by keeping a course with the wind the ark would easily outperform the shorter hulls 9 and 10 of the Hong study. Ask any mariner - ships aren't supposed to go side-on to the waves.

The most accurate way to gauge the conditions of the flood is to look at the specifications of Noah's Ark. If the water was very calm it could have been lower - maybe 2 decks which is easier. If the seas were confused it should have been shorter. To some extent Noah's Ark appears to have been designed for large wind generated waves traveling almost uni-directionally with respect to the ark. However it still has a wide enough base to handle some weather from other directions - and a smaller confused sea.

To ensure the Ark does not end up side-on to the waves, the stern should drag in the water and the bow should align with the wind. The usual trick would be a sea anchor. Since the typical sea anchor in the form of an underwater sail is likely to foul with floating debris and require attention, the stern drag might be generated by protruding features of the hull itself (logs, etc.). The bow would need the equivalent of a wind vane - perhaps a fin or raised area (forecastle).[20]

There are many feasibility studies on the Ark, though most are older and less complete than the ones cited here. Feasibility studies on the ark usually use a smaller cubit, around 17", assuming the smaller ark would be more stable. While there is a longer Egyptian royal cubit, the oldest cubit rods found, both stone and bronze, were very similar, varying only between 20.5" and 20.75". These cubit rods were Egyptian, Hebrew, and Mesopotamian.

[If you are interested in more information on how similar the ancient standards of measurement were, check The ark *information in the appendix for more references on that subject, p. 696.]*

The word cubit comes from the Latin noun *cubitum* "elbow." This shows the belief that a cubit was the tip of a man's longest finger to the end of the elbow when the arm was bent. It also assumes that the cubit was an inexact measurement since no two people have exactly the same elbow to fingertip measurement.

However, there are several ancient records which demonstrate that the cubit was a standardized measurement. Moving backwards in time, Ezekiel used a long cubit *And these are the measures of the altar after the cubits: The cubit is a cubit and an hand breadth;* Ezekiel 43:13 By pointing out the long cubit 20.6-20.75 inches (a cubit and a handbreath), it seems that the shorter cubit was more common in Ezekiel's time. There is an inscription in a tunnel built by the workers of Hezekiah to supply water to Jerusalem.

This inscription gives a measurement of the tunnel in cubits. By this standard, a cubit is slightly less than 18 inches. The Hezekiah tunnel cubit is often published as 17.6 inches. But we do not know if the tunnel is the same length today that it was when the inscription was written. If the tunnel was longer, then the cubit was longer. We can, however, reasonably assume that the tunnel is close to the same length. The cubit based on the tunnel length is close to 17.6 inches. This is where we get the standard shorter cubit. The cubit Solomon used to build the temple was larger than the cubit used later on in Hezekiah's day. *The length in cubits, according to the old standard was sixty cubits.* (2 Chronicles 3:3 NASB)

Moses was educated in all the learning of the Egyptians. Acts 7:22 NASB So Moses was familiar with a cubit of 20.6-20.75 inches. This is likely the cubit

Solomon used, which was shortened by Hezekiah's time. Moses writes that he was familiar with other sized cubits. *For only Og king of Bashan remained of the remnant of giants; behold his bedstead was a bedstead of iron; is it not in Rabbath of the children of Ammon? nine cubits was the length thereof, and four cubits the breadth of it, after the cubit of a man.* Deuteronomy 3:11 *ordinary cubit* (NASB)

The wider variations in lengths of cubits are found centuries later, usually by the order of a certain monarch. Since objects were taxed according to their size, reducing the size of measurements, including the cubit, was a way of raising taxes.

So the most reasonable assumption is that the cubit Noah used to build the ark was close to 20.6". The common, (in our time) smaller cubit of approximately 17" would result in an ark of 425'L x 71'W x 42.5'H (approximate). The larger cubit, which Noah probably used, of 20.75", results in an ark of 518.75'L x 86.5'W x 52'H (approximate). These are reasonable assumptions, not absolute facts.

Josephus said, "Now this ark had firm walls, and a roof, and was braced with cross beams, so that it could not be any way drowned or overborne by the violence of the water."

The Hebrew word translated into English as *gopher wood* could mean four-sided- or cornered- beam (from the *LXX*), planks (from the *Vulgate*) or cedar or cypress.[21] John Woodmorappe also suggests that *gopher* wood might mean teak wood or a method of hardening the wood something like modern pressure-treatment of wood, included in the appendix.

The ark had three stories and separate rooms. It was well-prepared for the number of organisms which lived on it.

An important point missed by many modern ark studies or reproductions is that the ark was covered, inside and out, with pitch. While the modern word pitch means asphalt, there is some question as to the exact meaning of this Hebrew word used this way in this verse. The KJV normally translates this word as *atonement*. So this is referring to completely covering and sealing rather than the type of material. The *LXX* and the *Syriac Peshitta* both use the word *asphalt*. Some ancient Egyptian coffins, made with ratios similar to the ark, 30L:5W:3H, are also covered inside and out with asphalt an example is included in the appendix] However, naval pitch was made from tree resin for thousands of years.

Since the pitch was used for waterproofing, it had to completely cover the bottom of the ark. The only possible way for the bottom of the ark to be completely covered in pitch, would be to put the ark on some type of scaffold, like a modern dry dock. Perhaps this might help explain why God closed the door of the ark instead of Noah. If the ark was sitting on a scaffold, the single door would have been an uphill ramp.

Fifteen cubits upward did the waters prevail; and the mountains were covered. (Genesis 7:20) This is all the Scriptures state. If the ark was built on top of a high mountain, perhaps the highest mountain, then the fifteen cubits are probably the draft of the ark. It is a reasonable assumption that the fifteen cubits was a combination of the scaffold the ark sat on and the draft of the ark.

Another reasonable assumption is that the fifteen cubit measurement was made after the ark ran aground. Noah could easily measure the mud line after he left the ark.

Also, the ark would have run aground on one of the highest mountains on earth. Since the Scriptures record that the waters receded very slowly and God sent a wind to remove the water, this wind blew the ark about constantly. This was a wind Noah could see as it evaporated the water. It is a reasonable assumption that this was a strong wind. Without any reefs or landmasses to slow the ark, the ark would rapidly travel great distances. Let us assume that wind propelled the ark at an average speed of twenty five knots in the same direction. It is possible that the speed would have been greater. Both the speed and directional assumptions are reasonable assumptions. The ark would then circumnavigate the globe in about one thousand hours, which is about seven weeks, less than 42 days.

From these reasonable assumption, we come to other reasonable assumptions. We assume that the mountains had not been uplifted yet, at least not to their present height. The mountains were roughly the same elevation as they were before the flood or slightly more. The ark would run aground soon after the water level was low enough for the ark to touch any mountain. So the ark would run aground one of the highest mountain ranges on earth, though not necessarily at the highest point.

If the draft of the ark was fifteen cubits (probably a little over 26 feet) and it was either built on a mountain before the Flood or rested on the highest mountain after the Flood, then all that Noah had to do was measure the waterline on ark after leaving the ark to know that *fifteen cubits upward did the waters prevails; and the mountains were covered.*

We are not even certain that the mountain we call Mount Ararat is where the ark came to rest. Many other mountain ranges today are much higher, such as the Himalayas. This indicates that the mountain ranges we see today were not uplifted until after the ark came to rest.

While no ancient document mentions protection from a Tsunami, it could be an important reason for building the ark on the top of a mountain. "The reason for the Japanese name 'harbor wave' (Tsunamis) is that sometimes a village's fishermen would sail out, and encounter no unusual waves while out at sea fishing, and come back to land to find their village devastated by a huge wave."[22]

"In deep ocean, Tsunami waves may appear only a foot or so high. But as they approach shoreline and enter shallower water they slow down and begin to grow in energy and height." [22]

The greatest danger from a tsunami is the crest as the wave approaches land. While waves can crest in deep water, tsunamis are much less dangerous when there is no land nearby.

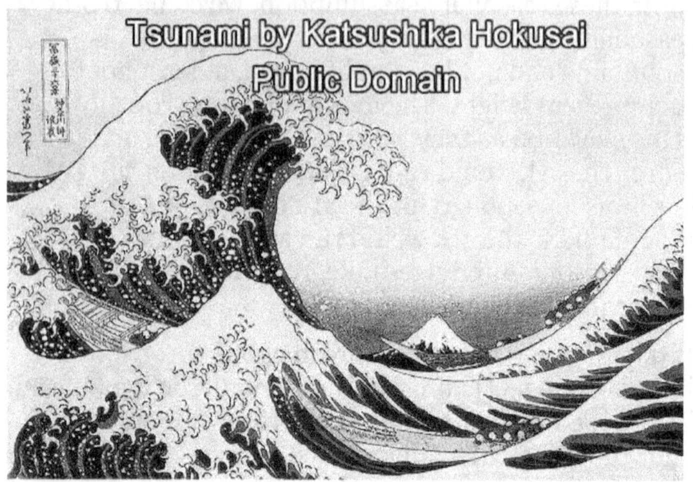

Building the ark on top of a mountain provided the greatest possible protection against shore breakers. There would be a minimal amount of land to form waves. Waves crashing against the shore were a much greater danger to the ark than the deep-water waves striking against the ark. If the ark was built on top of a mountain, that might also be a possible explanation for Noah entering the ark seven days before the flood. *It came about after the seven days, that the water of the flood came upon the earth.* (Genesis 7:10 NASB)

If the water was rising and Noah and the ark were on a mountain, the ark protected the occupants of the ark for a week before the floodwaters were high enough to float the ark. If floodwaters rose for a week before the rain started then this is additional support for the belief that the rain was caused by *the fountains of the great deep* and not extraterrestrial from a comet or collapse of a vapor canopy.

B. The Inhabitants of the Ark

All of the land animals and all birds we see today had ancestors on the ark. The last piece of information we can know for certain is that all of their genetic information adapted (not evolved, either micro or macro) into what we see today. Evolutionists usually define micro-evolution the same way they define macro-evolution, just with a shorter period of time. The problem for evolution is that the mutations we observe are not beneficial for the organism. The documented changes are not producing evolution. To state this another way, if we take observed changes and assume more of the same kind of changes, we do not get a new or improved species. The documented cases actually demonstrate devolution, or reverse evolution.

For one simple example, people have different kinds of hair. Some are blond. Others can be redheads, brown (light or dark), black or colorless. All of this information about natural hair color is genetic. Hair colors, as well as any other characteristics, can be dominant, recessive or the loss of information. Colorless hair appears white and can be the result of the loss of genetic information. When we examine all the possible genetic combinations of human beings, not just hair, the number of possible combinations are so great as to seem to be infinite. And all of the genetic information we see in land animals and birds today existed on the ark.

Noah and his family needed the smallest possible number of animals to take care of. We do not claim that every species we observe today existed on the ark. We do claim that all of the genetic information in existence today existed in the DNA of the organisms on board the ark. For example, all dogs seem to be descendants of the gray wolf. Then the only genetic representation of the dog needed on the ark was one pair of gray wolves.

Domestic dogs, jackals, foxes, dingoes and any other breed of dog would all be descended from that one pair of gray wolves. So domestic dogs, jackals, foxes, dingoes and other breed of dog were not on the ark. All of the necessary genetic information necessary to produce every possible breed of dog was in the single pair of gray wolves on the ark.

We are not given all the details about the ark so the following reasonable assumptions might not be accurate. These assumptions can be modified if we receive more information. The animals would be the smallest juveniles that no longer needed special attention. Perhaps some went into hibernation or estivation, requiring even less attention.

This comment from the *Book of Jasher* may or may not be accurate. However, the information supports the assumption made by feasibility studies on the ark that Noah took juveniles on board.

> And a lioness came, with her two whelps, male and female, and the three crouched before Noah, and the two whelps rose up against the lioness and smote her, and made her flee from her place, and she went away, and they returned to their places, and crouched upon the earth before Noah. And the lioness ran away, and stood in the place of the lions. And Noah saw this, and wondered greatly, and he rose and took the two whelps, and brought them into the ark. (The *Book of Jasher* 6:5-7)[23]

Image from PublicDomainPictures.net

We do not know the total number of organisms on the ark, but we know that there were seven pairs of clean animals and birds and a single pair of each kind of unclean animals.

> *Of every clean beast thou shalt take to thee by sevens, the male and his female: and of beasts that are not clean by two, the male and his female. Of fowls also of the air by sevens, the male and the female; to keep seed alive upon the face of all the earth.* (Genesis 7:2,3)

This tells us the ark had only land animals and birds. There were also likely insects which could not survive outside of the ark. There were few, if any, aquatic creatures; perhaps some seal pups, sea otters, and similar creatures. The insects or microbes on the ark required neither human care, nor food preparation by Noah.

The following is one example of the problem of knowing the number of animals on the ark. The *Book of Jasher* mentions a pair of lion cubs. Do all cats come from that (possible) pair? Or were there a pair of lions, a pair of tigers, a pair of leopards, a pair of cheetahs, a pair of domestic house cats, a pair of bobcats, a pair of mountain lions, a pair of ocelots, a pair of snow leopards, etc.? Or was there only one pair of the cat kind and all cats are descended from that single pair as all modern breeds of dogs are descended from the gray wolf?

While all dogs come from one pair of what we reasonably assume to be something like a gray wolf, there is no common ancestor for the lion and the gray wolf. The word "kind" in the Bible requires animals that naturally interbreed and produce fertile offspring. The Biblical word kind is closer to the genus level of Carolus Linnaeus' taxonomy system. Animals which are unable to interbreed naturally and produce fertile offspring are usually different kinds. The mule is an example of this limit. Did the ark carry a pair of donkeys and pair of horses? Or was there only a pair of horse colts, and donkeys are descended from horses? Or perhaps both donkeys and horses are both descended from an extinct common ancestor. Though we do not know for certain the exact limits, it is not difficult to know the approximate limits of genetic viability, or "kinds." If an animal is a different kind, then there is no genetic, reproductive link, no direct relationship. Organisms of the same kind have a direct, genetic, reproductive link.

The classification system originally developed by Carl Linnaeus is still the basic system used in taxonomy today. This system makes "kind" roughly equivalent to the genus, perhaps in some cases the family level. Above the level of "kind" (genus, perhaps family in certain cases), family, order, class, phylum and kingdom, the observed similarities do not indicate common ancestry. That is, there is no reproductive link. Without a reproductive link, there is no genetic link.

There is a common designer but not a common ancestor. In some fashion, everything is related because we have a common designer. Rocks and tree limbs are both solids made with chemicals, but have very few other similarities. Common features do not mean a common ancestor.

A common, and completely unwarranted, criticism of the ark is the difficulty of only eight people taking care of that many animals. Estimates for the number of animals on the ark range from 10,000 to 16,000. Trains and ships carrying animals to slaughter routinely transport many times that number with minimal provision for their survival. Modern livestock carriers (ships, not trucks or trains) can carry 7,000 full-size adult cattle along with 70,000 full-size adult sheep, though they rarely have the animals on board for even three weeks. Modern zoos also have routines worked out for taking care of captive animals and a few zoos have larger numbers than the largest estimates for the ark. The average number of animals in accredited zoos is more than 5,000 animals per zoo.[24]

The animals on the ark were not being led to slaughter, so they had to be cared for. At the same time, this was a rescue operation, not a permanent home, so provisions could be minimal, unlike a zoo providing a permanent home. There was minimal concern on the ark for exercise, birthing or even comfort. Provisions would be closer to an extended time on a modern livestock transport. A somewhat better analogy might be the extended, but temporary, transport of animals to a zoo.

> *And take thou unto thee of all food that is eaten, and thou shalt gather it to thee; and it shall be for food for thee, and for them. Thus did Noah; according to all that God commanded him, so did he. (Genesis 6:21,22)*

God gave this command to Noah 120 years before the floodwaters came. That is 120 years to gather the food, build storage units and fill the storage units. While the Bible is completely silent about both water storage and waste removal, it is completely reasonable to have roof storage tanks to catch and hold the rainwater. Animals with large amounts of waste removal would be kept above the water line. Opening and shutting doors into troughs could control water for both drinking and flushing. This is not significantly different from a modern feedlot. As both farmers and zoos sometimes do today, feed stored above the animal could be released as needed. It is also very likely that many animals hibernated or estivated in the extreme conditions.

Another possibility[25] has been used in cold countries for thousands of years. Manure is not removed for the winter; it is simply covered in straw. With three decks, feed and straw could be stored in the top deck, animals in the middle deck, and feed could be released by pulling on a rope and opening a gate to allow the feed and straw to fall. The manure would accumulate in the bottom and the straw would absorb (most of) the odors. Unlike a barn, which must be cleaned in the spring, the ark was simply abandoned. *Noah's Ark: A Feasibility Study* examines these issues in some depth.

Even so, the conditions on the ark for the first forty days were extremely difficult, while the "fountains of the great deep" were breaking up and adding subterranean water to the rainwater.

> And the ark floated upon the face of the waters, and it was tossed upon the waters so that all the living creatures within were turned about like pottage in a cauldron. And great anxiety seized all the living creatures that were in the ark, and the ark was like to be broken. (*Book of Jasher* 6:28, 29)[26]

This kind of stress would actually make providing food and water easier because some animals would either not eat or only eat a minimal amount. After the rains stopped and the seawater level stabilized, taking care the animals, though difficult, would be routine.

The dietary requirements were provided for in advance. So during the stay on the ark, and probably for months or even years afterwards, prepared fodder was distributed. Even today, animals which are normally carnivores, such as lions, have lived on entirely vegetation diets.[27] Smaller animals such as rodents and rabbits might have reproduced at rates to provide food for carnivores such as hawks or snakes.

Since the elephant was one of the largest, perhaps the largest, animal on the ark, (assuming dinosaurs were born quite small) it is easy to see how an unbeliever can inflate a difficult task of providing for animals to an impossible task.

The African Bull Elephant is a good example of the usual method used to exaggerate the problem of providing food for all the animals. A full grown adult African bull elephant consumes around 350 pounds of feed per day in the wild. Though 350 pounds per day is commonly reported, it is difficult to verify the exact amount a wild bull African elephant consumes per day. However, the exact amount is unimportant. The San Diego Zoo points out that this amount is greatly reduced when elephants are in captivity.

> "The elephants at the San Diego Zoo and the San Diego Zoo Safari Park eat less than their wild counterparts (about 125 pounds (57 kilograms) of food each day) because they don't have to burn as many calories looking for food."[28]

A juvenile[29] elephant rather than an adult bull would reduce this need even further. A full-grown African bull elephant can weigh up to 14,000 lbs (7 tons, 6,350 kg). A baby African elephant averages around 200 lbs ($\frac{1}{2}$ ton, 91 kg). Assuming that a pair of juvenile African elephants on the ark weigh around half a ton each is reasonable.

Fifty pounds of feed per day for a pair of caged juvenile elephants is a reasonable assumption. If anything, this is an overestimate. This reduces a 370-day total need from 259,000 lbs [11,748 kg](370 days * 700 lbs[317.5 kg]) of feed total down to 18,500 lbs [8391 kg](370 days * 50 lbs [23 kg]) for a pair of elephants. The average size for all animals, including birds, was considerably smaller. If we assume 15 lbs [7 kg] for the average weight of a pair of animals, collecting that much feed was a difficult, but possible task. These numbers are simply reasonable assumptions to allow you to understand that the total workload was *possible* for eight people. It is also a very reasonable assumption that many others helped collect the feed.

One possible method of feeding and taking care of the animals, which is still used in barns and feedlots today, is to store the feed on the top level, keep the animals on the second level, and use the bottom level for waste or bilge. If this method was used, the top storage would have massive amounts of straw to add to the bilge for odor control. The feed and straw would be controlled by gates which could be opened and closed. Once again, this is difficult but workable.

To examine these issues in greater detail, please see *Noah's Ark: A Feasibility Study*.

The health of each and every animal is very important to both zookeepers and livestock carriers. The Bible clearly teaches that God brought the animals to Noah. God also took care of the animals.

> *And God remembered Noah, and every living thing, and all the cattle that was with him in the ark: and God made a wind to pass over the earth, and the waters asswaged;* (Genesis 8:1)

The phrase "*God remembered Noah, and every living thing, and all the cattle that was with him in the ark*" has a double reference. First, it refers to ending the Flood (*the waters asswaged* or subsided or receded). It also refers to God taking care of the health of the animals. This phrase does not mean that Noah had no veterinarian responsibilities. It means that God miraculously took care of the health of the animals on the ark so that the health of the animals was not an insurmountably difficult task.

Public Domain image of camels

III. The Flood

A. The Timeline of the Flood, or the Sequence of Events

There are many books, such as the *Book of Jubilees*, that record the exact day of the month for every detail of the events of the Flood as recorded in the book of Genesis.

> "And Noah made the ark in all respects as He commanded him, in the twenty-seventh jubilee of years, the fifth week in the fifth year (on the new moon of the first month). And he entered in the sixth (year) thereof, in the second month, on the new moon of the second month, till the sixteenth;" (*Jubilees* 19:22,23).[30]

However, the timeline as recorded in Genesis is surprisingly simple. God spoke to Noah, commanding him to build the ark. One hundred and twenty years later the ark was completed. The animals entered the ark. The Lord shut the door of the ark. Seven days later, the rains started. *Then the Lord said to Noah, "Enter the ark...after seven more days, I will send rain on the earth..."* (Genesis 7:1,4 NASB) The rains lasted forty days. From that point the waters began receding. The waters covered all the earth another one hundred fifty days. The Lord God used two methods to cause the water to recede. First, "*God made a wind to pass over the earth.*" Second, the waters "*returned from off the earth continually.*"

> As the Psalmist said,
> *He established the earth upon its foundations,*
> *So that it will not totter forever and ever.*
> *You covered it with the deep as with a*
> *garment;*
> *The waters were standing above the*
> *mountains.*
> *At Your rebuke they fled,*
> *At the sound of Your thunder they hurried*
> *away.*
> *The mountains rose; the valleys sank down*
> *To the place which You established for them.*
> *You set a boundary that they may not pass*
> *over,*
> *So that they will not return to cover the earth.*
> (Psalm 104:5-9 NASB)

The sea floor dropped, *(The mountains rose; the valleys sank down)* allowing the sea level to drop. It is possible that some of the shifting of the mantle trapped some pockets of water at this time.

> "When Genesis says, 'the waters were dried': it happened this way. The wind evaporated the water from above and the water from below filtered back to where it came from, but the earth was still saturated and had the consistency of thick soup." *Seder Olam*[31]

> "And (on the new moon) in the fourth month the fountains of the great deep were closed and the flood-gates of heaven were restrained; and on the new moon of the seventh month all the mouths of the abysses of the earth were opened, and the water began to descend into the deep below." (*Book of Jubilees* 1:27)[30]

It is possible that the vast oceans of water currently under the earth's mantle consist of water reabsorbed after the flood. It is also possible that this is water which has existed since the Creation and was never part of the flood. "There may be more H_2O deep underground than in all oceans, lakes, and rivers combined." *National Geographic*[32]

On the seventeenth day of the seventh month the ark rested on the top of Ararat. On the first day of the tenth month the tops of the mountains were seen. Forty days later Noah released a raven, which did not come back inside the ark. *Yet another seven days* and Noah sent out a dove. On the first day, she returned without anything. A week later Noah released the dove again and she returned the same day with an olive leaf. After one more week, Noah released the dove a third time. This time the dove did not return and Noah opened the door of the ark.

> *And the LORD said, My spirit shall not always strive with man, for that he also is flesh: yet his days shall be an hundred and twenty years.* (Genesis 6:3)

> *For yet seven days, and I will cause it to rain upon the earth forty days and forty nights;* (Genesis 7:4)

And it came to pass after seven days, that the waters of the flood were upon the earth. In the six hundredth year of Noah's life, in the second month, the seventeenth day of the month, the same day were all the fountains of the great deep broken up, and the windows of heaven were opened. And the rain was upon the earth forty days and forty nights.
(Genesis 7:10-12)

The Scriptures do not give us any details about what triggered the beginning of the Flood. But this description in the *Book of Jasher* is in line with the brief words of Scripture. Concerning the beginning of the Flood;

And on that day, the Lord caused the whole earth to shake, and the sun darkened, and the foundations of the world raged, and the whole earth was moved violently, and the lightning flashed, and the thunder roared, and all the fountains in the earth were broken up...(*Book of Jasher* 6:11)[33]

The water levels began to rise and the rains began to pour. The reasonable question, "Wouldn't people outside the ark want to get on the ark once the rains began?" has a possible answer in the *Book of Jasher*.

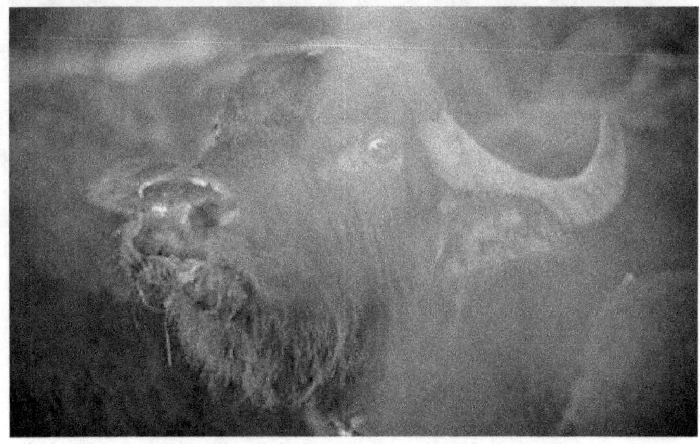

Public Domain image of a water buffalo

And the sons of man assembled together,
about seven hundred thousand men and
women, and they came unto Noah to the ark.
(*Book of Jasher* 6:17)

And the sons of men approached in order to
break into the ark, to come in on account of
the rain, for they could not bear the rain upon
them. And the Lord sent all the beasts and
animals that stood round the ark. And the
beasts overpowered them and drove them
from that place... (*Book of Jasher* 6:24, 25)[34]

For forty days there was catastrophic upheaval.
Volcanic activity was combined with additional water
from above the earth. The phrase *all the fountains of
the great deep* were *broken up* means geysers as well as
volcanoes. For a good visualization of the beginning of

this catastrophe, see Disney's 1940 original *Fantasia*, the section using Stravinsky's *Rite of Spring, Dance of the Adolescents*. Though Disney produced this as a propaganda piece for millions of years of evolution, it accurately depicts the catastrophic upheaval of the beginning of the Flood. The passage of time, the desert environment, and the lack of organisms, including the lack of people and mammals, are incorrect. But the violent, rapid uplifts, cracks in the earth, volcanic and geyser activity, the sudden death of animals, and the rain are all accurate depictions of the beginning of the Flood. In spite of its being Disney's propaganda piece for millions of years of evolution, it is a good visualization.

There are many reasonable hypotheses as to the origins of the water which rained down from above, but they are all hypotheses. Creationists used to believe that the water for the forty days of rain came from some extraterrestrial source, adding to the total volume of water on the earth. Two of these possible sources were the vapor canopy theory and comets. Most scientists today who understand that the earth was created about 6000 years ago theorize that all of the water in the Flood came entirely from subterranean sources. There is not enough evidence to be certain.

The vapor canopy requires a triggering mechanism, so some people hold to both comets and a vapor canopy. Genesis 1:20 says God created the sky where birds *"may fly above the earth in the open firmament of heaven"* (KJV). The English word *open* used to mean "unobstructed, unencumbered," which is the meaning of *open* in Genesis 1:20. *Open* has changed in meaning and is no longer clear to the average reader. The Hebrew means *the face of the expanse* and the LXX means *the foundation of heaven*. Flying creatures had a domain above the earth but below the expanse. This defines the expanse as the place of the stars. The canopy which God placed above the earth dividing the waters below, in the seas, from the waters above, might be the atmosphere.

If this view is correct, then there was water vapor above

the earth which collapsed during the flood. But another view has the waters above the canopy as the material God used to fashion the stars, planets and all celestial objects. The remaining water, if there is any, would be somewhere outside our solar system, or perhaps even a boundary at the edge of the universe. Dr. Russell Humphreys has written monographs on the boundary conditions of the universe, which include defining the canopy God created in Genesis One.[34] If you are interested in this subject, his book *Starlight and Time* is a good starting point.

It is possible that this water canopy is the source of comets.[35] If ice from a comet or some other extraterrestrial source triggered the flood, the ice probably would have melted as it traveled through the atmosphere. The water came down as rain. The possibility of a comet as a trigger for the Flood and the source of the rain is one possible theory of Creation scientists. If the rainwater began as steam, such as water from a geyser, then it cooled down to rain. If it began as ice then it warmed up to rain.[35]

The material thrown up by volcanic activity from cracks in the earth combined with rock and soil washing off the existing landmass to create most of the sediment we see today. This type of activity continued for forty days, sometimes violently stripping soil, rock and plant material from the earth, sometimes allowing sediment to settle. It created a variety of materials which settled down in many layers and continuously recombined into new materials depending on the location. Some of these layers were quite thick and others very thin. Some volcanic material would remain unmixed; some would dissolve partially and some would dissolve completely in seawater. Some would settle down on the bottom of the sea with more layers following on top, combine under heat and pressure with various other materials, and transform into completely different materials. Sometimes massive lava flows over the top of already deposited layers of sediment would harden the existing sediment, turning the soft sediment to stone.

After forty days the volcanic activity and steam geysers stopped adding water.

Simplified, one particular set of conditions produce one particular type of material. The turbidity of the seawater keeps this one type of material suspended in seawater. The volcanic activity slows. The turbidity of the water slows, allowing thousands of square kilometers, perhaps hundreds of thousands of kilometers, or even worldwide amounts of the same material, to settle and form a single stratum. The conditions change, adding different material to the seawater as turbidity once again increases, allowing this different material to remain suspended. Then once again the turbidity slows, allowing this different material to settle and form a different type of stratum. Sometimes the turbidity was violent enough to create sand. Sometimes there was enough volcanic activity and material to create a stratum of volcanic material that did seem to be mixed with seawater. This was very likely early on, before the floodwaters had risen and this volcanic material was deposited directly on land. Each stratum was laid down one at a time throughout the Flood, with most layers deposited in the first forty days. Various layers were still deposited for many years after Noah had left the ark, though at a greatly reduced rate.

The important point is that the strata we see today were formed by vast quantities of water and rapidly changing conditions, not vast quantities of time with nearly static conditions. The eruption of Mt. St. Helens proves that hundreds of layers can be deposited in minutes.

> *And the waters prevailed upon the earth an hundred and fifty days.* (Genesis 7:24)

> *God made a wind to pass over the earth, and the waters asswaged; The fountains also of the deep and the windows of heaven were stopped, and the rain from heaven was restrained; And the waters returned from off the earth continually: and after the end of the*

hundred and fifty days the waters were abated. (Genesis 8:1b-3)

Whatever mechanism caused it, a wind began evaporating water. This great wind initiated the current hydrologic cycle. The atmosphere absorbed some of the water. In the highest part of the atmosphere additional the water broke apart into separate hydrogen and oxygen atoms. This permitted the hydrogen atoms to dissipate into space. This massive evaporation of the waters was something Noah could see, regardless of how it happened. That certainly implies that the waters were warmer than the air, causing vapors or fog to be removed by winds. The air was visibly removing the water vapors.

We observe today that hurricanes gain strength over water. There was no land to slow these winds down. However, in a modern hurricane the clouds saturate and almost 100% of the water either stays in the atmosphere or precipitates back to earth. But almost 100% still allows for a tiny amount of water to radiate into space even today.

Water molecules are too heavy to escape the earth's gravitational field. So individual water molecules in the upper atmosphere must first break down into hydrogen and oxygen to permit the lighter hydrogen atoms to escape earth's gravitational field. Today, very rough estimates place this hydrogen loss around 95,000 tons each year. Though this seems to be a massive amount, it is such a small amount of the overall total that it is very difficult to measure. This hydrogen loss is entirely from the breakdown of water molecules in the upper atmosphere.[36]

To be powerful enough to help dry the earth, these winds at the end of the Flood had to be able to transport considerably more water into the upper atmosphere than anything we are familiar with, except tornadoes (waterspouts) and hurricanes (typhoons). These winds had to allow for the water molecules to break down and the hydrogen atoms to radiate into space.

The other mechanism which lowered the water level was deeper ocean basins forcing the lighter continents to rise. Seabeds continued to fold throughout this process. These bent, twisted, and often-distorted layers make up the continents we see today. So continuous plate tectonics were moving the continents after the major volcanic and geyser activity stopped. At the end of the forty days of violent activity, the waters calmed down and began the slow process of subsiding. It is also possible that Noah took soundings, which let him know that the water was receding.

While all volcanic activity that Noah could see ceased, that does not even imply the end of 100% of all volcanic activity. It only means that the volcanic activity which Noah could observe ceased. The common reading of the text is that the massive volcanic and geyser activity which Noah could detect ceased. The important point was that the earth was reabsorbing the water, not adding more to the total volume of surface seawater. The volcanic activity was no longer visible from the surface of the water. This does not imply that the continents were anything like what we know today. The Antediluvian single continent broke apart during the Flood, but the major movement of continents into the position that we know today might have waited for another three- to three- and-a-half centuries.

> *In the seventh month, on the seventeenth day*
> *of the month, the ark rested upon the*
> *mountains of Ararat. The water decreased*
> *steadily until the tenth month; in the tenth*

month, on the first day of the month, the tops of the mountains became visible. (Genesis 8:4, 5 NASB)

And it came to pass at the end of forty days, that Noah opened the window of the ark which he had made: And he sent forth a raven, which went forth to and fro, until the waters were dried up from off the earth. Also he sent forth a dove from him, to see if the waters were abated from off the face of the ground; But the dove found no rest for the sole of her foot, and she returned unto him into the ark, for the waters were on the face of the whole earth: then he put forth his hand, and took her, and pulled her in unto him into the ark. And he stayed yet other seven days; and again he sent forth the dove out of the ark; And the dove came in to him in the evening; and, lo, in her mouth was an olive leaf pluckt off: so Noah knew that the waters were abated from off the earth. And he stayed yet other seven days; and sent forth the dove; which returned not again unto him any more. And it came to pass in the six hundredth and first year, in the first month, the first day of the month, the waters were dried up from off the earth: and Noah removed the covering of the ark, and looked, and, behold, the face of the ground was dry. (Genesis 8:6-13)

Raven image from www.publicdomainpictures.net

Before the mountaintops were visible, the ark ran aground. With such great winds propelling the ark, it likely covered vast distances in brief time periods. However, at this point in time, towards the end of the Flood, the seafloor the ark rammed into would be very soft, loose, silt and mud.

Two-and-a-half months after the ark ran aground, the mountaintops were visible. Since the draft of the ark was probably about twenty-six feet, it seems that the water was receding at a rate of approximately one foot per day at this point. This was the most dangerous time for the ark. The ark had stopped moving, yet winds and waves pounded it.

At some point the winds had to die down enough to allow Noah to release the birds. Perhaps waiting for the winds to die down is why Noah waited so long. Forty days after the mountaintops were visible, Noah sent out a raven as a test. The raven did not return. This means the raven found enough to eat and someplace to sleep at night. Noah then sent out a dove, which returned that evening. He sent the dove out a week later. It returned with an olive leaf in its mouth. Another week later, Noah released the dove and it never returned. So Noah removed the cover of the ark and God spoke to him, telling him, his family, and the animals to leave the ark. *The surface of the ground was dried up*.

From the time the ark ran aground to the day Noah opened the door of the ark was 75 days until the tops of the mountains became visible (approximately), 40 days until the raven was sent out, and 21 more days until Noah actually opened the door. That is approximately 96 days from the day the ark ran aground until the day the door was opened.

God originally created the stars for seasons, *And God said, Let there be lights in the firmament of the heaven to divide the day from the night; and let them be for signs, and for seasons, and for days, and years.* (Genesis 1:14)

As Noah and his family left the ark, God established what we know as seasons. *While the earth remaineth, seedtime and harvest, and cold and heat, and summer and winter, and day and night shall not cease.* (Genesis 8:22)

There certainly were seasons in the antediluvian world. But somehow, something changed. This seems to imply that in the antediluvian world, seeds would grow any time they were planted. Now seeds would only grow in certain seasons. Also, animals are now given as food. This does not mean that no one ever ate meat before this, or that animals did not eat one another, but now God gave men permission to eat meat. While conditions seem to be harsher than the antediluvian world, the deltas, coastlines, and rivers in the new postdiluvian world were ideal for game. The evidence indicates that the Ice Age saw an explosion in wildlife and edible wild plants.

As new ocean depths were created, the continents continued to move and uplift. The sea floor dropped. *The mountains rose; the valleys sank down* (Psalm 104:8) allowing the sea level to drop. Some of the newly added water was trapped under the ocean floor by this activity. This slower activity likely continued for hundreds or thousands of years. Oceans heated by the volcanic activity were very warm, perhaps even hot. This caused an ocean evaporation rate which saturated the atmosphere. The atmosphere was also so filled with volcanic ash as to darken the sun. As the water levels dropped, the mountains pushed increasingly higher. The new mountaintops pushed upward above the warm waters of the oceans and warm rivers. This likely took place in stages.

"Therefore, to cause an ice age, rare conditions are required: warm oceans for high precipitation, and cool summers for lack of melting the snow. Only then can it accumulate into an ice sheet,"[37] says Michael Oard.

The *Seder Olam* describes the oceans as "thick soup" (they contained volcanic ash and sediment).[38] These waters greeted Noah as he emerged from the ark. They were warm, perhaps hotter than any other time in earth's history. At the same time, the volcanic ash and aerosols in the atmosphere blocked out more of the sun's rays, making the summers cooler than any time in earth's history. The warm oceans provided both the moisture and the salt particles to create abundant snow. The summers would be too cool to melt all of the abundant winter snow, allowing the snow to compact into ice, forming glaciers. These new mountaintops became glaciers as the saturated air precipitated out with snow. This also forced civilizations to stay near the oceans for warmth. As the sea level dropped, most men continually followed it to lower altitudes, both to escape the growing ice and to follow the growing food supply. This was the beginning of the Ice Age, and this single Ice Age probably ended at the time of Joseph.

"Although a major mystery of uniformitarian history, the Ice Age is readily explained by the climatic consequences of the Genesis Flood: it was a short Ice Age of about 700 years, and there was only one Ice Age. We do not need the hundred thousand years for one ice age, or the few million years for multiple ice ages, as claimed by uniformitarian scientists." (from *Where Does the Ice Age Fit?*, referenced above)[163]

So we add approximately 700 years, based on Michael Oard's estimate of the Ice Age for a corresponding event in the Bible. That would be approximately 1650 BC. The seven years of plenty followed by the seven years of famine is very close to Michael Oard's estimate for the end of the Ice Age. That was 1708-1694 BC, Old Julian Calendar, according to Ussher. This is just an estimate which might change with more information. It is also very likely that the ice grew and shrank repeatedly during this more than six-hundred-year period. The initial decades after Noah and his family left the ark were not part of the Ice Age, which is the reason for the more than six-hundred-year period. All of these numbers are very rough estimates, except for the time of Joseph.

It is possible that the weight of the ice was the triggering mechanism which caused the continental break-up. If that was the case, the Ice Age might be divided into two periods, before and after the breakup of the continents. It is also possible that the continents were in place, the sea levels were four hundred feet lower, and the division of the continents resulted from a rapid ice melt that flooded many passageways, causing a division of continents by water.

This continual decrease in lifespan stopped just after the time of Jacob (Israel) at around 120 years, as Josephus said, "cutting short their lives, and making their years not so many as they formerly lived, but one hundred and twenty only."[39]

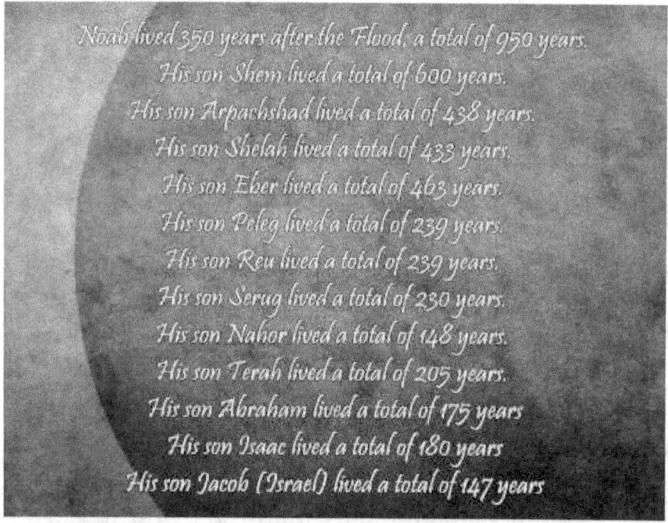

The length of the human lifespan stabilized for about 450 years then declined again, stabilizing for several generations around 225 years. It then resumed its decline again until it stabilized with the lifespan we are familiar with. This stabilization took place sometime around the time of David (approximately 1000 BC) at something around 70 years. Though the environmental conditions were far harsher than the antediluvian world and might contribute to a temporary reduction in lifespans, only some form of genetic mutations which would make the reduction in lifespan permanent. While there are many theories as to the cause of these mutations, the most likely causes are radiation, chemicals, and/or disease. Diet, temperature, and other temporary environmental changes would not cause the permanent changes which resulted in a shorter expectancy for the entire human race.

Also, every human on earth was descended from the shipbuilders Noah and his sons Shem, Ham, and Japheth. So every human on earth knew about shipbuilding. Humans certainly had the opportunity, if they chose to do so, to build ships and to travel by ship all over the world. The subsequent worldwide lack of shipbuilding skills and the inability to navigate during the middle ages was a loss of skills. The voyages of Columbus, Magellan and Henry Hudson simply rediscovered lost abilities and skills. They did not invent new skills.

At the time Noah left the ark, the water tables were much higher than any time in history. The sea levels continued to drop until the sea level was four hundred feet below our current sea level. Water pressure forced ocean floors lower, which forced mountains higher; As the mountains rose, they collected snow, which formed glaciers and ice sheets.

At first travel was much easier. The limited amount of land was easily accessible by ship. Great distances could be traveled because food would be readily available worldwide. Areas such as the Gobi and the Sahara, which are now deserts, were rich with game. Vast amounts of fresh water in glaciers kept rivers flowing year round. And the higher water table made the interior areas more accessible by ship. Areas of the far north such as the Yukon, Alaska, and Siberia were warmer and inhabited.

While modern archaeologists deride these people as unintelligent and lazy, hunting and finding food was easy during this time period. They founded civilizations, invented what we know as writing, developed astronomy, and built buildings with great stones which we can only copy with great difficulty. We are unable to duplicate these great buildings today at any reasonable cost.

B. The Geology of the Flood

To repeat our goal, it is not to answer every possible problem in detail, but to reveal to you, the student, the correct questions and how to think the problem through to the correct conclusion.

1. What Is Geology?

Geology compares the information from special revelation (the Word of God) with general revelation (the material universe). With empirical science, we examine the evidence and allow the evidence to show us the proper conclusions. However, uniformitarians not only reject the evidence of special revelation, they also refuse to allow any interpretation of general revelation which supports special revelation.

Geology is frequently described as "a science that deals with the history of the earth and its life especially as recorded in rocks" *(Merriam-Webster)*. That is a basic, workable definition if we understand the limits of Geology. However, many prefer more pretentious definitions such as "The scientific study of the origin, history, and structure of the earth" (definition from *The Free Dictionary*). This is pretentious because the information necessary for understanding the origin of the earth is not to be found in the "structure of the earth." The facts of many and massive catastrophic events make understanding the earth's history exclusively from the record left in rock impossible.

James Hutton (1726-1797) was a Scottish farmer who traveled about observing rock strata. Geology before James Hutton was founded on catastrophic explanations. Also, before Hutton and Charles Lyell, many geologists believed in a young earth created about 4000 BC. James Hutton laid a foundation for the idea of vast periods of time without God and without being formed by worldwide catastrophes. Today this is called deep time. He based this solely on his belief that the processes he observed could be projected into the past. Radiometric dating was more than one hundred years in the future. He believed that the amount of coal, the vast number of fossils and rocks in the various strata, and the marking in the rocks were best explained by vast periods of time and not catastrophic causes. Uniformitarian doctrine was, from the very beginning, a choice, a religious doctrine, and not science.

Painting of James Hutton by Henry Raeburn 1776, from the Scottish National Gallery. Engraving of Charles Lyell, Public Domain, Wikimedia Commons

James Hutton is credited by Secular Humanists with being the "Father of Modern Geology." His name, along with Charles Lyell's, is likely to show up on tests, even in graduate school, so these are names worth remembering. He was the first modern person to openly reject the application of special revelation to geology. He published a work with the lengthy title *Theory of the Earth; or an Investigation of Laws observable in the Composition, Dissolution, and Restoration of Land upon the Globe,* published in *Transactions of the Royal Society of Edinburgh,* 1788, which included the now infamous statement "from what has actually been, we have data for concluding with regard to that which is to happen thereafter." Charles Lyell, in 1830, took this and other statements and rephrased it as the familiar "the present is the key to the past". Though there are many other definitions, that is a concise and popular definition of uniformitarianism. James Hutton's paper concluded with "The result, therefore, of our present enquiry is, that we find no vestige of a beginning: no prospect of an end." Soon after publication, Richard Kirwan pointed out, in print, that James Hutton's ideas were illogical as well as atheistic.

A closer and more thorough examination of the evidence has forced geologists today to accept the fact that both floods and other catastrophes shaped the earth's geologic history. But they still believe in atheistic deep time, so they place the obvious catastrophes in the distant past.

The Missoula Glacial Lake[40] represents perhaps the most famous example of a massive catastrophe. Examining the evidence showed comparisons between the collapse of the Missoula Glacial Lake Ice Dam and the November 5, 1996 collapse of a modern ice dam in Iceland. In Iceland a volcano erupted beneath the Vatnajökull ice cap. This collapse of an ice dam is certainly not common. It does, however, have a name, *jökulhlaups,* literally, "glacier burst." Based on this comparison with the Vatnajökull ice cap *jökulhlaups*, it is believed that an enormous ice dam formed the Missoula Glacial Lake.

While there are disagreements about the size of the ice dam, the number of floods, and other details, most geologists believe that the ice dam was 2,500 feet high. The high water points of water flow give us the measurement for the height of the dam. The near-instantaneous release of water caused by the collapse of the ice dam allowed water from Lake Missoula to flow down part of the existing Clark Fork River into the Columbia River and Snake Rivers, forming the existing Columbia/Snake River Gorge. This 2,500 foot high wall of water flowed at an average speed of 60 mph.[40]

Lake Missoula is only one example of our catastrophic past. With overwhelming evidence for a massive flood, or floods, with Lake Missoula, there are only two disagreements between secularists and creationists. When did these floods take place? And was there a worldwide flood that destroyed all air-breathing life (except for aquatic animals)?

In addition to examining the surface, we have core samples, mines, naturally-exposed layers of mountains, and mountains which humans have cut into. With very minor exceptions, this is all of the evidence we have. Over 99% of all geologic evidence is buried, most of it deep beneath the sea. While we are able to examine the entire surface of the earth, including the ocean floors, this is still far less than one percent of all geologic evidence. We can make reasonable estimates of the unseen buried material based on the available evidence and the measurement of seismic waves, but we do not even know for certain what is buried between two core samples. The geologic evidence we have is valuable, but, as more information becomes available, our conclusions might need to be modified.

2. A Biblical Model For Geology

The geology of the Flood begins with the original Creation. Soil was created before any life. Later upheavals allowed for a very limited number of organisms to burrow into or be buried in this material. The vast majority of these are microorganisms. Many microorganisms were created on the Third Day of Creation when plants were created, which allowed them to exist in the lowest layers of soil. Uniformitarians call these layers that essentially have no fossils of life forms Pre-Cambrian. The standard names for geologic layers are listed under the section on the geologic column. There is disagreement as to the exact names for each stratum among uniformitarians so finding a "standard list" for the entire geologic column is impossible. The International Commission on Stratigraphy sets official nomenclature for the geologic column. However, not only do they make periodic changes, there is considerable disagreement about what the geologic column should be based on. The fossil record does not always match the stratigraphy, which does not always match up with physical sciences such as magnetic alignment sequences.

We recommend the Walker/Klevberg model, which avoids the problems of the "standard model."

Time-Rock Transformation

Adapted from http://biblicalgeology.net/General/geologic-column.html

Time Scale

Event/Era	STAGE	DURATION	PHASE
Postdiluvial (4300 years)			
		4000 years	Modern
		~300 years	Residual
2300 B.C.	Recessive	ca. 220 days	Dispersive / Abative
The Deluge	Inundatory	ca. 110 days	Zenithic / Ascending
		40 days	Eruptive
Antediluvian (1700 years)		1700 years	Antediluvial
	Formative	2 days	Biotic
		2 days	Derivative
Creation Week	Foundational	2 days	Ensuing
		0 days	Primordial

(The endnote also sources the graphic above.)[41] The Walker/Klevberg model is superior for aligning the known strata into understandable categories. It labels original geological material for the Creation Week "Creation Event". This event is divided into Foundational and Formative Stages.

- The Foundational Stage is further divided into the Primordial and Ensuing Phases, covering the first two days of Creation.

- The Formative Stage is subdivided into the Derivative and Biotic Phases for the rest of the Creation Week.

This geological model then labels the Antediluvian Era without subdivisions as the Antediluvial Phase. It then labels the Deluge Event.

The Deluge Event is subdivided into Inundatory and Recessive Stages.

- The Inundatory Stage is further subdivided into Eruptive, Ascending, and Zenethic Phases.

- The Recessive Stage is further subdivided into Abative and Dispersive Phases.

The Walker/Klevberg model then labels as Postdiluvial Era everything after the Deluge. The Postdiluvial Era is not broken down into stages, but it is further subdivided into Residual and Modern Phases.

This geological model is vastly superior to categories in existing mainstream geological models. Due to the number of observed strata, however, this model could benefit, in my opinion, from splitting the Antediluvian phase and the Postdiluvial Residual phase into more phases.

Except for the time when each stratum was deposited, there is considerable agreement with the observations of mainstream geologists. There might have even been geologic catastrophes during the antediluvian period.

> And every man made his god and they bowed
> down to them, and the sons of men forsook
> the Lord all the days of Enosh and his
> children; and the anger of the Lord was
> kindled on account of their works and
> abominations which they did in the earth. And
> the Lord caused the waters of the river Gihon
> to overwhelm them, and he destroyed and
> consumed them, and he destroyed the third
> part of the earth, and notwithstanding this,
> the sons of men did not turn from their evil
> ways, and their hands were yet extended to do

> evil in the sight of the Lord. And in those days
> there was neither sowing nor reaping in the
> earth; and there was no food for the sons of
> men and the famine was very great in those
> days.
> (*Book of Jasher* 2:5-7)[42]

Antediluvian catastrophes might have changed the
conditions of soil layers. But far more likely, the later
cataclysmic changes have eradicated all evidence of any
antediluvial catastrophes.

3. Transformation from Antediluvian Geology: an
overview.

The antediluvian[43] world was watered by the river
which left Eden and split into four parts. For a single
river to water most of the earth, the earth would have
to be a single continent (perhaps there were islands in
addition to the single continent). It would also need a
gentle, shallow slope with an overall gradual change in
elevation from sea level to Eden, the highest watered
point on Earth. That is similar to the Missouri-
Mississippi River in North America today. The
Missouri-Mississippi River in North America is 6,275
kilometers long beginning at Brower's Spring in
Montana, with an elevation of 2,629 m (8,626 feet).
That is somewhat shorter and lower than the total
length of the Nile (6,650 km), which drops 2,700 m
(8,858 ft); the Amazon (6,400 km), which drops 5,170
m (16,962 ft); and the Yangtze (6,300 km), which drops
more than 5,000 m (16,000 ft).

Like these rivers, the antediluvian river system might
have had waterfalls and a few steep rises. The climate
of Eden, the highest watered point on Earth, was
comfortable when Adam and Eve were naked. This
means that Eden, the highest place that was watered in
the antediluvian world, had a low elevation, probably
lower than the Missouri-Mississippi or Nile Rivers, and
certainly lower than the higher elevations of the
Amazon or Yangtze River sources. This also indicates
that the entire Antediluvian earth had a mild climate
(cool summers and warm winters). These conclusions

are in line with findings of what secularists call the Devonian period. Geologic periods are more properly called systems since the term system more accurately describes a physical set of conditions and does not imply a time period. "According to creationists, the geological systems represent different ecological zones, the buried remains of plants and animals that once lived together in the same environment."[44]

To repeat an earlier statement; every geologic period from the Cambrian to *at least* the Jurassic co-existed at the same time. Each of these made up different aspects of the Antediluvian world. The Devonian system was one aspect of the Antediluvian world.

Perhaps there were earth tremors, wind, ash clouds, or similar indicators some time before the rains started. But the Flood began with the fountains of the great deep breaking up, cracking, shattering, and the sluices of heaven opening wide. The geologic evidence indicates that much or all of this coincides with volcanic activity. For those who question where the water came from, even today large volumes of water are stored deep underground, both beneath the oceans and the land.[45]

The fossil evidence indicates possible volcanic activity. The four conditions necessary for the creation of fossils are found in volcanic activity. (click the image for source information)[46]

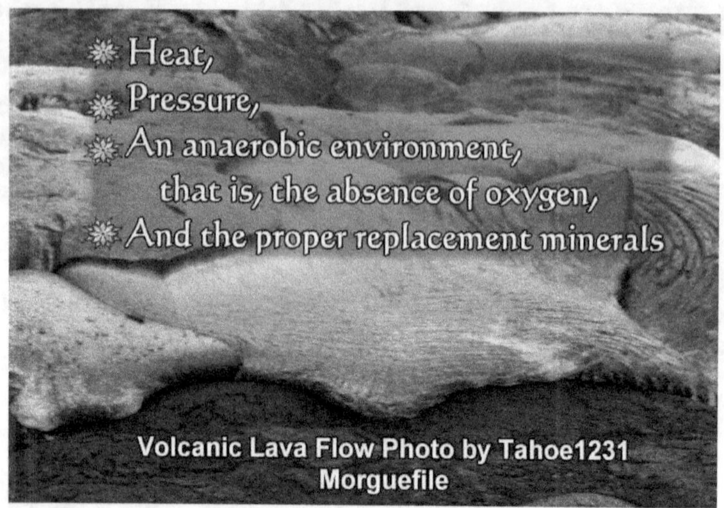

Volcanic Lava Flow Photo by Tahoe1231
Morguefile

The bread, garbage, and waste fossilized in the AD 79 eruption of Mt Vesuvius show us one way fossils can be created.

There is considerable disagreement as to how much volcanic activity took place and when. The evidence is the thousands of sequential layers found all over the earth. (Click on the image below for source information.)[47]

This canyon, including all of the layers you see, was formed in less than one day by the Mt. St. Helen eruption.

The following picture of Mt. St. Helen and definition of a phreatic eruption is by the USGS.

Photograph by D.A. Swanson on 4 April 1980

Click here for sources on volcanic activity, Mt St Helens, and Underground Oceans[48]

Phreatic eruption:

> "Phreatic eruptions are steam-driven explosions that occur when water beneath the ground or on the surface is heated by magma,

lava, hot rocks, or new volcanic deposits (for
example, tephra and pyroclastic-flow
deposits). The intense heat of such material
(as high as 1,170° C for basaltic lava) may
cause water to boil and flash to steam, thereby
generating an explosion of steam, water, ash,
blocks, and bombs."

The entire Western chain of the American Continents is
volcanic, covered with volcanic soil, from Alaska and
the Yukon to Chile. Were *the fountains of the great
deep* which broke up phreatic eruptions? Assuming
that the Flood of Noah originated with massive
phreatic eruptions is a reasonable assumption.

The single Antediluvian continent broke apart, creating
many volcanic eruptions along fault lines at the same
time. Nor was it a continuous, even eruption. As
modern eruptions can change over time so the
eruptions during the Flood changed. Geysers and
phreatic eruptions were predominant during the period
that the "fountains of the great deep were broken up,"
that is, were venting water.

Geologist Andrew Snelling, PhD, theorizes that there
was no additional extraterrestrial water. He believes
that the Phreatic eruptions and geysers put water into
the upper atmosphere, where it cooled and precipitated
as "the sluice gates of heaven." So all of the water of the
Flood, according to the theory of Dr. Snelling,
originated beneath the oceans.

This volcanic activity formed fossils. Not directly,
because the molten rock would destroy organic
remains. But there were many kinds of volcanic
activity, throughout the Flood period, just as we
witness many kinds of volcanic activity today. We
reasonably expect the different kinds of volcanic
activity to produce various kinds of sediment to bury
the organic remains and the heat to fossilize organisms
almost instantaneously where they lived. Rapid burial,
likely instigated by volcanic activity, was also necessary
keep the organic material in an anaerobic (oxygen free)
environment. Like creatures today, they lived in

groups. The entire antediluvian world teemed with life, billions more organisms than live on earth now. Those organisms normally lived together with similar kinds of organisms. Today we see these of groupings of organisms that lived together and were fossilized together as different strata. The different strata were formed by a variety of different volcanic processes.

After forty days the flood-gates of heaven were restrained and the fountains of the great deep were closed. At this time it is likely that the volcanic activity changed over from geysers and phreatic eruptions to magma eruptions.

> And (on the new moon) in the fourth month
> the fountains of the great deep were closed
> and the flood-gates of heaven were restrained;
> and on the new moon of the seventh month all
> the mouths of the abysses of the earth were
> opened, and the water began to descend into
> the deep below. *(Book of Jubilees* 5:29)[49]

> When Genesis says "the waters were dried: it
> happened this way. The wind evaporated the
> water from above and the water from below
> filtered back to where it came from, but the
> earth was still saturated and had the
> consistency of thick soup. They did not plant
> seed until fresh rain came because they
> considered the Flood waters to be a curse and
> no blessing could come from something that is
> cursed." *Seder Olam*[50]

The various geologic strata were originally large pools of material from volcanic eruptions. Lava, magma, pyroclastic flow, and tephra combine in different ways with water. There would also be different kinds of water, such as

- rapidly rushing water,

- slow or even stagnant water,

- turbulent water

- hot and cold areas.

Each of these combined in different ways to make different layers which hardened into vastly different strata. There were times when the turbulent, rushing water turned the much of the material to sand. At other times the volcanic activity slowed and allowed the water to settle and the sediments to precipitate out. Sometimes volcanic ash settled out on top to add a thin layer between layers. Though each eruption, or series of eruptions of similar or identical volcanic material, would mix together to form a massive layer, few of these would be world-wide. Mats of trees and other plant material floated before becoming waterlogged and covered in volcanic ash and perhaps even other volcanic material such as magma. They sank down to become layers of coal. These covered far less than half of the earth.

As a result of volcanic eruptions, turbulent, water-formed plastic (mud) layers created massive, irregular-shaped areas which were moved about, twisted and deformed as the continents moved. The process of layer formation changed and slowed after Noah left the ark, but there is no indication that it stopped at that time. The continued slow formation of thin layers today is the basis of uniformitarian dogma. The ammonite fossils on top of the Himalayas and the twisted, distorted strata found everywhere on earth mean that the mountains were uplifted after the fossil layers were laid down, but the fossils were still surrounded by soft mud that protected them from being crushed. While other explanations might be possible, the only logical answer seems to be that they were uplifted into their current location before being heated to the point that they were fossilized. Perhaps the mountains uplifted near the end of the Flood to allow for deeper ocean basins and allow the sea level to drop. Perhaps the mountains uplifted later, after the Flood.

There are two possible times for this later uplift or even perhaps these later uplifts. The division of the languages and perhaps continents which occurred during the time of Peleg, 340 years after the Flood, is one possibility. Another possibility is the seven years of plenty and seven years of famine in Egypt during the time Joseph, about 650 years after the Flood. Perhaps mountains uplifted near the end of the Flood, the end of Peleg's life, during Joseph's lifetime and perhaps there were more uplifts and mountain-building due to volcanic activity later.

IV. Material Results of the Flood

The Geologic Column

A. The Geologic Column

Though secular humanists use the geologic column for dating, that was not the original purpose of the geologic column. It surprises many secularists to learn that creationists usually begin the examination of general revelation (the material world) in the area of geology with the geologic column. Beginning in the 1700s, many people, not just James Hutton and Charles Lyell, examined the strata all over the earth and noticed the similarities in strata and the similarities in the relationships of strata.

That is, one type of strata, Devonian for example, was found in England, North America, Australia, and other continents. On top of the Devonian was a different stratum, which is commonly labeled today as Carboniferous. The concept of the geologic column relies on strata B to be on top of strata A, the same way, wherever it is found, even on different continents around the world. These relationships were compared worldwide and these comparisons became the "standard" geologic column. The following points (in the graphic) are from the ICR article *Ten Misconceptions about the Geologic Column* by Steven

A. Austin, Ph.D.[51]

Since these are standard terms that appear on standard tests all over the world, it is worthwhile to memorize these in order. Cambrian is the oldest fossil stratum (individual layer: stratum is singular, strata is plural). If it is simply a sedimentary accumulation of mud, it is properly called a layer. Strata (plural) and stratum (singular) are the proper terms for these layers which have turned to rock. Precambrian, according to uniformitarian terminology, begins with the formation of the earth and lasts until the Cambrian explosion. Precambrian strata have virtually no fossils. Some people put the Ediacaran Biotas in the Precambrian; others include them in the Cambrian. The Ediacaran Biotas are fossils which do not fit into either system. They are "older" according to uniformitarians and different from Cambrian fossils. We simply acknowledge that the Ediacaran Biotas lived at the same time as all other antediluvian organisms, just in a separate environment.

Quaternary is their term for the current time, which they claim goes back the beginning of humans and comes after the Tertiary system. There are subcategories to each system. Also, each of these ten (or twelve if you include Quaternary and Precambrian) systems is a subdivision of what they call an era. Depending on who is dividing up the eras, there are usually four eras.

It is also difficult to grasp the number of times the "standard" systems have been modified. Please compare the 1984 standard Dr. Austin used with the 2010 USGS standard. While the major points have not changed, the USGS pdf file lists a number of changes with this warning; "Advances in stratigraphy and geochronology require that any time scale be periodically updated. Therefore, Divisions of Geologic Time[52] is intended to be a dynamic resource that will be modified to include accepted changes of unit names and boundary age estimates."

Going from the most recent to the oldest,

- The Cenozoic is the current era, which is made up of the Tertiary and Quaternary systems. The Cenozoic is preceded by

- the Mesozoic, which is made up of the Triassic, Jurassic, and Cretaceous systems. The Mesozoic is preceded by

- the Paleozoic, which is made up of the Cambrian, Ordovician, Silurian, Devonian, Carboniferous, and Permian systems. The Paleozoic is preceded by the Precambrian.

According to eras, the oldest era is Precambrian. Normally, there are few or no fossils found in the layers which make up this era. The Ediacaran Biotas are an exception to this.

The reason for the word "system" was the collection of subcategories of strata into one "system." That is, many different strata fit into the Devonian system (not period). Also, the word "system" matches the facts. There is no implication of time with a system. You can take a few pounds of rock from each system and pour them into a very large aquarium, one at a time, allowing one layer to settle before pouring in the next one. In less than an hour you will have a scale model of the geologic column.

The following indented paragraphs are quoted from the icr.org article "Ten Misconceptions about the Geologic Column."[53] The material is not quoted in its entirety. Reading the whole article is highly recommended, and it referenced in the appendix/endnotes.

> "...(T)he standard geologic column was devised before 1860 by catastrophists who were creationists. Adam Sedgewick, Roderick Murchison, William Coneybeare, and others affirmed that the earth was formed largely by catastrophic processes, and that the earth and life were created. [53]

The geologic column was never intended to be proof of evolution, deep time, or anything else. It was simply an observation of the fact that the layers were often, though not always, in the same order.

> "The geologic column was not composed by assembling a chronology of "periods," "eras" or other supposed measures of time, but by superposition of objectively defined sequences of sedimentary strata called 'systems.' The 'periods' and 'eras' were later appended to the system nomenclature of the 'geologic column' transforming it into a 'geologic time scale.'"

> Keeping with the term "system" for a layer of sedimentary strata "...approximately 77% of the earth's surface area on land and under the sea has *seven* or more (70% or more) of the strata systems missing beneath..." and "an estimated 99.6% (of the entire earth surface including seafloor) has *at least one* missing system."

> "The entire geologic column, composed of complete strata systems, exists only in the diagrams drawn by geologists."

> "Hundreds of locations are known where the order of the systems identified by geologists does not match the order of the geologic column." [53]

Probably the most well-known example of visible strata deposited in the most nearly complete order is the Grand Canyon. The first issue, though, is *What part of the Grand Canyon are you examining?* Though the layers of the Grand Canyon are in the main consistent, there are some dramatic changes in the strata as you travel down the canyon. There is not a single place on earth where more layers are visible to more people in one place than the Grand Canyon. Yet even here in the Grand Canyon only part of the standard Geologic Column exists.

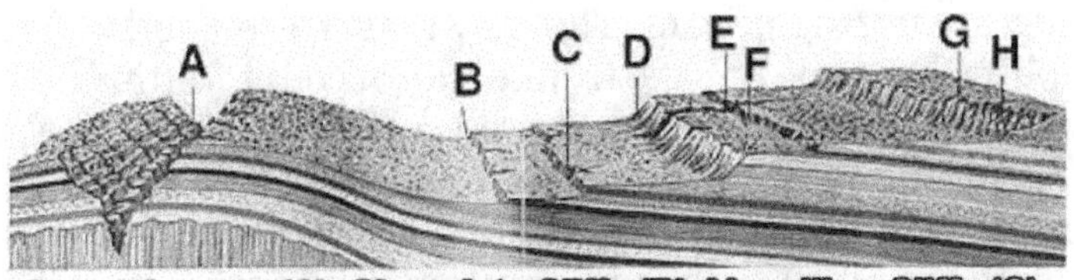

Grand Canyon (A), Chocolate Cliffs (B), Vermilion Cliffs (C),
White Cliffs (D), Zion Canyon (E),
Gray Cliffs (F), Pink Cliffs (G), Bryce Canyon (H)
The "Grand Staircase"
Public Domain

The standard cross-section of the Grand Canyon strata jumps from the Cambrian to the Devonian systems. The Ordovician and Silurian systems are missing completely. There are no systems which are above (considered more recent than) the Permian system. The explanation given is that these more recent systems eroded away when the entire Kaibab Plateau was uplifted. That is a very reasonable catastrophic explanation. It also fits the facts, as we see when we examine the entire region of the Grand Staircase.

The strata of the Grand Staircase begin at the lowest elevation with the Precambrian system (approximately 1500 feet), located at the bottom of the Grand Canyon. They climb to the top of the Bryce Canyon in Utah with the Eocene System (approximately 9000 feet).

These geologic columns made by geologists must not only account for missing systems, but they must also account for systems in incorrect places. There are also missing strata and missing information between strata. These "unconformities" or "discontinuities" are expected in a catastrophic formation, but do not easily fit into uniformitarian assumptions. Please note that these catastrophic explanations do not have to be recent catastrophes. The missing strata,[54] incorrect order of strata and unconformities demand catastrophic explanations. But these catastrophes do not come with labels explaining when these catastrophes occurred.

Uniformitarians readily admit to these "unconformities" or "discontinuities" but claim that they are not significant. They say that erosion and uplifts, one type of catastrophe, can account for the missing information. The overall column, according to this position, is not affected by these "unconformities" or "discontinuities." This *assumes* "unconformities" or "discontinuities" to be unimportant. And the *assumption* that they are unimportant *implies* that "unconformities" or "discontinuities" are rare, or at least unusual.

Using this *assumption*, the most recent strata should be the most accurate. Examination of existing evidence works from the present to the past. This means that the most recent evidence is likely to be the most accurate, as well as the highest elevation. Any type of erosion, volcanic activity, uplift or any other drastic geologic activity would hide or eliminate earlier evidence. However, that is not what a serious examination of the strata reveals.

> "Two-thirds of Earth's land surface has five or fewer of the ten geological 'periods' in place. *Only 15-20% of Earth's land surface has even three geological periods in correct order.*" Michael Oard (emphasis added)[55]

This article by Michael Oard *The Geologic Column Is a General Flood Order with Many Exceptions* is an excellent introduction to the next section, types of strata.

B. Types of Strata

Before we continue with types of strata, we must be reminded of an important recurring theme. The use of true science to organize knowledge should result in information which is easier to understand and easier to explain. When people, even geologists with earned Ph.D.s, use terms and explanations which are difficult to understand and even harder to explain, examine their words very carefully. Sometimes they are simply explaining difficult concepts. However, complex explanations are often clever attempts at deception. This type of deception is common with geologic strata and much of the deception is unintentional because the person making the statement sincerely believes the falsehood he is putting forth.

Geology, more than any other branch or division of science, was developed on different continents with different people unknowingly using different terms to describe the same phenomena. Combine these differences in terminology with the deliberate uniformitarian bias and the complex field of geology becomes even more complicated. Understanding Geology calls for great skill and discernment.

While there are an almost infinite number of subcategories, classifying rock strata depend primarily on two pieces of information.

- What kind of fossils does the stratum contain?

- What kind of material is the stratum made of?

The fossil evidence requires a very detailed explanation, which is covered in its own point, *Fossils in Geologic Strata*. We will begin with the type of material contained in the strata. Once again, we are only examining the basics.

Rocks making up these strata fall into several categories.

1. Sedimentary

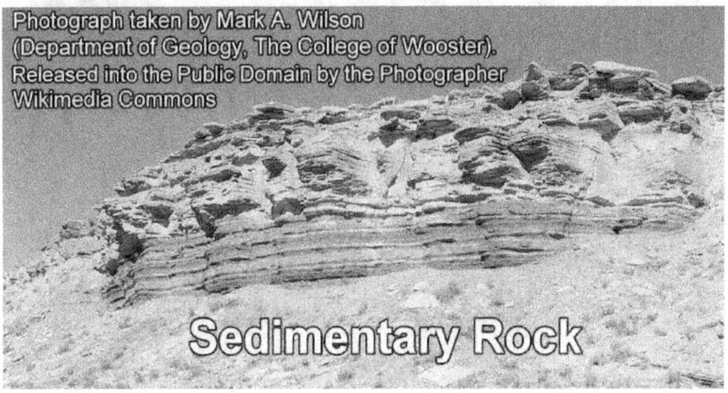

First, there are strata formed by material deposited in water, allowed to settle as sediment, then hardened into rock. Rocks making these strata are called sedimentary rocks. Perhaps they hardened to rock under water, but more likely they were uplifted before heat hardened the material into rock.

Sedimentary rock requires heat and pressure to become stone. Sandstone is one example of sedimentary rock. Flint is another. Flint is made up of the mineral quartz and usually found in chalk and limestone strata. Common coal (both bituminous and anthracite) is also sedimentary. Shale and oil shale are both sedimentary. These are only a few examples.

2. Igneous

Second, there are strata formed by some type of direct volcanic activity. Rocks making up these strata are called igneous. A few examples are obsidian, pumice and basalt. Obsidian, like flint, easily chips into sharp edges. Both obsidian and flint (sedimentary) are commonly used to make arrowheads and spearheads. The igneous rock scoria is filled with holes formed by gas bubbles as the material hardened and is what many people think of when they see volcanic rocks. The common countertop material granite is an igneous rock.

3. Metamorphic

Third, there are strata formed by transformation. Metamorphic rocks began as something else and were modified or transformed by heat, pressure and chemical processes. Some examples of common metamorphic rocks are marble, quartzite, gneiss, slate, soapstone, and schist.

Though strata can be, and usually are, made up of a combination of types of rock and fossils, there is usually one identifying rock for each stratum. For example, the Carboniferous System is made up of coal. Since there are many types of coal, such as bituminous and anthracite, and these different types of coal can be combined with other rocks and fossils, exact correlations between strata in different geographic regions can be difficult.

These difficulties led Whitcomb and Morris in their 1961 book *The Genesis Flood* to make a new geologic column based on the same rock strata, but using a catastrophic flood model instead of a uniformitarian model.

Meteorologist Michael Oard believes that the later 1994 Walker model is better. This model uses the same catastrophic flood foundation as Whitcomb and Morris. It was later modified by Klevberg. The title of Michael Oard's article clearly explains his position: *The*

Geological Column Is a General Flood Order with Many Exceptions.

C. Scientific Results of the Flood

Karl Popper, Richard Dawkins, Stephen Hawking, and many other secularists have transformed the word "science" in the mind of the average scientist. The Christian definition of science is the observation and classification of knowledge. It goes through several steps:

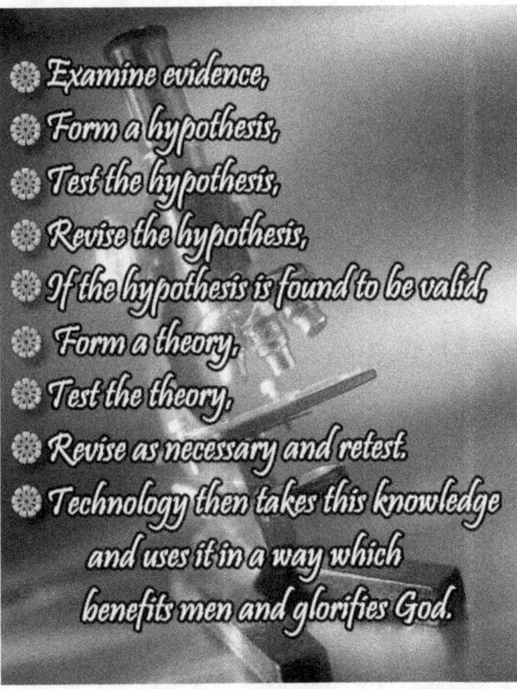

This was first detailed and applied to all branches of learning by Isaac Newton. It became the universal definition of science until the concept of God ruling in the affairs of men was rejected. Newton repeatedly emphasized that true science benefits men and glorifies God.

The relativistic redefinition of science has taken over as the only definition of science. This redefinition explains the origin of the universe and life as entirely material. There is neither a need for nor any room for God or even some unknown kind of Intelligent Design. It ignores any knowledge or observations which contradict its preconceptions. Secular Humanism also ignores or attacks any observations which do not support its claims. Instead of drawing conclusions from the data, it begins with beliefs and attempts to force preconceived conclusions from the data.

Nowhere is this more evident than with the Flood and the *results* of the Flood.

1. Gemstones

Today, corporations produce gems, especially diamonds, under the proper conditions, in days, weeks or months, depending on the size and quality. The Federal Trade Commission wants the term laboratory-grown or laboratory-created instead of synthetic because the final product is identical in

- chemical composition,
- durability,
- gem quality and
- industrial usefulness

to geologic diamonds. Laboratory-created diamonds can be superior to geologic diamonds in industrial applications because the diamond-growing process allows control. One common application is an almost microscopic thin coating of diamond on eyeglasses. According to the FTC, Synthetic diamonds are imitations and chemically different from diamonds. According to the FTC, Synthetic diamonds are not diamonds.[56] In the real world, not everyone follows the FTC guidelines and laboratory produced diamonds are sometimes referred to as synthetic diamonds.

A rose-cut synthetic diamond created by Apollo Diamond using a patented chemical vapour deposition process. May 2006 Source http://www.flickr.com/photos/jurvetson /156830367/ Author Steve Jurvetson Wikimedia Commons

This is evidence of a rapid formation *process*. The time of geologic gem formation is indicated by the presence of ^{14}C (Carbon 14). The presence[57] of ^{14}C in measurable amounts means that the diamonds which were tested were formed less than 55,000 years ago. We should understand that even this date is far too old because it is based on a belief that there were no changes in the past 55,000 years.

2. Petroleum

Petroleum[58] can be produced from a variety of original sources in hours. Petroleum from algae has proven so successful that it is in commercial production.

3. Petrified Wood

Wood can be transformed into petrified wood in less than a week.

Artificial petrified wood,[59] artificial geodes, and artificially-produced fossils are produced cheaply and easily and are available for purchase in stores worldwide. These are also identical to the geologic variety in both chemical composition and appearance.

Artificial Petrified wood under a scanning electron microscope
Wikimedia Commons

4. Coal

Artificial coal[60] has been produced on a small scale for hundreds, perhaps thousands, of years. Artificial coal has been in commercial production since 1910. It is not as popular today because liquid fuels have replaced most of the demand for artificial coal. Geologic or natural coal is so abundant that it is less expensive to mine geologic coal than to convert wood to coal.

Like diamonds, this is evidence of a rapid formation *process*. The time of geologic gem formation is indicated by the presence of ^{14}C (Carbon 14). The presence of ^{14}C in measurable amounts means that the coal which was tested[62] was formed less than 55,000 years ago. We should understand that even this date is far too old because it is based on a belief that there were no changes in the past 55,000 years.

5. Stone

Brick manufacturers have created artificial stone since the 1700s. People have wanted decorative sandstone, granite, marble, slate, shale, and many other stones where natural stone was expensive and difficult to obtain. Artificial stones save on transportation and cutting expenses. Artificial stone can be produced in the desired finished shape. The demand for artificial stone is fueled by cost savings. On the commercial market, cement or concrete made to look like natural stone is even less expensive and is often used in place of commercially produced artificial stone. Cement is materially different from geological stone, but commercially-produced artificial stone is made of identical material to geologic stone. One major difference is that the commercially-produced stone can be manufactured without any blemishes, so is considered superior for countertops, etc. There are three types of artificial stone. First, cement, either painted to look like natural stone or covered with a layer of natural stone.

Second, natural stone is turned to powder then combined with polymers. This technique is commonly used with marble. It is then poured as a liquid into a mold and mass-produced into items such as marble chess pieces. This is the most common technique and the end result is commonly known as "cultured" as in cultured marble or cultured granite.

Third, inexpensive and abundant minerals are transformed using heat and pressure into artificial stone. Like laboratory-produced gems, they are identical to natural stone, so the term "artificial" is misleading.

6. Fossils

Artificially-produced fossils can be so accurate that even the National Geographic Society has purchased them as geologic fossils. Like laboratory-produced gemstones, artificially-produced fossils[63] are recognized because they are "too perfect."

- Diamonds,

- gems,

- petrified wood,

- fossils,

- geodes,

- petroleum,

- coal, and

- stone

can be produced and are being mass-produced today under the proper conditions. The proper conditions are usually

- the correct starting materials,

- enough heat and

- enough pressure.

The proper amount of time varies, depending on what is produced, but is usually a few hours to a few weeks. The tremendous heat and pressure needed to make these transformations not only do not need vast amounts of time. Longer periods of time under extreme pressure with extreme temperatures actually cause the laboratory-produced products to break down.

Observable, verifiable, repeatable science produces diamonds, other gemstones, petrified wood, fossils, geodes, petroleum, coal, and stone today in hours to months. What is the proper word for a belief system which demands that when no one was observing, these items took millions of years to form?

D. Radiohalos: a Very Tiny Mystery

(For more complete information on radiohalos, please go to the referenced books and articles in the "How Much Is Enough?" section.)

The media called the 1981 trial *McLean v Arkansas Board of Education* in the Federal District Court in Little Rock, Arkansas, the "Scopes II" trial. During the trial Dr. G. Brent Dalrymple, who was at that time Assistant Chief Geologist of the US Geological Survey, was the expert witness for the ACLU. Under cross-examination he was asked if he had read Mr. Gentry's work on radiohalos and replied that he had not. Then

Dr. Dalrymple said, "also in Gentry's work, he's proposed *a very tiny mystery*[63] which is balanced on the other side by an enormous amount of evidence. And I think it's important to know what the answer to that little mystery is. But I don't think you can take one little fact for which we now have no answer, and try to balance, say that equals a preponderance of evidence on the other side. That's just not quite the way the scales tip." (Please continue reading for more information about this court case and its significance.)

The term *a very tiny mystery* is an effective propaganda term for those who choose to not think. It implies that the tiny size means tiny in importance or insignificant.

So what is this "very tiny mystery," this "one little fact for which we now have no answer..."? And why is it so important?

   1. What are radiohalos?

The electron microscope was invented in 1931 by two Germans, Max Knott and Ernst Ruska. This allowed men to see for the first time ever, small objects on the molecular level. But men had already viewed with very powerful light microscopes strange, colored, concentric circles found in mica contained in Vosges granite when they were sliced open. *The Genesis of Pleochroic Haloes,* published in 1918, is a record of what J. Joly examined and understood by 1916.

The concentric circles were observed on the smooth surface of cut granite. The radiohalos are actually in biotite, a mica which cooled inside the granite.

It is so thin that each individual slice is translucent. This allows examination of the same set of concentric circles, in different layered slices. The change in diameters in the various layers indicates that what we see as concentric circles on the cut surfaces of the flat slices are actually concentric spheres or concentric shells.

When first viewed, there was some question as to how these beautiful, colored, concentric shells were formed. We are not aware of any serious disagreement that these concentric shells, which are viewed as concentric circles when they are cut open, were formed by radioactive decay. The careful measurement of the size of each shell reveals not only the original element but the exact amount of total radioactive decay. As radioactive isotopes decay, they go through a series of stages. Each stage of radioactive decay emits subatomic alpha particles and each energy level causes the alpha particle to travel a different distance. The decay process emits individual particles, but each one travels in a different direction and each individual particle leaves a tiny visible trail. The visible trail of each one of the millions or more particles in each stage of radioactive decay eventually form a visible spherical shell. Because each particle travels outward from the central core, the inner spheres are darker than the outer spheres. The particles which travel the greatest distance leave a visible trail through each of the older, inner shells. The smallest sphere is the densest and the largest sphere is most transparent. The greatest amount of discoloration is caused by the point at which the alpha particle stops.

Extremely careful measurements reveal both the type of particles and the element. The smallest part of an element is an atom. Atoms are made of subatomic particles. These alpha particles, two protons and two neutrons, are too small to be seen with a light microscope. The radiohalos created by the alpha particles are much larger. Radiohalos can be viewed with a light microscope.

Microscopic radiohalos are common in granite, zircons and other igneous rocks worldwide. Zircons are crystals.

The following is the most common example of a radioactive ^{238}U decay chain.
U = Uranium, Th = Thorium, Ra = Radium, Rn = Radon, Po = Polonium, Pb = Lead

^{238}U is the original material with a half-life of 4,470,000,000 years
^{238}U decays into ^{234}U with a half-life of 245,500 years
^{234}U decays into ^{230}Th with a half-life of 75,400 years
^{230}Th decays into ^{226}Ra with a half-life of 1599 years
^{226}Ra decays into ^{222}Rn with a half-life of 3.823 days
^{222}Rn decays into ^{218}Po with a half-life of 3.04 minutes
^{218}Po decays into ^{214}Po with a half-life of 163.7 microseconds
^{214}Po decays into ^{210}Po with a half-life of 138.4 days
^{210}Po decays into ^{206}Pb which is stable.

In chemistry, the word *stable* is used for an element which is not radioactive and will not change into another element over time by radioactive decay. This means they will not change into another element. Chemical changes such as oxidation which produces rust and fire can still cause changes, but they will still be the same element. Chemical reactions can make various compounds by bonding with other elements but only radioactive changes actually alter the element.

    2. Why are radiohalos important?

Radiohalos exist everywhere we look for them. They are in granite, which makes up every continent and can even be found under the sea. While we include several quotes to give a skeleton overview, the astounding conclusion is explained in detail on both the *Answers In Genesis* and *Institute for Creation Research* websites.

Dr. Snelling's conclusion for the paired uranium/polonium radiohalos found everywhere on earth:

> "So unless the granites cooled quickly, no polonium radiohalos could be present. Thus, the existence of the polonium radiohalos implies that **granites crystallized and cooled within just six to ten days,** not millions of years!"[64] (emphasis mine)

Dr. G. Brent Dalrymple testified under oath in 1981 that radiohalos were a "very tiny mystery" for which "we now have no answer." More than thirty years later, believers in deep time still have no reasonable answer. While creation science in general and Dr. Gentry, the expert witness for the creationist position at the same trial, are vilified, paper after scientific paper have actually supported many of Dr. Gentry's specific conclusions. They simply choose to believe, without evidence, that the formation of radiohalos took place millions of years ago.

Examine this evidence carefully and draw your own conclusions based on the evidence. To do this thoroughly will require looking at more material than we can possible include in this module. Each point is sourced.

> "Biotite flakes[65] consist of layers and layers of ultra-thin crystal sheets, stacked on top of one another like the pages of a book. Wedged between these sheets are tiny zircons (like bookmarks between pages of a book).

> "An additional characteristic of zircons is that they are radioactive. None of the atoms of

pure zirconium silicate are radioactive. However, uranium atoms (which are radioactive) are so similar in size and electric charge to zirconium atoms that they can 'play the part' of zirconium atoms. When zircon crystals form, any uranium atoms in the vicinity can replace zirconium atoms in the zircon's crystal structure."[65]

Radiohalos are found in igneous rock everywhere on the earth's surface, including the deepest boreholes. The tested radiohalos referenced in the above articles are all from biotite samples. Biotite is a mica often found as small black flecks within granite. The majority of granite is found above sea level, because it is lighter than basalt, though some granite is found on the sea floor, particularly the continental shelves.

Here is a part of an open letter[66] written by Dr. Andrew Snelling to Dr. Robert Gentry in 2002. This summary explains in semi-technical language what the evidence is for the current creationist position.

> "... we can provide you with the precise location details (even GPS coordinates in most instances) of every granite sample we have collected..."

> "... let us summarize (all too briefly) the main lines of evidences that convince us (and most other creationist geologists):

> 1. Sedimentary basins ought to be places where granite magmas were generated. Copious phase equilibria laboratory studies demonstrate that, at c. 735°C and 5 kbar in the system $NaAlSi_3O_8$-$KAlSi_3O_8$-SiO_2-H_2O, the minimum point on the liquidus surface upon further cooling produces crystals in the ratio of approximately quartz 30% orthoclase 35% and albite (plagioclase) 35%, which is the exact normative mineral composition of thousands of granite plutons. In many sedimentary basins the deposited sediments with fossils buried in

them can be thousands of meters thick. At depths of 5-10 km, especially in tectonically active zones, the pressures and temperatures can reach 5 kbar and 735°C respectively. These phase equilibria experiments indicate that, under such conditions, the fossiliferous sediments would partially melt to form granitic magmas. Less dense than the surrounding residues, the magmas would then rise through fractures to intrude into the overlying fossiliferous sediments. Subsequent erosion has exposed at the Earth's surface the cooled granite bodies intruded into those fossiliferous sediments.[66]

2. Regional relationships provide evidence for an igneous origin of granites. In the field it is possible to literally walk over the outcrops from fossiliferous sedimentary rocks through zones of metamorphosed sedimentary rocks, whose mineral constituents reflect the increasing temperatures and pressures of regional metamorphism (these temperatures and pressures being verified by many phase equilibria experiments), to where the felsic minerals in the metasedimentary rocks have melted to form migmatites, and then finally to where at temperatures around 735°C and pressures of 5 kbar and above the whole rock melted to form granite (with the Qz 30% Or 35% Ab 35% composition). One classic example is the Cooma Granodiorite in the centre of the Cooma metamorphic complex in southeastern Australia. Other examples abound, in Scotland, Germany and elsewhere, including the Zoroaster Granite in the Grand Canyon, and the Harney Peak Granite in South Dakota.

3. Local boundaries argue for an igneous origin of granites. In the field, and in three dimensions within mines (both open cast and underground), the effects on the host rocks of the intrusion of hot granitic magmas can be observed, including veining, stoping and contact metamorphism. The most spectacular examples of the latter are skarns, where granitic magmas have metamorphosed limestones to produce new minerals under high temperature and pressure conditions which have been verified by phase equilibria experiments. And the hot magmatic fluids from the granites have introduced metals into the resultant skarns, such as W at Grassy, King Island, Tasmania and Cu at Grassberg, West Papua, Indonesia. I spent weeks mapping the boundary of the Bathurst Granite west of Sydney for my B.Sc. (Honours) thesis in 1974, noting the veining, stoping and contact metamorphism of the host fossiliferous sedimentary strata in outcrops and in cuttings along the main western railroad from Sydney.[66]

"Bob, when we found Po radiohalos alongside U radiohalos in the same biotite flakes in the Cooma Granodiorite we had to rethink what the radiohalos are telling us. We fully agree with you that the Po radiohalos formed exceedingly rapidly, so this granodiorite must have formed rapidly during the Flood. This is exciting evidence that granites intrude and cool rapidly (within days). It is also thus evidence that the U radiohalos formed rapidly, so U decay had to have been accelerated during the Flood year."[66]

While the letter to Dr. Gentry is an excellent summary of the evidence, most people will not understand the significance of these points in this letter. The following quotes come from the third part of a three-part series published by *Answers In Genesis*. The conclusion is so astounding that he uses three pages of explanations and foundational material before writing it. The conclusion is based on the same evidence that was written in summary to Dr. Gentry.[67]

"The implications are astounding. At least 500 million uranium-238 atoms had to alpha decay within a few hours or days. The equivalent of '100 million years' of uranium-238 decay had to occur within hours!

"Thus, the decay rate of uranium had to be nearly a billion times faster in the past than it is today! And if uranium decayed at such an accelerated rate, then other radioactive elements, which are even less stable, must have also decayed much faster.

"Yet long-age dating methods assume that the radioactive decay rates have never changed. The very existence of the polonium radiohalos is evidence that the radioactive rates were accelerated in the past. This means that dates for rocks of billions of years must be questioned, as the rocks are in fact only thousands of years old." (material skipped)

"The rapid formation of polonium radiohalos has another astounding implication for earth history.

"The granite masses that contain the radiohalos are typically cubic miles in size and originally formed under ground from molten magmas at temperatures between 650°C and 705°C (1200-1300°F). It is usually claimed that they thus take millions of years to crystallize and cool. [67]

"4. Since radiohalos can survive only at and below 150°C (302°F), based on observed evidence,

"5. The radiohalos had to be generated very
late in the granite formation process
(Figure 2). By this time, though, most of
the polonium would have decayed away.
Any polonium halos that might have
formed would be destroyed by the heat."

"So unless the granites cooled quickly, no
polonium radiohalos could be present. Thus,
*the existence of the polonium radiohalos
implies that granites crystallized and cooled
within just six to ten days, not millions of
years!*[emphasis added]

"Uranium and polonium radiohalos found
together in the same biotite flakes thus
provide startling evidence of past catastrophic
geological processes acting on a young earth.
During Day Three of Creation Week (about six
thousand years ago) and again during the
year-long Genesis Flood (about 4,300 years
ago) sediments were eroded and deposited
catastrophically on a global scale.

"6. Rapid earth movements pushed up
mountains and melting of rocks formed
granite bodies quickly.

"7. Inside these granites, super-fast
radioactive decay generated uranium and
polonium radiohalos rapidly.

Though the radiohalos are so microscopic they
could easily be overlooked, their abundance in
granites all around the world cannot be
ignored."[67]

For extremely helpful charts and graphs, please see the
original article series on the *Answers in Genesis* (AiG)
website. There are many similar articles throughout the
AiG website. *The Institute for Creation Research* (ICR)
helped fund this project and also has many helpful
similar articles.

Once again, the Word of God does not tell us what
triggered the Flood. Like the statement of Dr. Snelling

in the letter to Dr. Gentry says, we "had to rethink what the radiohalos are telling us." That is the responsibility of science. As more evidence becomes available, we might have to once again rethink what the evidence is telling us.

An extremely important point is the phrase, "Uranium and polonium radiohalos found together." (The endnote also sources the graphic.)[68]

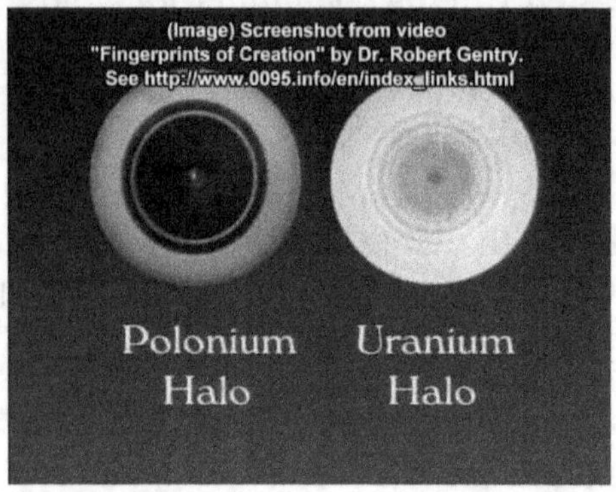

While the referenced articles explain in detail, this means that while the rocks we see were forming (a process which required great heat), water carried the core of the decaying radioisotope, which began as uranium, a tiny distance while it was radon gas. As the radioisotope decayed further to polonium, the same core formed a second radiohalo, usually less than a micron from the original radiohalo.

> "The problem is that polonium[69] is never found alone in rocks. It is a rare, unstable element that appears quickly during the decay of uranium and then decays into stable elements, such as lead. The only possible source of the polonium was the decay of uranium."

> "Yet under normal conditions, like those we see in the earth today, that migration would be impossible."

It is interesting to note that this observation was first made and published by uniformitarians to discredit Dr. Robert Gentry's work. Dr. Gentry concluded that radiohalos were formed during the original creation. As Wakefield's paper attacking Dr. Gentry says [see the next section]"I will hypothesize that the uranium, and hence the polonium, were deposited by precipitation from circulating fluids." He also said, "The geology of the sites shows that the uranium, and most likely the polonium, were deposited via postmagmatic hydrothermal fluids."

These comments, though written to attack the creationist position, actually support the thesis that they were formed during the Flood. They have backtracked and now say they were formed from a "secondary" fluid transport, that is, the Po halo was transported twice. For a detailed explanation of why this is not possible please see the ICR article "Polonium Radiohalos Still A Very Tiny Mystery."[70]

> "The right conditions for the formation of the granite containing the biotite mica and zircons filled with radiohalos which we observe today, lasted only 6-10 days. Granite is found on every continent. Radiohalos as described in these articles are found in abundance throughout the surface of the earth. **They are not rare.**"[71]

The following is based on the best current information, but we might have to "rethink what the (future discoveries) are telling us."

Radiohalos indicate that radiometric clocks did not begin at creation, but that the radioactive material which is used for radiometric clocks was formed during the Flood. It is easy to understand why this seems so difficult to accept. Is this evidence is being interpreted correctly? The material that all radiometric clocks are based on are assumed to have an "origin point." The evidence points to a worldwide "origin point" for all radiometric clocks with the flood, not creation.

3. The Uniformitarian Answer?

More complete information is available in The Uniformitarian Answer Appendix.

Author's Note: Wikipedia is usually considered an inferior reference source and many discourage quoting from it. We quote it here, however, because it presents in clear, complete fashion, the position of secularists on radiohalos, and is the easiest way to show how biased and anti-scientific that position is. It is also a common position held by the majority of scientists.

In a 2013 article on radiohalos Wikipedia[72] says, "The most widely accepted explanation is that the discolouration is caused by alpha particles emitted by the nuclei; the radius of the concentric shells are proportional to the particle's energy (Henderson & Bateson, 1934) The phenomenon of radiohalos has been known to geologists since the early part of the 20th century, but wider interest was prompted by the claims of creationist Robert V. Gentry that radiohalos in biotite are evidence for a young earth (Gentry 1992). These claims are rejected by the scientific community as an example of creationist pseudoscience (Wakefield, 1988)."

The sentences are juxtapositioned to imply that creationists either do not believe the Henderson & Bateson paper or that creationists arrive at different conclusions from the Henderson & Bateson paper. Neither is true. The understanding that "the discolouration is caused by alpha particles emitted by the nuclei; the radius of the concentric shells are proportional to the particle's energy" is foundational to a creationist understanding of radiohalos. It is also explained and expounded on in great detail in creationist literature, including Dr. Gentry's book *Creation's Tiny Mystery*.

The cited Wakefield paper frequently calls Creation Science "pseudoscience," but never proves its point or even presents hard evidence. Wakefield simply makes a lengthy series of gratuitous assertions. Calling Creation Science "pseudoscience" without hard evidence is the standard secular humanist position. The same false charges were made in the 1981 *McLean v Arkansas*

Board of Education trial. The Wakefield paper follows the *McLean v Arkansas Board of Education* excerpt.

Here are a few brief excerpts from testimony by Dr. G. Brent Dalrymple, the ACLU expert testifying in *McLean v Arkansas Board of Education* 1981. He testified under oath in December 1981 representing the ACLU. The text of the trial transcript is from *Creation's Tiny Mystery* by Dr. Robert V Gentry, p. 122 and following. A longer excerpt is available in the Uniformitarian Answer appendix.

A. "But, you know, the scientific literature and even the Creation Science literature, which I do not consider scientific literature. It's outside the traditional literature. There is an enormously complex business. There is a lot of it. And we can't review it all."

"...given the limited amount of time that I have to put in on this, reviewing the Creation Science literature is not a terribly productive thing for a scientist to do."

Q: How many articles or books have you reviewed, approximately?

A: You mean in Creation Science literature?

Q: Creation Science literature.

A: I think it was approximately twenty-four or twenty-five, something like that, as best I can remember. I gave you a complete list, which is as accurate as I can recall.

Q: And if there were articles in the open scientific literature: Excuse me, in refereed journals which supported the Creation Science model, would that not be something you would want to look at in trying to review the Creation Science literature?

A: Yes, and I did look at a number of those. And I still found no evidence.

Q: But you didn't look at any from Mr. Gentry?

A: No, I did not. That's one I didn't get around to. There's quite a few others I haven't gotten around to. I probably never will look into all the creationists' literature. I can't even look into all the legitimate scientific literature. But I can go so far as to say that every case that I have looked into in detail has had very, very serious flaws. And I think I've looked at a representative sample.

And also in Gentry's work, he's proposed *a very tiny mystery* which is balanced on the other side by an enormous amount of evidence. And I think it's important to know what the answer to that little mystery is. But I don't think you can take one little fact for which we now have no answer, and try to balance, say that equals a preponderance of evidence on the other side. That's just not quite the way the scales tip.

THE WITNESS: Well, basically what he has found is there is a series of radioactive haloes within minerals in the rocks. Many minerals like mica include very tiny particles of other minerals that are radioactive, little crystals of zircon and things like that, that have a lot of uranium in them.

And as the uranium decays, the alpha particles will not decay, but travel outward through the mica. And they cause radiation damage in the mica around the radioactive particle. And the distance that those particles travel is indicated by these radioactive haloes. And that distance is related directly to the energy of the decay.

And from the energy of the decay, it is thought that we can identify the isotopes.

That's the kind of work that Gentry has been doing.

And what he has found is that he has identified certain haloes which he claims are from Pollonium-212 [sic, polonium-218; correct form of the chemical elements used hereafter]. Now, polonium-218 is one of the isotopes intermediate in the decay chain between uranium and lead.

Uranium doesn't decay directly from [sic, to] lead. It goes through a whole series of intermediate products, each of which is radioactive and in turn decays.

Polonium-218 is derived in this occasion from radon-222. And what he has found is that the polonium haloes, and this is what he claims to have found, are the polonium-218 haloes, but not radon-222 haloes. And therefore, he says that the polonium could not have come from the decay of radium, therefore it could not have come from the normal decay change [sic, chains].

And he says, how did it get there? And then he says that the only way it could have gotten there unsupported by radon-222 decay is to have been primordial polonium, that is polonium that was created at the time the solar system was created, or the universe.

Well, the problem with that is polonium-218 has a half-life of only about three minutes, I believe it is. So that if you have a granitic body, a rock that comes from the melt, that contains this mica, and it cools down, it takes millions of years for a body like that to cool.

[p. 126]

> So that by the time the body cooled, all the polonium would have decayed, since it has an extremely short half-life. Therefore, there would be no polonium in the body to cause the polonium haloes."

Though Dr. G. Brent Dalrymple makes *several very important technical mistakes*, he correctly states the basic issue. With trillions of polonium radiohalos next to uranium radiohalos found worldwide and such a short half-life, where did the polonium come from?

The Geology of Gentry's "Tiny Mystery." 1988 by J.R. Wakefield is the source cited by *Wikipedia, Talkorigins* and others as "proof" of "creationist pseudoscience." The opening abstract of the article says,

> "The unusual polonium halos described by Robert Gentry have been a problem for some years now. Gentry claimed that the polonium halos show that the Precambrian granite they are hosted in were 'instantly created.'"

(Some quote material omitted)

> "Some research on the halos has been carried out by other scientists, but most of it has been aimed at solving the problems of the peculiar configuration of these halos. Fortunately, Gentry provided two specific site locations in the Canadian Shield where his samples came from. The geological setting of these sites shows conclusively that Gentry's notion of an 'instantly created' earth composed of granite is false. Specifically the samples came from crystallized rocks which can be shown to crosscut several sedimentary and other plutonic rocks. Some of the sedimentary rocks contain stromatolites. The geology of the sites shows that the uranium, and most likely the polonium, were deposited via postmagmatic hydrothermal fluids. Besides ignoring the geology at his collection areas, Gentry also makes numerous grossly erroneous

generalizations about the origin of plutonic rocks."

After three pages of attacks on creationists, he finally states his thesis.

"I do not intend to discuss the physics of halos in this paper. What I will describe here is the geology of three of the locations where some of Gentry's biotite samples came from: the Fission Mine, the Silver Crater Mine and the Faraday Mine, all near Bancroft in southern Ontario (see Figure 1). On the basis of the geology of the sample sites. I will hypothesize that the uranium, and hence the polonium, were deposited by precipitation from circulating fluids."

All of J.R. Wakefield boils down to

1) He is not going to "discuss the physics of halos" and

2) "the uranium, and hence the polonium, were deposited by precipitation from circulating fluids."

The rest of this paper is immaterial because his second point, which is his thesis, is exactly the position of almost all creationists today. We completely agree with his thesis, "the uranium, and hence the polonium, were deposited by precipitation from circulating fluids." The mechanism of *how* that happened, which determines *when* it happened, is the issue, but that is not discussed in this paper. So nothing in the cited source supports Wikipedia's false assertion that Creationism is pseudoscience.

Longer quotes from Wakefield and *McLean v Arkansas* are available in the Uniformitarian Answer appendix.

This material is included in this text because these are the standard arguments Secular Humanists use to promote their religion. You will encounter these arguments and you should understand that these arguments are erroneous.

We could examine thousands of pages of similar material by many different authors, but every uniformitarian paper I am aware of handles the issue of radiohalos the same way. The lengthy, complex arguments can always be boiled down to one or more of these three points.

> Uniformitarians are in the majority. The majority is right because we are the majority. Creationism is wrong because we, the majority, say so.

> Other unnamed evidence proves deep time so whatever evidence radiohalos have must be brought into line with the concept of deep time.

> On occasion, uniformitarians will discuss certain individual aspects of radiohalos. Whenever uniformitarians actually "discuss" any individual aspect of radiohalos, these extremely narrow studies agree with creationist theories on those individual points.

4. What Triggered the Flood?

The answer to the question of what triggered the Flood is probably the same answer as what created radiohalos and accelerated nuclear decay. As stated many times, this work is based on the best information available today, but might need to be altered in the future when more or better information becomes available. Massive volcanic activity could produce this type of heat. But is the volcanic activity a cause or simply a result?

Svend Buhl Chelyabinsk Meteorite Recon fragment Wikimedia Commons

On February 15, 2013, a meteor (or comet) exploded over Chelyabinsk,[73] Russia, east of Moscow and over the Ural mountains. The meteor (or comet) left a trail thousands of miles long before breaking apart in an explosion 16-19 miles above the mountains. The mass was estimated to be at least 10,000 tons. 20 infrasonic monitors were triggered, including a station in Alaska, after the shock waves had circled the globe three times. The explosion was at least the equivalent of 460 tons of TNT. Thousands of small fragments were recovered.

> "What's remarkable about the Russian mega-meteor is how little of it has been found. According to Buhl and Wimmer, the combined mass of the submitted finds is just 117 pounds (53 kg)."[199]

The largest fragment was found at the bottom of Chebarkul Lake. This fragment had a total mass of 654 kg (1,442 lb).[74]

There was a far more powerful explosion over Tunguska, [75] Siberia, Russia, in 1908.

> "Through comparison of old seismograms of the Tunguska event and seismograms of the decaya [probably should be Navaya Zemlya] Zemlya and Lop-Nor nuclear-weapon tests, Ben-Menahem (1975) determined that the Tunguska projectile had "the effects of an Extraterrestrial Nuclear Missile of yield 12.5 ± 2.5 megatons." This is approximately 3 orders of magnitude greater than the Hiroshima A-bomb and about one-fifth the energy of the largest hydrogen bomb explosion (McWhirter and McWhirter 1974). The height at which the explosion occurred was estimated to be approximately 7.5 km, with a total energy release of approximately 3×102^{3} ergs, 5×10^{18} ergs of which was changed into seismic energy (Ben-Menahem 1975). More energy went into the air blast than the earthquake. F.J.W. Whipple (1930) estimated the energy of the air blast wave to be 3.2×10^{20}

ergs. The seismic activity measured on the Richter scale was 5.0; and the air compression wave went twice around the world, according to recordings at meteorological stations."[75]

(Material skipped)

"The temperature at the center of the fireball was estimated by one source to be up to 30 million degrees Fahrenheit (LeMaire 1980). Some storage huts in the nearby vicinity of the focus were found devastated by fire and the silverware and tin utensils within were deformed by intense heat. "Preceding the front of the shock wave there arises a heated zone whose radiating surface area is far larger than that of the shock wave itself." (Stanyukovich and Bronshten 1961). This is substantiated by Semedec who first felt the heat wave, then was thrown to the ground by the air shock wave.

The inhabitants of Central Siberia saw the fall and explosion of the meteorite over an area with a radius of 600-1000 km. Eighty million trees in the taiga (coniferous forest) were uprooted and blown down for a radius of 30-40 km (F.J.W. Whipple 1934). Some trees on the leeward side of hills were somewhat protected, yet still had their branches broken off and bark stripped to leave them standing naked, resembling telegraph poles.

After the impact, forest fires broke out and ravaged an area of 10-15 km in radius (Astapowitsch 1934). Kridec (1960) describes these forest fires as being unnatural. The trunks of trees and their branches were not burned through but were only scorched on the surface. Apparently a searing heat wave caused the scorching, yet a conventional forest fire was not present. Some trees were entirely scorched in standing position, but were bent away from the epicenter. In normal fires in the Vadecara area, trees remained vertical with fire damage occurring at the lower sections while the tree tops remained untouched. It is also interesting to note that some trees which had been stripped of bark showed no signs of scorching (Kridec 1963)."

"The Tunguska explosion is indeed unique and mysterious. Of the possible causes it appears that the present consensus favors the comet hypothesis. However, suggesting a consensus is quite tenuous. Though the other theories have plausibility, they have difficulty explaining the observed event and the resulting physical evidence." [201]

Only a few small fragments were ever found, and a small impact crater.

By contrast, near Winslow, Arizona is the most well-known and best-preserved impact crater in the world. It is almost a mile across and almost 600 feet deep. Impact was estimated to be 26,000 mph with a force more than 20 million tons of TNT. Over the years, estimates of the size of the impact meteorite have changed considerably, but the current estimate is 300,000 tons.[76]

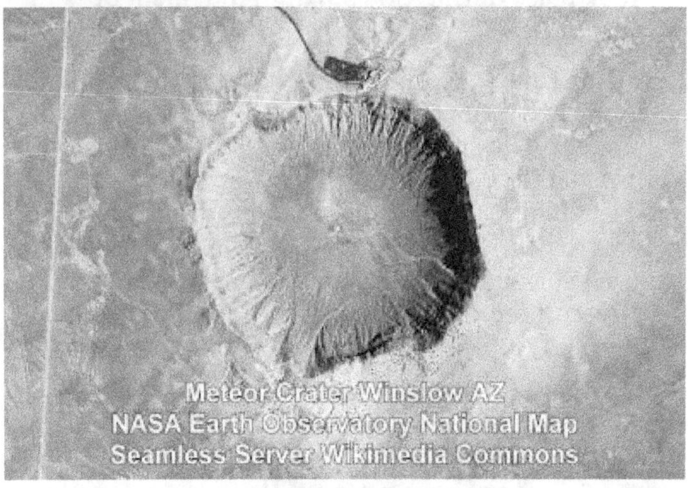

In 1960 "the minerals coesite and stishovite, rare forms of silica found only where quartz-bearing rocks have been severely shocked by an instantaneous overpressure" were found in the crater. "It cannot be created by volcanic action; the only known mechanism of creating it is through an impact event (or artificially through a nuclear explosion)."[77]

"The kinetic energy of the meteorite is estimated by scaling to have been from 1.4 to 1.7 megatons TNT equivalent."[77]

> "According to the Flood model, the first 71 of these 110 impacts would have occurred during the year of the Flood, and the other 39 were spread out over the 4,500 years since the Flood."[78]

> Material skipped

> "We cannot be certain whether God used an asteroid or swarms of asteroids to begin the Flood event and the resulting breakup of the earth's crust into plates. However, we do find evidence that asteroids were striking the earth at catastrophic rates during the Flood and that these asteroids were spread over the earth's surface. Asteroids surely contributed greatly to the horrific and violent geologic events that took place during God's year of judgment of the earth."[78]

Wikipedia lists 44 "confirmed"[79] impact craters and 14 "unconfirmed" craters between 20 and 600 kilometers in diameter. The smallest of these 58 impact craters is 20 times larger than the meteor crater in Arizona. The smallest of these would cause massive destruction. If these were nearly simultaneous, the impacts and the resulting volcanic activity would almost certainly trigger a continental breakup, flood, massive volcanic activity, and would certainly be an extinction level event (ELE).

E. Radiometric Dating

Radiometric dating combined with fossils in strata are the foundational pillars of "evidence" used by uniformitarians to support their beliefs. Since all forms of radiometric dating are based on foundational assumptions we will examine those assumptions in detail. We will also introduce several of the more popular dating methods, though each of these methods makes the same assumptions.

There are many of types of radiometric dating. Carbon-14 is fraught with potential pitfalls, but is still very usable. Neither rocks nor fossils should have any ^{14}C (Carbon-14). Since ^{14}C is used to date organisms which were once alive, it will be the subject of future modules.

1. Foundational assumptions

The foundational assumptions of radiometric dating[80] might be somewhat difficult to grasp. The following illustration of an hourglass by Mike Riddle is simple, easy to understand, and at the same time accurately communicates. You walk into a room and an hourglass has about half of its sand in the top and about half in the bottom. The first piece of information you need is how much time is the "hourglass" designed to run for? That is, how much time will elapse from the first grain of sand falling from the top until the last grain of sand empties into the bottom? One minute? One hour? Twelve hours? To know the current time based on the hourglass in front of you, then you must know the following:

Radiometric dating has many similarities to the hourglass illustration. An original amount of material is carefully measured as it changes from one state to another state. Like the hourglass, an accurate reading depends on certain assumptions.

a. Original had no daughter material

First and most important is the assumption that the sample being tested began its existence with no daughter material. (There was no "sand at the bottom of the hourglass" in the beginning). The testers assume it only contained parent material. If this one assumption is incorrect, then the age of the sample is drastically younger. For example, if the tested sample began its existence with only $\frac{1}{2}$ of parent material and $\frac{1}{2}$ daughter material, then the calculations for the age of the sample would only go back $\frac{1}{2}$ as far. So whatever age was calculated by the test of the sample, the actual age would be no more than $\frac{1}{2}$ of the tested age.

So just taking this one assumption into account, if the sample tested came back with a result of 800,000 years old, but this sample began its existence with parent material being only half of the entire mass of the material, then the actual age would be only 400,000 years old. Yet no one can know the original condition of the material.

b. Samples Are Rarely, or Never, Contaminated

The second assumption is nothing contaminated the sample during its existence. (Sand was neither taken out nor added to the hourglass) The uniformitarians correctly point out that samples from the same strata all over the world test the same so any possible contamination would have to be worldwide. This worldwide contamination does not have to be the Flood, but for their radiometric clocks to be accurate uniformitarians have the burden of proof to prove that such contamination never happened. Localized, recent contamination, such as rocks near nuclear blasts, is well-known and well-documented. Simply to assume that such contamination never occurred is not science. This is especially bad science in light of the uniformitarian belief that "extinction events" ended five of the supposed geologic periods.

c. The Rate of Decay Is Inviolate

The third assumption used to be considered inviolate, that nothing can alter the rate of radioactive decay. (Nothing could increase or decrease the rate of the sand falling)

A Forbes article based on a combined Stanford/Purdue study:

"Radioactive Decay Rates May Not Be Constant After All"[81]

One of the researchers observed, "What we're suggesting is that something that doesn't really interact with anything is changing something that can't be changed."

Neutrinos from the sun seem to be slightly altering decay rates on earth.

> "Checking data collected at Brookhaven
> National Laboratory on Long Island and the
> Federal Physical and Technical Institute in
> Germany, they came across something even
> more surprising: long-term observation of the
> decay rate of silicon-32 and radium-226
> seemed to show a small seasonal variation.
> The decay rate was ever so slightly faster in
> winter than in summer." [81]

The decay[82] rate change noticed by the Stanford/Purdue study is very small, yet quite noticeable. The variations are seasonable and coincide with variations in recorded neutrino output from the sun. Neutrinos travel through the entire earth without any known variations. As the article states, neutrinos do not "really interact with anything," and that includes traveling through the earth's core.

The only known way of detecting neutrinos is to observe Cherenkov light[83] in tanks of water deep underground. That is not an observation of neutrinos directly, or even secondary interaction. It is an indirect result of interaction of other actions as they pass through the water. (Please see the image from the Idaho National Laboratory below.)

The important fact is that neutrinos in some unknown indirect way alters radioactive decay rates. They can do this even after they have traveled through the earth. It is now understood that even without contamination from what is traditionally considered to be outside sources, decay rates can alter. We acknowledge that these neutrinos might be considered contamination from an outside source. However, at this point in time, there is no evidence that the solar neutrino output is directly affecting the rate of radioactive decay.

"Samples from Idaho National Laboratory's
Advanced Test Reactor (ATR) core
will be sent to Argonne's ATLAS
particle accelerator for analysis to learn
the characteristics of the nuclear material.
Powered up, the fuel plates can be seen
glowing bright blue. The core is
submerged in water for cooling. "

This is an image from the Idaho National
Laboratory's ATR.
8 April 2009 Matt Howard Wikimedia Commons

A far more massive, but less well-known, alteration in radioactive decay rates was documented with ^{187}Re-^{187}Os.

"... Decay has been experimentally demonstrated in the rhenium-osmium (^{187}Re-^{187}Os) system. (The Re-Os method is one of the isotopic 'clocks' used by uniformitarian geologists to supposedly date rocks.) The experiment involved the circulation of fully-ionized ^{187}Re in a storage ring. The ^{187}Re ions were found to decay to a measurable extent in only several hours, amounting to a half-life of only 33 years. This represents a staggering

117

billion-fold increase over the conventional half-life, which is 42 Ga! (Ga = giga-annum = a billion (10^9) years)."[84]

While we readily acknowledge that future discoveries might change our understanding, it seems that no longer is the issue "can decay rates change?", but "how much do they change and why?"

2. Problems and Failures of radiometric dating

Mt Ngauruhoe[85] in New Zealand has erupted dozens of times since Europeans first recorded a steam eruption in 1839.

> "Eleven 2-3 kg samples were collected two each from the February 11, 1949, June 4, 1954, and July 14, 1954 lava flows and from the February 19, 1975 avalanche deposits, and three from the June 30, 1954 lava flows."
> by Dr. Snelling

> The *Answers In Genesis* article is a semi-technical, detailed "abstract" of the technical ICR article. The information is the same in both articles. If you are simply interested in easier reading or if you have difficulty understanding the original ICR article, the AIG article is excellent.

> "The samples were sent progressively in batches to Geochron Laboratories in Cambridge, Boston (USA), for whole-rock potassium-argon (K-Ar) dating: first a piece of one sample from each flow, then a piece of the second sample from each flow after the first set of results was received, and finally, a piece of the third sample from the 30 June 1954 flow. To also test the consistency of results within samples, second pieces of two of the 30 June 1954 lava samples were also sent for analysis.[85]

> "Geochron is a respected commercial laboratory, the K-Ar lab manager having a Ph.D. in K-Ar dating. No specific location or

expected age information was supplied to the laboratory. However, the samples were described as probably young with very little argon in them so as to ensure extra care was taken during the analytical work."

(Material skipped)

"The "ages" range from <0.27 to 3.5 (± 0.2) million years for rocks which were observed to have cooled from lavas 25 -50 years ago."
By Dr. Snelling[85]

There is a table at the end of each article which details samples, how they were prepared and analyzed, and the results.

The final sentence of the twenty-page article concludes "There may, in fact, be some pattern or systematic way in which 'excess ^{40}Ar' has been trapped in rocks and occluded in minerals at different levels (depths and relative ages) in the geological record. If so, then K-Ar and ^{40}Ar/ ^{39}Ar "dating" would irrevocably be discredited."[85]

Dr. Andrew Snelling

by Dr. Snelling[86]

While the whole-rock potassium-argon (K-Ar) dating example above is very solid and properly documented, it is also a very tiny tip of a very large iceberg. Here are just a few more brief examples.

"A 1986 dacite lava dome at Mt St Helens volcano gave a (K-Ar) 'date' of method as 0.35 ± 0.5 million years old."[87]

Samples were taken from Mt. St. Helens.

> "In June of 1992, Dr Austin collected a 7-kg (15-lb) block of dacite from high on the lava dome. A portion of this sample was crushed and milled into a fine powder. Another piece was crushed and the various mineral crystals were carefully separated out. The 'whole rock', rock powder, and four-mineral concentrates were submitted for potassium-argon analysis to Geochron Laboratories of Cambridge, MA a high-quality, professional radioisotope-dating laboratory. The only information provided to the laboratory was that the samples came from dacite and that 'low argon' should be expected. The laboratory was not told that the specimen came from the lava dome at Mount St Helens and was only 10 years old."[88]

> Because the preceding example uses only one laboratory , Geochron Laboratories of Cambridge, MA, and only one radiometric method, K-Ar, some might mistakenly *assume* that there is either a problem with an incorrect reading from one particular laboratory or a problem with just one particular method. Further examination of the evidence proves this to be an incorrect assumption. Please understand that this brief module can only provide a very limited number of examples, though many other examples exist.

One serious issue which is commonplace yet never mentioned in radiometric dating is the same sample is tested using different methods with vastly different results. The following is just one of many examples. The Cardenas Basalt lava flows in the Grand Canyon were tested several ways.

"The claimed age of 1,103±66 million years was obtained using the rubidium-strontium isochron method with 10 samples and has been regarded as the best radioactive dating result for any Grand Canyon rock unit. Nevertheless, potassium-argon model "ages" for each of 15 individual Cardenas Basalt samples range from 577±12 to 1,013±37 million years, while the potassium-argon isochron "age" obtained using 14 samples is only 516±30 million years. This is less than half the rubidium-strontium isochron "age" of 1,111±81 million years obtained using 19 samples. It is also less than the claimed Cambrian age of the Tapeats Sandstone that sits on top of, and well above the Cardenas Basalt lavas (Figure 4). Worse still, the samarium-neodymium isochron "age" obtained using 8 samples is 1,588±170 million years: more than three times the potassium-argon isochron "age" of 516±30 million years!"[89]

"During several raft trips through Grand Canyon, many samples of these 'Brahma' amphibolites were collected from various outcrops in the Inner Gorge. These included seven samples from a single amphibolite body."[91]

Footnote 6 "These samples were collected with a Scientific Research and Collecting Permit issued by the Grand Canyon National Park, as part of the RATE (Radioisotopes and the Age of The Earth) project." [216]

"All the samples were sent to two well-respected commercial laboratories for radioisotope testing."

Footnote 8 "'Whole rock' samples were analyzed in all cases: K-Ar at Activation Laboratories, Ancaster, Ontario, Canada; Rb-Sr, Sm-Nd and Pb-Pb at the PRISE Laboratory, Research School of Earth Sciences, Australian National University, Canberra, Australia."

"The 'black, metamorphosed basalt flows called amphibolites' were metamorphosed approximately 1,700 million years ago based on U-Pb dating.

"The results of the new tests 'for each of the 27 amphibolite samples from Grand Canyon' for the time they were metamorphosed ranged from 'potassium-argon (K-Ar)' '405.1 ± 10 Ma (million years) to 2,574.2 ± 73 Ma.' That is a six-fold difference, for samples that should be of similar age."

"Rb-Sr "age" of 1240 ± 84 Ma from 19 of the 27 samples,"

"Sm-Nd "age" of 1,655 ± 40 Ma from 21 samples"

"Pb-Pb "age" of 1,883 ± 53 Ma from 20 samples"

"the 'isochron discordance' is pronounced. Figure 8 graphically illustrates how that, even when the calculated error margins are taken into account, the different radioisotope dating methods yield vastly different 'ages' that cannot be reconciled."[216]

Please remember that these are just examples. The discrepancies are far greater than these few examples can begin to illustrate. The problem of vastly different dates from the same sample using different radiometric methods is usually not noticed because of the tremendous cost of radiometric testing. Usually a geologist makes an estimate based on other factors, then has the sample(s) tested by the one method he believes to be the most reliable. So it is unusual to find a geologic area, feature or stratum ever tested by more than one radiometric method.

> "It should be noted that dates obtained by different (radiometric) methods commonly show some discrepancies... As the Committee on the Measurement of Geological Time said in 1950, 'These figures are, as railway timetables say, subject to change without notice.'"[91]

3. Compared to Helium diffusion rates

While there are several indicators of altered decay rates in the past, one is helium diffusion rates in zircons. Zircon crystals usually vary in size from microscopic to grains of sand. In these zircon crystals there are both uranium atoms and helium atoms. The helium atoms are present in the zircon crystals as a result of the decay of the uranium isotopes. Since helium defuses out of the zircons naturally, the question is why is there so much helium still in the zircon crystals? There are only four possible answers.

a. Physics involved is not understood

This is always a possibility, but in this case is highly unlikely. If "We do not understand the physics involved" is the correct answer, then we need to develop new theories of physics to explain our observations.

b. samples tested are anomalies

The zircons tested are anomalies, and retesting other zircons from other locations will provide different results. Since the original tests were performed, other zircons from other locations were tested with similar results, proving these were not anomalies.

c. test results contaminated

The test results are due to contamination, misreading the data, or some other human error. These issues have been examined repeatedly for over a decade and there is no indication that there was any contamination, misreading of the data, or any other type of human error.

> d. zircons are less than 6000 years old

The zircons are less than 6000 years old and something altered the decay rate of the Uranium. The original test samples were from a borehole near Los Alamos varying from 700 to 4,310 meters.

> "Two decades ago,[92] Robert Gentry and his colleagues at Oak Ridge National Laboratory reported surprisingly high amounts of nuclear-decay-generated helium in tiny radioactive zircons recovered from Precambrian crystalline rock, the Jemez Granodiorite on the west flank of the volcanic Valles Caldera near Los Alamos, New Mexico (Gentry, Glish, & McBay, 1982). Up to 58% of the helium (that radioactivity would have generated during the alleged 1.5 billion year age of the granodiorite) was still in the zircons. Yet the zircons were so small that they should not have retained the helium for even a tiny fraction of that time. The high helium retention levels suggested to us and many other creationists that the helium simply had not had enough time to diffuse out of the zircons, and that *recent accelerated nuclear decay had produced over a billion years worth of helium within only the last few thousand years*, during Creation and/or the Flood. Such acceleration would reduce the radioisotopic time scale from megayears down to months."[92] [emphasis mine]

Dr. Russell Humphreys

The following is a response[93] by Dr. Russell Humphreys to criticisms of the original paper.

"In 2001 we commissioned one of the world's most respected experimenters in this field to measure the diffusivity of helium in the same-size zircons from the same borehole in the same rock formation. We used an existing mining company as an intermediary, and we asked it to not tell the experimenter about us or our goals. The experimenter, being a uniformitarian (believer in long ages) and not having read our prediction, had no idea what results we were hoping for. It was a truly "blind" experiment, and we (the RATE team) were eagerly awaiting the data."[93]

(Paragraph omitted)

"To our great delight, the data fell right on the '6000 year' prediction! This alignment validates the young-age model even for readers who are not experts in this field, because the probability of such a lineup by accident is small. The data resoundingly reject the "1.5 billion year" model. The experimenter, whose name is in one of our articles, stands by his data, even though as a uniformitarian he does not like our interpretation of them. (Even after several years, he has not offered an alternative interpretation.)

This sequence of events places the burden of disproof on the critics, because they must explain how, if there is no truth to our model, the data "accidentally by sheer coincidence just happened by blind chance" to fall right on the predictions of our model." [93]

There are other indicators of altered radioactive decay rates, but these two examples were chosen because:

- Everyone involved in the Stanford/Purdue study was a uniformitarian. The information is readily available to anyone who wants to examine the evidence.

- The Helium Diffusion Rate information matches the conclusions of the Polonium radiohalo data. The important data from the Helium Diffusion Rate study has been viciously attacked for more than a decade, yet the 2005 Dr. Humphreys answer to criticisms not only apply to the specifics of the following letter of Kevin Henke, but to all of the criticisms of Helium Diffusion Rates that I am aware of.

Dr. Humphreys wrote in an open letter to Kevin Henke: "The first thing to notice about Henke's issues is how few of them there really are. For example, of the fifteen items above, six of them (4, 5, 6, 8, 9, 12) boil down to only one issue, how much helium was deposited in the zircons. Several other items repeated themselves similarly.[93]

"The second thing to notice is how peripheral they are. Not one of them has any chance of solving Henke's real problem: how to keep helium in leaky minerals for over a billion years.

"Third, notice how petty most of them are. One of my challenges in answering those charges was to find different words describing their basic character: "molehill, not a mountain ... distinction without a difference ...

haggling ... ridiculous quibble ... inconsequential ... majoring on minors ... irrelevant". Eight of the items (1, 2, 3, 6, 7, 10, 11, 12) fall into that class.

But despite his scarcity of significant issues, Henke chose to puff them up to enormous proportions with a torrent of hot air: fifty single-spaced pages using up my printer supplies. Why? Well, of course he is trying to bluff his readers. Unless the reader is technically well-informed in this specialty and wants to take the time to examine Henke's monograph carefully, he is apt to think that where there is so much verbal smoke there must be some factual fire." [219]

(All the previous material is from the Humphreys response.)

4. Types of Radiometric Dating

The basic fallacies[94] of radiometric dating apply to all forms of radiometric dating. However, since these dating methods are likely to be included among questions on standardized tests, familiarity with the following six methods will be useful for answering test questions. The following is an incomplete list of the most popular radiometric dating methods and the materials they are used on. The numbers are the half-life of the radioactive isotope. While each method is different and has different applications, they are all founded on the above three assumptions listed at the beginning of this section. Any other method we list will be founded on the same three fallacious assumptions. Methods 1 (K-Ar) and 6 (U/Th-Pb) are the best known.

1. The Potassium to Argon (K-Ar) method is used on igneous rock and minerals. It has a half-life of 1,280,000,000 years.
2. The Rubidium to Strontium (Rb-Sr) method is used on igneous rock and minerals. It has a half-life of 48.8 billion years.
3. The Samarium to Neodymium (Sm-Nd) method is used on igneous and metamorphic

rocks, minerals, lunar rocks and meteorites. It
has a half-life of 106,000,000,000 years.
4. The Lutetium to Hafnium (Lu-Hf) method
is used on gneiss and basalt. It has a half-life
of 37,800,000,000 years.
5. The Rhenium to Osmium (Re-Os) method is
used on sulfide minerals, molybdenite ore and
metallic meteorites. It has a half-life of 42.3
billion years.
6. Uranium/Thorium to Lead (U/Th-Pb)
method is used on igneous and metamorphic
rocks, minerals. It has a half-life of 4.47 billion
years (U).[94]

Fossils In Geologic Strata

F. Fossils In Geologic Strata

As problems with radiometric dating become more well
known among more educated uniformitarians, there is
a renewed emphasis on the fossil record. While the
subject of fossils in geologic strata can be quite
complex, the uniformitarian arguments primarily fall
into two categories. These two beliefs are the bedrock
foundations of uniformitarianism and evolution in
general. If either of these two *assumptions* (beliefs) are
in error, then there is not enough time for evolution to
be possible.

• To deposit the material we observe today
throughout the geologic column, the present rate of
deposition would take millions of years of
accumulations. The very word "uniformitarian" is
the belief that there has not been a significant
change in the rate of deposits. Uniformitarians
believe that there were slight changes in the recent
past and there are local or regional catastrophes
which temporarily changed the rate, even
"extinction level events." But the overall rate of
deposits is still an overall accurate and dependable
rate of deposits in the fossil record.

- There is a progression of fossils from simple organisms in "older" strata to increasingly complex, or at least more "modern" organisms in more "recent" strata.

1. The Rate of Fossil Deposits

The rate of fossil deposits in the present was the driving force behind James Hutton's belief in deep time.

a. Belief in a Constant Rate

James Hutton observed billions of fossils segregated into strata. He observed the same world around him that we can observe. He firmly believed that the organisms lived and died, then were deposited, in the various strata at the same rate that he observed in the late 1700s. He firmly believed fossils were deposited throughout all time at the same rates he observed. Those he corresponded with confirmed this belief.

One example: he simply *assumed* a continuous and constant death rate and rate of deposit for the calcium carbonate of the billions of dead bodies of microorganisms he observed whose shells made up the White Cliffs of Dover. He also *assumed* the same rates on a global scale. These calcium carbonate strata, commonly known as chalk, are found in Kansas, Colorado, Malta, mainland Europe, the United Arab Emirates, and many other places throughout the earth.

Using calcium carbonate as an example, the *assumption* that the present rate of deposit of calcium carbonate from the shells of dead organisms, primarily microorganisms into the oceans, is responsible for the existing thicknesses of fossil stratum, means the existing carbonate strata were deposited with 70-100 million years of deposits.

Unlike James Hutton's assumptions, there is actually little or no evidence that calcium carbonate fossils are being produced today, even in small quantities. Different conditions, not more time, are needed to produce multiple chalk strata.

  b. The rate was much greater in the past.

A serious examination of the evidence does not show a continuous rate of deposit of the same calcium carbonate shells. Instead, the evidence shows that the population growth rate of organisms we observe today as fossils was much greater in the past.

> "For the chalk formations[95] to have reached the thickness they are today in a few thousand years, the production of microorganisms would have had to greatly increase sometime in the past. In fact, under the right conditions, rapid production and accumulation of these microorganisms on the ocean floor is possible. These conditions include turbulent waters, high winds, decaying fish, and increased temperature and nutrients from volcanic waters and other sources.

> "With catastrophic volcanic activity warming the oceans and releasing large amounts of CO_2, and with the torrential rains and the churning and mixing of fresh and salt waters, the Flood of Noah's day produced the right conditions for a "blooming" production of microorganisms and the chalk's rapid accumulation. The three major sections of the White Cliffs of Dover give evidence of three major "blooms" in chalk formation, which

would have taken place during the year-long Flood."[95]

"The purity of the chalk itself also points to rapid accumulation. One cannot imagine a scenario where deposits over millions of years could maintain such purity without accumulating some contaminating sediments from other events."

"Additional evidence for a global Flood in the White Cliffs of Dover includes the layering of the chalk in alternating thin, hard layers and thick, soft layers. In these hard layers, called hardgrounds, we find fossils of mollusk shells and other sea creatures, some as large as 3 feet (1 m) across (ammonites), which could not have been buried alive slowly! The same chalk formation in the Netherlands has yielded a very large Mosasaurus skull."[95]

The White Cliffs of Dover are just one example. The type of chalk which makes up the White Cliffs of Dover is found all over the world. The same type of chalk is found in Kansas, Europe, and many other places. Throughout the world the principles hold true: proper conditions can produce "blooms."

Blooms are enormous,[96] explosive growth of specific types of organisms. Localized blooms, especially of microbes, are common where rapid, drastic changes increase the food supply and other environmental factors favor a particular organism. This is especially true of marine saprophyte microbes, even today. Hurricanes, tsunamis, and any other types of wide-ranging disasters see blooms of saprophyte organisms. The well-known "red tides" of the Gulf of Mexico are deadly blooms of a single kind of phytoplankton, dinoflagellates, commonly known as red algae. Oil spills usually have blooms of bacteria. In four months "bacterial blooms had dissolved some 200,000 tons of methane" in a 2011 Gulf of Mexico drilling spill. Blooms are often beneficial.

Immediately after the Flood[97] drowned all air-breathing land organisms on earth, conditions were perfect for a massive bloom of saprophyte microbes. Such a bloom would easily account for the various chalk strata we observe today.

How fast can a bloom grow? Look at the growth rate of a Paramecium. A Paramecium is a microscopic organism which lives in marine, brackish and fresh water. Over 99% of the organisms which make up the calcium carbonate strata are microorganisms. For those of you who find this difficult to understand or believe, the following statement, made by a uniformitarian, might put some perspective on this issue. A once a day division rate is a very low estimate.

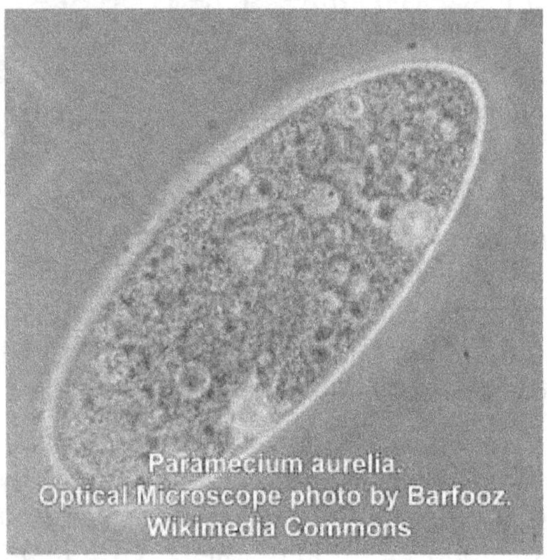

"One scientist calculated that if all the progeny of a single Paramecium survived, assuming a division rate of once a day, then after 113 days, the mass of paramecia would equal the volume of the Earth![98]

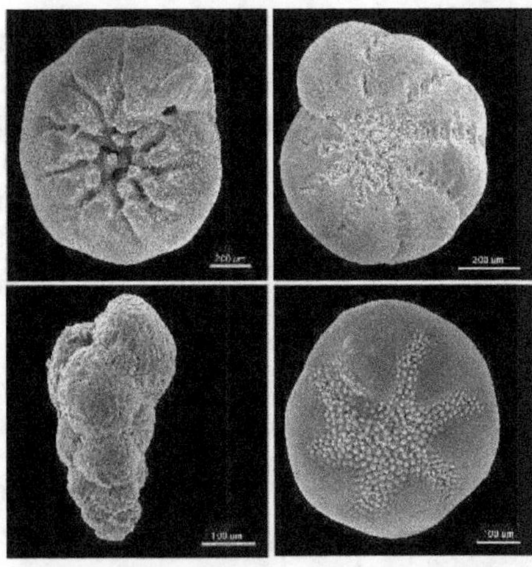

SEM micrographs of four benthic foraminiferans (ventral view) from the USGS. Clockwise from top left: Ammonia beccarii, Elphidium excavatum clavatum, Buccella frigida, and Eggerella advena.
Above caption copyright en:User:Hadal, and released under the GFDL with English Wikipedia disclaimers per this history log entry: 01:59, 20 February 2004 Hadal (Talk | contribs) (caption)

For a brief period of time, the natural predators of the saprophyte microbes nearly died off and their food supply exploded. This is exactly what we expect from a catastrophic event like a worldwide flood. The bloom of saprophyte microorganisms would take place after the fossils were buried, the turbidity had slowed and the remaining carcasses were either floating or exposed at the bottom of the sea. These strata were likely formed near the end of the Flood or after Noah had left the ark.

The Walker/Klevberg model places the formation of these calcium carbonate strata during the Deluge Event. But understanding the historic reality using the standard uniformitarian geologic scale is difficult. These strata are labeled Cretaceous by uniformitarian geologists. According to their dating system, the Cretaceous system immediately precedes the Tertiary System.

The worldwide catastrophe known as the Flood of Noah ended all of the systems from the Cambrian to at least the Jurassic in a matter of weeks, days or in some cases even hours. Every stratum from the Cambrian to at least the Jurassic was deposited during the flood. The organisms lived during the Antediluvian period and died in the flood. That is the 1656 years which started after the Fall and ended with the Flood. The best name for it is the Antediluvian Period.

Just as one example, according to uniformitarians, the extinction event which ended the Devonian System was followed by the Carboniferous System, which is commonly divided into the Lower Carboniferous System (Mississippian; the older system) and Upper Carboniferous System (Pennsylvanian; the more recent system). Many geologists divide these two systems even further. The Carboniferous System which formed the coal mankind has mined for over four thousand years was created catastrophically, though there are no tags describing the Flood as the catastrophe which formed the Carboniferous System.

All of the fossils we find in theses strata died during the flood or later. All were deposited during the Flood and represent organisms which also lived during the antediluvian period. While this represents the approximate order as they are found in the field, the uniformitarian arrangement of including the Cambrian through the Devonian, the Carboniferous and the Permian into the same era (Paleozoic) then putting the Triassic and Jurassic into a different era (Mesozoic) is both misleading and confusing. The Mesozoic Era, like the Paleozoic Era strata was deposited during the Flood. The organisms in these strata which became fossils during the Flood lived in the Antediluvian period. The Flood created or caused the conditions which formed all of these strata.

Many strata consisting of the shells of deceased calcium carbonate organisms are part of the Cretaceous System. These shell deposits are just one example of how a stratum can be formed. The rate of deposition of the material making up *all* the strata and the reproductive rate of organisms in the fossil record was massively greater in the past compared to the reproductive rates and rate of deposition of organisms today. Also, some kind of protection against oxygen, both atmospheric and water, was essential to permit fossilization. Volcanic activity is one possibility which could both seal vast numbers of organisms from oxygen and at the same time provide the minerals and heat necessary to fossilize them.

The organisms which make up each of these strata, at least up to the Jurassic, lived at the same time during the Antediluvian period.

c. Multiple Strata Laid Down Rapidly.

Strata containing fossils are on every continent. Multiple layers of strata do not have signs telling us that they were formed over millions of years. Nor do these strata have signs informing us that they were laid down rapidly by means of a catastrophe or even a series of catastrophes. We do find volcanic activity today, but on a greatly reduced scale.

The conditions which laid down the materials of the individual stratum were different than conditions today. These different conditions allowed a stratum to be formed quickly, often in hours, through catastrophic, usually volcanic processes. Several recent volcanic eruptions, on a much smaller scale, allow current examination of similar catastrophic processes. So much of the strata which can be observed today were either formed directly by volcanic activity or indirectly triggered by volcanic activity. Volcanic activity can create or move vast amounts of sand, cause turbidity, tsunamis, and mix a combination of ash, seawater, and other materials such as clay. The resulting strata can be measured, the minerals can be analyzed, fossils can be cataloged and the geographic coverage can be estimated. But there is no verifiable method for determining the age of any strata or how rapidly it was deposited.

Uniformitarians primarily use index fossils and radiometric methods to date strata. In the few cases where it is possible to verify strata formation by other methods the evidence points to rapid formation. One example is trees trunks without roots or branches, which proves that the trees did not grow in that location but were transported to their existing location. These trees are found throughout the world upright, through multiple geologic strata. Often these are multiple strata of coal. This type of formation is well-known and well-documented. The following *Journal of the Geological Society,* London article shows the need for very rapid burial of the upright logs and the need for those same logs to be cut off from oxygen or fossilized quickly, almost instantaneously. The upright trees through multiple strata are referred to in this article as T° assemblages.

> "To be preserved, not only must T° assemblages be buried rapidly, they must also occur in settings subject to high rates of accommodation that permit a longer-term escape from exposure by post-burial erosion. Following burial, their preservation follows a pathway similar to that of any other deposit containing terrestrial organic matter (Behrensmeyer et al. 2000). First, in the shorter term, the entombed plants must be removed from the effects of aerobic decay in the vadose zone (Gastaldo & Demko 2010); this may occur rapidly following sea-level rise, tectonically driven earth movements, or even compaction, in the case of a substrate such as peat."[99]

According to Occam's Razor, the simplest explanation is most likely the correct explanation. A massive, global flood that put down layers of plant material rapidly, transporting upright trees into these layers is the simplest explanation. Then as continental movements and volcanic activity continued, additional strata were laid down. Sometimes these were additional strata of coal.

The important points of this article are
1) The upright trees "must...be buried rapidly"
2) The upright trees "must also occur in settings subject to high rates of accommodation that permit a longer-term escape from exposure by post-burial erosion..." That means that the combined strata in which they are buried must be thick enough to protect them from future erosion.
3) "...the entombed plants must be removed from the effects of aerobic decay..." The fossilization process is anaerobic. The entombed upright trees must be isolated from oxygen, either atmospheric or groundwater.

A fourth major point which the article does not state is the need for the proper conditions, usually extreme heat and pressure, as well as an environment free from oxygen, with the proper minerals to fossilize "the entombed plant." Without these conditions, "the entombed plant" will not fossilize.

Known volcanic activity demonstrates examples of the proper conditions to bring this about. Known volcanic activity has fossilized material in hours. Probably the most famous example is the fossilized bread and garbage in Pompeii resulting from the A.D. 79 eruption of Mr. Vesuvius. The bread was fossilized almost instantly.

The *Geological Society* article about upright trees in coal formation follows the above quote with this sentence: "Second, in the intermediate term of millions to tens of millions of years (or much less were the deposit to have formed at high elevation), the deposit must be buried to a depth sufficient to ensure it will escape erosion..."

The original scientific observation is stated "To be preserved, not only must T° assemblages be buried rapidly ..." And rapidly in this context means almost instantaneously. But that is followed by the unsupported leap of faith without evidence, "in the intermediate term of millions to tens of millions of years..."

An important point which I did not find in this particular article are the instances where several upright trees are grounded in different strata at different heights and the total combined height of the various trees includes multiple strata. Creationist literature calls these upright fossilized trees through multiple strata *polystrates*. Polystrates is considered "not a standard geologic term" by uniformitarians. Polystrates exist and we would gladly use the "standard geologic term" instead of calling these fossils through multiple strata *polystrates*. But there is no "standard geologic term" for the well-known and common polystrate. So, for lack of a so called "standard geologic term," we are forced to use the word *polystrate*.

The individual stratum which immobilized the upright tree is evidence that the stratum was deposited almost instantaneously. All the remaining strata entombing the tree, from top to bottom, were deposited fast enough to prevent the tree from decaying and slow enough to keep it from toppling over.

Fig. 34.—*Section of middle part of Subdivison XV. in which the Dendrerpeton, Land Shells, etc., have been found.*

1. Underclay, with rootlets of *Stigmaria*, resting on gray shale, with two thin coaly seams.
2. Gray sandstone, with erect trees, *Calamites*, and other stems: 9 feet.
3. Coal, with erect tree on its surface: 6 inches.
4. Underclay, with Stigmaria rootlets.

    (*a*) *Calamites.*
    (*b*) Stem of plant undetermined.
    (*c*) Stigmaria roots.
    (*d*) Erect trunk, 9 feet high.

(From Dawson 1855; other editions 1868, 1878, 1891.) *The Geology of Nova Scotia, New Brunswick and Prince Edward Island, or Acadian Geology*, Oliver and Boyd, Edinburgh. Public domain.

There are drawings of areas before they were mined. These drawings were made before photographs were readily available.

To repeat a question: Why does the evidence we can verify (strata with fossilized upright trees) prove that those strata were laid down very rapidly, but other strata with no additional dating evidences, are claimed to take millions of years? In these other strata, the only evidence to date the age of the individual stratum are radiometric dating and index fossils. And why are the fossils *assumed* to be fossilized before they were placed in the various strata where we find them today? Is it because the fossilization process requires an anaerobic environment, which would *require a very rapid, nearly immediate* formation of every single stratum containing fossils? Every single stratum from the Cambrian system to the present has fossils. Not a few fossils, but billions upon billions of fossils.

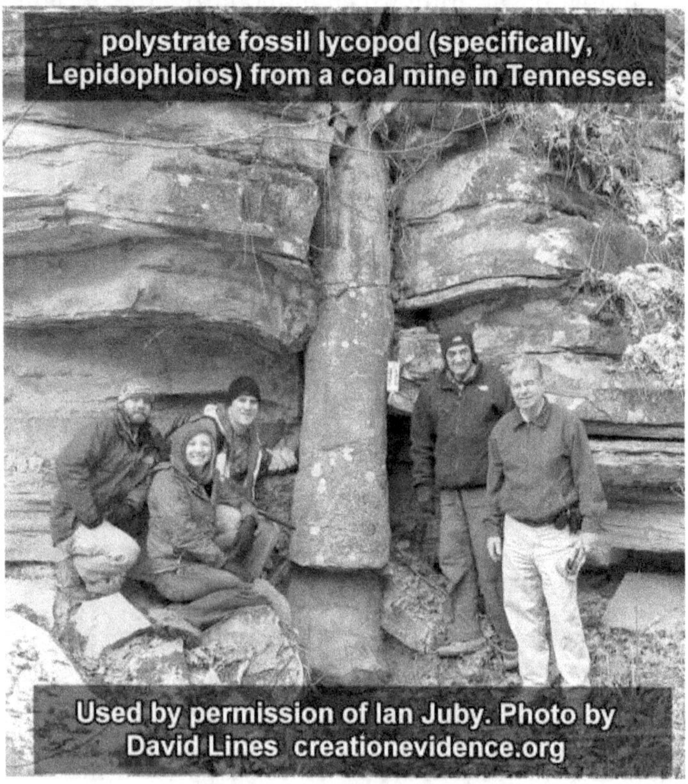

Polystrate Tree in a Tennessee Coal mine.[100]

The very evidence that convinced James Hutton of uniformitarianism is actually, when properly understood, evidence of rapid catastrophes. The thickness of individual stratum does not indicate a continuous process similar to what we observe today, but a process catastrophically different from anything we observe today.

d. Massive simultaneous fossilization

Not only were the strata laid down rapidly, but vast numbers of organisms were fossilized at the same time. Fossil graveyards all over the world can only be explained by the simultaneous death of all the organisms in the graveyards. Educated uniformitarians readily agree with this. That is why they insist on five separate mass extinctions and numerous minor extinctions. Each of their *assumed* extinction events occurred rapidly, because that is what the evidence says. Their beliefs force them to *assume* that there were many unrelated extinction events millions of years apart.

The billions upon billions of fossils do not have tags or any other method of scientifically identifying these extinction events. When we carefully examine the evidence, the science of examining and organizing the evidence reveals that these catastrophic extinction events are actually connected to one another and not separated by millions of years. These nearly identical kinds of extinction events are most likely separated by hours, days or at the most years, not millennia.

In 1982,[101] uniformitarians Jack Sepkoski and David M. Raup wrote a paper proposing that extinction events cycled, with five major mass extinction events controlling earth's history. Though this belief is just a belief and not science, standardized test questions assume that these five "extinction events" are facts. The following is a list of the *assumed* five major mass extinction events. Uniformitarians believe in many, many extinctions. These are, according to their beliefs (assumptions), *assumed* to be the largest. In order from *assumed* oldest to the *assumed* most recent.

- Ordovician-Silurian: 450-440 - two stages

- Late Devonian: 375-360 Ma

- Permian-Triassic: 251 Ma

- Triassic-Jurassic: 200 Ma

- Cretaceous-Paleogene: 66 Ma

This "cycle of extinction events" is essential to their belief system. They must invent some type of "explanation" because the billions of fossils worldwide appear just as a reasonable person who understands the geology of a worldwide catastrophe expects to find them. For example, regardless of Secular Humanist complaints, human fossils from a catastrophe like the Flood should not be expected.

The lack of human fossils indicates that the humans were able to escape the initial catastrophe which entombed so many organisms. If they were able to put something together which floated, they still died of exposure or starvation. We would not expect to find the dead bodies because they were not entombed. Dead bodies floating in a worldwide flood would have almost no chance of becoming fossilized. Human corpses floating in the Flood were eventually devoured by saprophyte organisms, from microbes to fish. When those saprophyte microorganisms died, their shells became chalk. So the answer to the question, "Where are the human fossils?" is most likely, "In the Cretaceous stratum."

Of the fossils viewed by humans, less than one percent of these fossils are viewed *in situ*, literally "in position" fossils. The vast majority are viewed in museums, in photographs and other "staged" or variously altered settings. *In situ* fossils are viewed in the stratum where they were deposited in the same way they were deposited. Other nearby fossils and the surrounding material are not disturbed in any way. Public lands with true *in situ* fossils are often not available for viewing by the public. Even photographs of *in situ* fossils are very difficult to come by.

Even when *in situ* fossils are available for examination, the *in situ* fossil must be "interpreted". There is no question as to the science of the fossils, what they look like, measurements, taxonomy (perhaps some disagreement about taxonomy, but not usually), physical location in the stratum, relationship to other fossils in the same stratum and chemical composition of the fossil. But when we depart from the physical, observable evidence and begin making *assumptions,* such as the manner and time of death, all agreement ceases. So Secular Humanists very much want to control *in situ* fossil sites and carefully feed interpretations to the public. Only the indoctrinated priesthood are allowed to "properly" examine and, to the extent possible, even *see* fossils *in situ.*

Public Domain image of marine fossils

In the United States many, many fossil beds are part of state or national parks. Looking at the websites of these parks is somewhat discouraging, since only "perfect" fossil examples are shown, and there are no groupings that might disturb the secularist insistence that these creatures lived in different eras.

Fossils range from individual organisms, such as microbes and insects trapped in amber, to the organisms fossilized *en masse* in places such as the Florissant Fossil Beds, CO, and Dinosaur National Monument. We find fossils beds of many different organisms jumbled together, such as Dinosaur

National Monument in Utah. We also find large numbers of fossils of the same kind of organism together, such as the Ammonites in the yellow band of the Himalayas or the fossilized horses of the Hagerman Fossil Beds, National Monument, ID.

The World's a Graveyard[102] by Dr. Snelling points out the sheer number of fossils around the world, and the combinations of kinds, including plants, that don't fit the uniformitarian schemes.

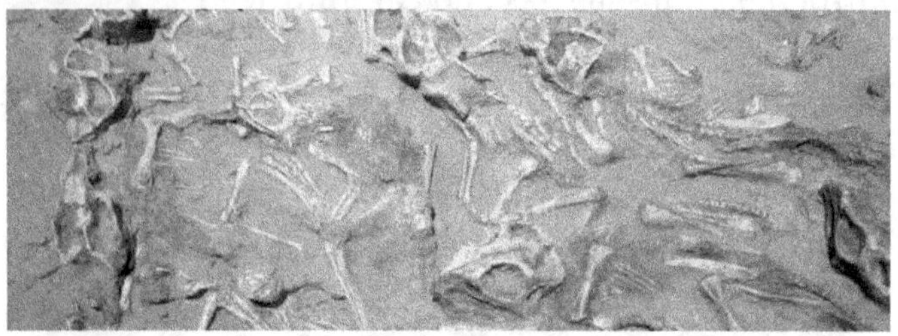

Canadian fossil bed

An Ankylosaur[103] fossil was found near Ft McMurray in Alberta, in a spot where marine fossils have been found, but not land animals. This article cites multiple examples of mixed fossil beds of creatures from what uniformitarians consider to be different geologic eras. Morrison Formation at Dinosaur National Monument (Colorado and Utah) and Two Medicine Formation (a sandstone formation east of the Rocky Mountains extending into Edmonton, Alberta, in Canada, are only two places such fossils have been found. Dr. Carl Werner said in this article that "We visited 60 museums but did not see a single complete mammal skeleton from the dinosaur layers displayed at any of these museums."

Carnegie Museum fossil graveyard exhibit

The Shandong[104] quarry is described as "one of the largest concentrations of dinosaur bones in the world". It contains specimens of a T-Rex like dinosaur, 30 feet long, six tons. Uniformitarians concede these dinosaurs were swept into the bed by a flood, but how big of a flood would be necessary to overcome a dinosaur of that size, and such a huge number of others as well?

Uniformitarians have found a way to explain mounting evidence that flooding killed dinosaurs,[105] as evidenced in this article about a new book. The formal description of one such "discovery" was published in a book titled *New Perspectives on Horned Dinosaurs*. Co-editor David Eberth, Senior Research Scientist at the Royal Tyrrell Museum, stated in a museum news release, "Data from this mega bonebed provide pretty clear evidence that these, and other dinosaurs, were routinely wiped out by catastrophic tropical storms that flooded what was once a coastal lowland here in Alberta, 76 million years ago."

Uniformitarians are quick to dismiss these out-of sequence fossils, explaining them away as somehow intruded[106] rather than admitting they might actually belong there. But it's hard to dismiss the examples collected by the *Center for Scientific Creation*. Everything from plant features that shouldn't have evolved yet to tracks of mammalian species or even human coexisting with dinosaurs. Can all this evidence be wrong?

They can explain away any difficulty because they control the fossils, and can set up "interpretative"[107] exhibits to repeatedly stress the geologic column, and millions of years, and simpler to complex. Interpretative in this case is synonymous with manipulative and indoctrinating. The link in the appendix goes to an article about Paleoanthropology and is a good example of how uniformitarians interpret the fossil record based on their beliefs.

(Note: The following lengthy quote is from an Andrew Snelling article about fossil graveyards.)[108]

> "Billions of straight-shelled, chambered nautiloids (figure 2) are found fossilized with other marine creatures in a 7 foot (2 m) thick layer within the Redwall Limestone of Grand Canyon (figure 1). This fossil graveyard stretches for 180 miles (290 km) across northern Arizona and into southern Nevada, covering an area of at least 10,500 square miles (30,000 km²). These squid-like fossils are all different sizes, from small, young nautiloids to their bigger, older relatives."

> "Hundreds of thousands[108] of marine creatures were buried with amphibians, spiders, scorpions, millipedes, insects, and reptiles in a fossil graveyard at Montceau-les-Mines, France. More than 100,000 fossil specimens, representing more than 400 species, have been recovered from a shale layer associated with coal beds in the Mazon Creek area near Chicago. This spectacular fossil graveyard includes ferns, insects, scorpions, and tetrapods buried with jellyfish, mollusks, crustaceans, and fish, often with soft parts exquisitely preserved."

> "At Florissant, Colorado, a wide variety of insects, freshwater mollusks, fish, birds, and several hundred plant species (including nuts

and blossoms) are buried together. Bees and birds have to be buried rapidly in order to be so well preserved."

"Alligator, fish (including sunfish, deep sea bass, chubs, pickerel, herring, and garpike – 7 feet [1-2 m] long), birds, turtles, mammals, mollusks, crustaceans, many varieties of insects, and palm leaves (7-9 feet [2-2.5 m] long) were buried together in the vast Green River Formation of Wyoming."

"At Fossil Bluff on the north coast of Australia's island state of Tasmania (figure 3), many thousands of marine creatures (corals, bryozoans [lace corals], bivalves [clams], and gastropods [snails]) were buried together in a broken state, along with a toothed whale (figure 4) and a marsupial possum (figure 5). Whales and possums don't live together, so only a watery catastrophe would have buried them together! In order for such large ammonites (figure 8) and other marine creatures to be buried in the chalk beds of Britain (figure 6), many trillions of microscopic marine creatures (figure 7) had to bury them catastrophically. These same beds also stretch right across Europe to the Middle East, as well as into the Midwest of the USA, forming a global-scale fossil graveyard. In addition, more than 7 trillion tons of vegetation are buried in the world's coal beds found across every continent, including Antarctica."[108]

How do the collection of organisms in these fossil graveyards differ from the way organisms congregate today? Today there are herds, swarms, hives and flocks of the same type of living organisms. Some of these, especially insects and marine creatures can gather in the billions. There are also lone individuals, such as hawks, bears, tigers, sharks, scorpions and frogs. Large groups of mixed organisms congregate daily in oceans, ponds, at watering holes, grazing in fields, flocking in updrafts and fighting. These are exactly what we find in the fossil record.

Many of the kinds of organisms contained in the fossil record are extinct. There is nothing similar to the extinct organisms alive today. Tyrannosaurus rex is one familiar example of a kind of organism which used to live but is extinct today. But all organisms alive today are descended from organisms from the past. The changes from organisms in the past to the organisms observed today is neither macro- or micro-evolution. The proper term is adaptation.

While every organism on earth is a result of adaptation, we only have room for one example. Probably the best-documented case of adaptation is *Canis lupus*, the gray wolf. While we cannot know with absolute certainty, it is widely believed by both creationists and uniformitarians that every kind of dog which is observed today is a descendant of the gray wolf. Dingoes, jackals, hyenas, foxes, coyotes and all breeds of domestic dogs from chihuahuas to great Danes descend from *Canis lupus*. Over half of the various breeds descended from the original *Canis lupus* were developed as separate or distinct, individual breeds within the last 500 years.

Canis lupus becoming the many breeds observable today is an example of adaptation, not evolution, either micro or macro. They can grow deep, thick fur and even adjust their blood flow to not only survive, but thrive in the coldest winters. They can also shed their under layer of fur, some of their outer fur, adjust their blood flow and survive in the heat of Mexican summers. With parents of two different breeds, every pup might be a different size and shape with different markings. Yet all of this genetic information was contained in the *Canis lupus* pair which lived on the ark.

Image from IMSI Hijacks's Masterclips Collection

People can be short, tall or something in between. There is a wide range of hair types and colors, skin tones, types of features such as nostrils, eyebrows, knuckles, etc. There are even different temperaments, athletic abilities, susceptibility to illnesses, etc. All of this genetic information was contained in six people onboard the ark. So the ability to survive in various climates, hot vs cold, high altitude vs sea level, humid vs dry is adaptation.

Certain adaptations, perhaps a longer tail, a white coat in snow, a camouflaged coat/feather pattern in dense forest are a result of breeding over time to retain useful traits. Science has attempted, without success, to develop a working definition of the term "breed." The simple, nonscientific definition for a breed is animals with similar characteristics which retain these same characteristics over multiple generations when interbred with animals of the same breed.

One obvious example of a breed is a longhorn cow. Longhorn cattle have very long horns. The longhorn breed is also very hardy and capable of surviving in regions on diets which kill many other cattle breeds. They also have slightly longer gestation periods and lower quality beef, so their meat is worth slightly less than that of other breeds, such as Black Angus.

Understanding the differences in various breeds helps us compare living organisms with similar organisms in the fossil record. We can compare organisms alive today, the total numbers and types of breeds with the types and total number of organisms in the fossil record. This is especially true of fossil graveyards. The total number and variety of organisms that died at the same time in these graveyards indicates a variety of different conditions on earth. These graveyards tell us when and where these organisms died. It does not indicate any kind of a continuity for millions of years.

e. Different fossils in the same strata

Examination of fossils in various strata begins in one location. When that examination is complete, the examination moves to another location, then another location. As the examination moves away from the geographic starting point, the correlations of similarities in local fossil beds are replaced by "progressively greater differences."

> "As one moves from local[109] all the way to global correlation by fossils, correlations become increasingly less empirical and more conceptual. This is because there are progressively greater differences (such as lithology, local fossil succession, and overall faunal character) as one moves even further geographically from a reference section in the type areas."

Michael Oard's main point in this quote is that correlating fossils in local fossil beds is possible. But as you move away from your starting point, you will have "progressively greater differences." That means that the basic, foundational *assumption* of James Hutton, that the strata he observed in England were uniform worldwide, was an erroneous *assumption*. While uniformitarians frequently admit to a "limited" number of "out of place" fossils for whatever reason, they hold fast to the belief that fossils determine the time period of the individual stratum.

This belief is so firmly entrenched that the *primary* method used to identify and date individual stratum are "index fossils." These are fossils which are *assumed* to have lived only at certain times. Therefore, finding a

certain fossil or certain types of fossils, clearly
identifies the time period of the stratum the "index
fossil" is found in.

The USGS[110] clearly defines "index fossil" in this
caption to a chart with two dozen "index fossils" and
the *assumed* time period each type of organism lived.
The link in the appendix will take you to the actual
chart.

> "Keyed to the relative time scale are examples
> of index fossils, the forms of life which existed
> during limited periods of geologic time and
> thus are used as guides to the age of the rocks
> in which they are preserved."[110]

An examination of the evidence gives a very different
story.

2. Progression of Fossil Deposits

Uniformitarians use the term "progression of fossil
deposits" to mean that the oldest strata have the
simplest, least-developed fossils and that life develops
according to a general evolutionary standard. They
teach that evolution can be observed in the progression
of fossil deposits as strata progress from oldest to the
present. At each stage, according to uniformitarians,
there are fossils identifying these developments.

a. Uniformitarians Need Fossil Progression

When all other forms of "proof" fail, the first recorded
observations of James Hutton are still the foundational
fallback. Without a progression of fossils from "simple"
single-cell organisms to the highly complex modern
organisms we observe everyday, there is neither deep
time nor time for evolutionary development. To a
uniformitarian, fossil progression is sacrosanct.

It does not matter if a position is sacrosanct. If it
contradicts the evidence, it is still in error.

b. Most living organisms are in the fossil record

The fossil record,[111] just like the world around us, has
far more microorganisms than all other organisms
combined. The fossil record, just like the world around

us, has far more plants than all multicellular animals combined. The fossil record, just like the world around us, has far more multicellular marine creatures than all land and flying creatures. The fossil record, just like the world around us, has far more insects than all amphibians, birds, reptiles and mammals combined. In every possible comparison, the fossil record to the extent we know and understand it mirrors the world around us.

The following is a sample list of a small number of organisms which exist today with little or no change from the samples we have in the fossil record.

1) Trapped In Amber:

Amber[112] is a sticky liquid resin which trapped billions of organisms before turning into clear, usually golden-tinted, solid. Since oxygen would degrade the resin, they had to be rapidly cut off from oxygen and heated, to become amber. Either a volcanic eruption or explosion from a comet/meteor can easily cause a tree to release the resin, capturing an organism inside. The heat of the pressure wave of the eruption or explosion of a comet/meteor would then solidify the viscous resin, entombing the organism in amber as we see today. Organisms trapped in amber are a separate category because they are almost always preserved complete, not simply skeletons or just an impression.

A tiny sample list of a few of the organisms trapped in amber that appear to be identical to the same organism today, except for size (some of the organisms entombed in amber are much larger); dragonfly, oak flower, mushroom, mosquito, biting black fly, fig wasp, ants, rock louse, hollow shelled snail, spider, conifer branch, centipede, millipede.

Northern Cordillera, Dominican Republic Mosquito in amber
Photographed by Archaeodontosaurus Wikimedia Commons

2) Plants:

The Wollemi[113] Pine, *Wollemia nobilis* belongs to a group of plants thought (from fossils) to have been extinct since the so-called Jurassic Period.

Where do ferns go[114] when they die? A better question might be, what do they look like when they have died and been buried and turned into fossils? The picture below should help illustrate the point of the AiG article about fern fossils and how they are formed.

Image of curved fern superimposed over dead ferns. Both images from Morguefile

"Oak,[115] willow, magnolia, sassafras, palms, and other such common flowering plants. "ground pine" (*Lycopodium)* and "horsetail" (*Equisetum*) the algae are recognizable from their first appearance in the fossil sequence as

153

greens, blue-greens, reds, browns, and yellow-browns, the same groups we have today."

"Summarizing the evidence from fossils' plant studies, E. J. H. Corner, Professor of Botany at Cambridge University, once put it this way (even though he believed in their evolution): '. . . to the unprejudiced, the fossil record of plants is in favor of special creation.'"

Living liquidambar (*Liquidambar styraciflua*), just one "living fossil", like the coelacanth unchanged from the fossil versions.[116]

Comptonia peregrina from North America. LEBENDIGE VORWELT (Living Ancient World) is a German faith ministry museum of living fossils like this type of fern.[117]

3) Fish, marine creatures:

Flying fish, *Exocoetidae*[118]

Flying fish image from NOAA

"*Triops australiensis*" "...the tadpole shrimp Triops. Fossils of this remarkable little creature are found in rocks which evolutionists date at 200 million years old. Yet it is alive and unchanged today."[120]

horseshoe crabs, *Limulus polyphemus*.[121]

(genus *Penaeus*) is essentially the same as the fossil shrimp (*Antrimpos*).[122]

The fossil *Busycon contrarium* (a seashell fossil pictured in the AiG article in the link) from Pliocene rock (alleged evolutionary age of 5.3-1.6 million years ago) was found in Sarasota, Florida, in the United States. Yet a modern *Busycon contrarium* was also found in Florida.[123]

The fossil *Pleurotomaria* shell, shown in the AiG article linked, was found in England in Jurasic deposits (supposedly 135-205 million years old on the evolutionists' time-scale). Yet the modern-day version from Japan, shown in the photo on the left, is virtually identical.[125]

4) Insects (also see amber):

A Polistes wasp was found in Tertiary deposits at Willershausen and was supposedly millions of years old. Yet a nest of Polistes wasps living today in southern Europe has individuals of identical appearance.[125]

5) Reptiles, Amphibians:

Sea Turtles, salamanders.

"Despite its Bathonian age, the new cryptobranchid [salamander] shows extraordinary morphological similarity to its living relatives. This similarity underscores the stasis [no change] within salamander anatomical evolution. Indeed, extant cryptobranchid salamanders can be regarded as living fossils whose structures have remained little changed for over 160 million years."[126]

6) Mammals:

A group of mammals called *diatonyids* has modern representatives among Guinea pigs and porcupines. One squirrel-like rodent was thought to have gone extinct 11 million years ago and is found in the fossil record. However, the *kha-nyou* or Laotian rock rat belongs to the *diatonyids* family, appears identical to the fossil "rat", and is alive today in Laos. When it was discovered it was thought to be an unknown, new species by uniformitarians. Now they protest that it is not unchanged and "hasn't stopped evolving", though they don't say how it is different.[127]

7) Summary:

Author Kurt Wise[128] has an article about species preservation in the fossil record. The AiG reprint link appears in the appendix along with Wise's sources for the article.

> "Scientists have named more than 1.3 million species of living animals, and they have named only about 250,000 in the fossil record."

> "In one study Björn Kurtén determined that 88% of the mammal species living in Europe today are also present in the fossil record in Europe, and 99% are present in the fossil record somewhere on earth."

> "In another study, James W. Valentine, in his PhD dissertation, found that 76.8% of the marine mollusk species currently living along the southern California and Baja California coast are also found in the fossil record."[128]

c. Do fossils progress in successive strata?

"Evolution predicts[129] that new groups of creatures would have arisen in a specific order. But if you compare the order that these creatures first appear in the actual fossil record, as opposed to their theoretical first appearance in the predictions, then over 95% of the fossil record's "order" can best be described as random.

"…If these organisms were buried by the Flood waters, the order of first appearance should be either random, due to the sorting effects of the Flood, or reflect the order of ecological burial. In other words, as the Flood waters rose, they would tend to bury organisms in the order that they were encountered, so the major groups should appear in the fossil record according to *where* they lived, and not *when* they lived. This is exactly what we find, including this fossil record within the Grand Canyon-Grand Staircase.

"You can also see another interesting pattern that confirms what we would expect from a global flood. You would expect many larger animals to survive the Flood waters initially, leaving their tracks in the accumulating sediment layers as they tried to escape the rising waters. But eventually they would become exhausted, die, and get buried.

"What do we find? In the Tapeats Sandstone are fossilized tracks of trilobites scurrying across the sand, but fossilized remains of their bodies do not appear until higher up, at the transition into the Bright Angel Shale (Figure 4).

"Similarly, we find fossilized footprints of amphibians and reptiles in places that are much lower (in the Supai Group, Hermit Shale, and Coconino Sandstone, Figure 5) than the fossils of their bodies (in the Moenkopi Formation).[129]

Conclusion

"At the Grand Canyon-Grand Staircase strata sequence, both the column of sedimentary rock layers and the fossils are observable and real. The stacked layers throughout this region appear in a definite order. They contain fossils in a recognizable order, too, reflecting the order in which the organisms were buried during the Flood.

"Indeed, the pattern of first appearances doesn't fit the expected evolutionary order but instead is consistent with the rising flood waters, as they inundated the continents. Furthermore, even the pattern of finding tracks before bodies is consistent with creatures surviving in the initial flood waters before eventually perishing." [129]

In an evolutionary/uniformitarian system, there is no explanation for the explosion of life in the Cambrian system. The multicellular fossils found by the billions in Cambrian strata on every continent on earth, including Antarctica, have no evolutionary explanation. The evidence certainly indicates some form of a creation event at the beginning of the Cambrian system, even if you reject the concept of Creation.

Even more perplexing to evolution are the Ediacaran Biotas. The Ediacaran Biotas,[130] which uniformitarians believe to be older than Cambrian strata, are complex multicellular organisms which do not fit into an evolutionary scheme. These organisms do not seem to have any relationship with any supposed later, simpler organisms.

As we progress from the lowest (elevation) to the higher systems, the simplest and most logical explanation based on observation is that all of these organisms were alive at the same time and were covered by successive catastrophic waves of various materials. The difference was location and circumstances, not vast amounts of time. Most organisms survived the cataclysm which deposited the initial system. Some more organisms died in the next catastrophe. Even uniformitarians recognize the overlap of index fossils from one system to the next.

When more evidence becomes available, theories might need to be revised based on that evidence. Just as the eruption of Mt. Vesuvius fossilized bread in the ovens of Pompeii, each strata rapidly fossilized the entombed organisms in the worldwide flood.

1) The Walker/Klevberg model

Throughout[131] the explanation of fossils in the Geologic Strata, there were many explanations "forced" into a geological model that does not fit the evidence. The Walker/Klevberg model might need some minor modifications, but it fits the evidence.

The Creation Event created the original foundation materials, including the clays and soils for plants. One serious question many creationists ask: "Did the strata of the Creation Event include minerals and/or stones near the surface where men would see/use them or was the original surface of the earth entirely or almost entirely clay/soil?" Put another way, is stone completely, or almost completely, from the Flood period and later? These modules have no answer for this. Perhaps this is an area you would like to research.

The sorting of fossils according to strata are best explained by hydrodynamic sorting, ecological niches and attempts by various organisms to escape the rising floodwaters. It is possible that some Cambrian organisms (for example) were trapped and entombed in one location at the same time Devonian organisms (for example) on the other side of the globe were trapped and being entombed.

This sounds complicated, until we turn to the Walker/Klevberg model which has earth's entire geologic history divided into four simple Eras: Creation Week, antediluvian Era, the Deluge Era and

Postdiluvial Era. The antediluvian Era (1656 years) may or may not have left evidence in a stratum. It is followed by the Deluge Era (370 days) which produced most of the strata observable today. This is simply followed by the Postdiluvial Era, which is divided into residual and modern. The Postdiluvial Era/residual phase is the Ice Age(s) and the continents settling into their approximate modern locations.

A 370 day flood[132] is based on Bodie Hodge's timeline, *Biblical Overview of the Flood Timeline.*

The Walker/Klevberg model clearly recognizes the catastrophic formation of the geologic strata and permits the massive variety which is clearly seen in the field observations. It even allows for a version of "the present is the key to the past," as long we understand that the past was catastrophic.

    2) Total Number of Species

A commonly-raised objection to this evidence is the total number of species found in the fossil record. Uniformitarians claim that the massive number of different species in the fossils record proves some type of progression from one species to another, even if is not evolution as evolution is presented today. By that they mean that evolution is proved by the variety of species in the fossil record, even if our understanding of evolution is flawed.

There are two parts to the answer to this objection.

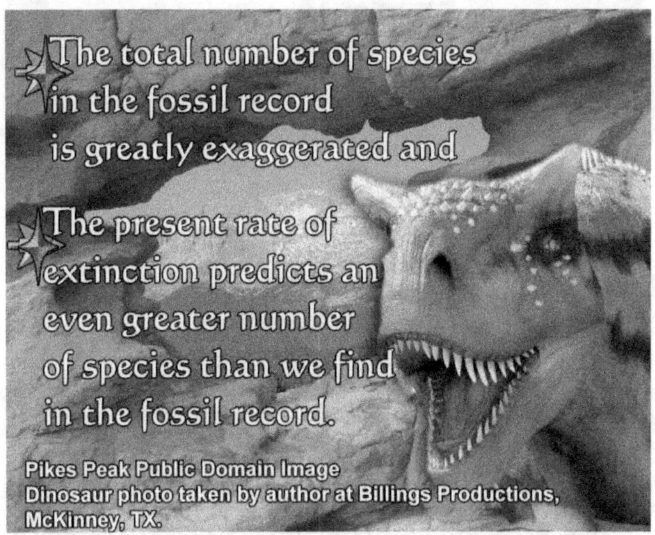

Pikes Peak Public Domain Image
Dinosaur photo taken by author at Billings Productions, McKinney, TX.

The total number of fossils not represented by living organisms is massively exaggerated.

> "According to[133] a new analysis of dinosaur fossils by University of Pennsylvania researchers, specimens once thought part of three distinct species of the genus *Psittacosaurus* all derive from a single species. The case of mistaken identity arose not from the anatomical variety among different animals, but rather the differences in how the fossil remains of each were buried and compressed."

(Material skipped)

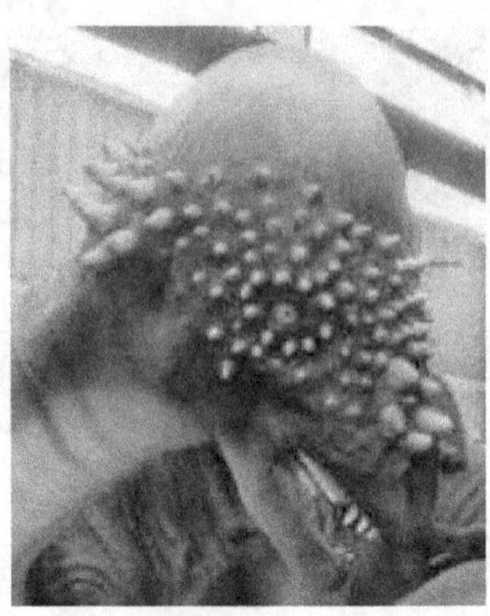

Dinosaur photo by the authors taken at Billings Productions in McKinney, TX.

"In a story similar to the three species of *Psittacosaurus* consolidated into one, in 2009 two species of dome-headed dinosaur, one of which was named *Dracorex hogwartsia* after Hogwarts in the Harry Potter series, were wiped out of existence. What was once thought to be distinct animals were in fact juvenile and nearly sexually mature specimens from the same species.

"One of the study's authors, renowned paleontologist John 'Jack' Horner, suggested that as many as a third of named dinosaur species could be cleared from the record books as they might simply be juvenile versions of another identified dinosaur."[133]

John Horner's suggestion for dinosaur species is just as valid for all species, not just dinosaurs. Compare this to the article by J. W. Valentine, "How Good[134] Was the Fossil Record?" J. W. Valentine believes "The bulk of the marine invertebrate fossil record [which is the majority of the fossil record] does not represent a series of unusual skeletal accumulations, but rather the preserved remnants of an excellent original record formed through ordinary though episodic processes." As long we understand that "episodic processes" were very rapid, part of the Flood and the following Ice Age, we agree with this statement. However, J. W. Valentine believes that "episodic processes" were millions of years.

According to Valentine's article, "At least 85% of durably skeletonized living species (families of bivalves and gastropods of the California Province [ocean, continental shelf]) may have been captured in the [fossil] record."

Today we observe the extinction of species. The extinction rate of species for the past 200 hundred years is known, studied and tested. Using the basic uniformitarian *assumption*, that the present is the key to the past, they project that extinction rate of the past 200 years into the distant past. If that were accurate, we would expect very many more species than we observe in the fossil record.

Saying that what we see in the fossil record are species that became extinct over millions of years is a uniformitarian *assumption*. It depends, according to Valentine, on there being large numbers of species that would represent the intermediary stages of evolution. He admits that not all are represented in the fossil record but explains that some were lost because of erosion, decomposition before fossilizing, etc. In other words, he *believes* there are more species that would fill in the fossil record completely, based on his assumptions that the 200-year observed extinction rate continued back into antiquity at the same rate. He does not have the physical evidence of these unaccounted-for species.

The actual number of observed species today compared to the number of species in the fossil record is best explained by a massive, recent, catastrophic event such as the Flood.

The fact is that all modern species were preserved with ancestors on board the ark. Extinctions have occurred for the last four thousand years since the Flood, not evolution. Another word for this devolution. These extinctions make the foundation of uniformitarianism, vast periods of time or deep time extremely unlikely, if not completely impossible.

3) Coal formation

The Flood is well under way. The strata are loose and plastic enough to move about as continents move, to fold and bend, though there was enough heat and pressure to either form fossils or preserve the bones for later fossil formation. Larger air-breathing land animals have moved to higher ground and still survive.

Then something changed. Through some type of destructive force or forces thousands of times more powerful than the combined destructive power of the comet/meteorite exploding over Tunguska and the eruption of Mt. St. Helens, trees from all over the planet were ripped from their soil and washed into the rising sea. With this hypothesis, these trees were either waterlogged, which is unlikely, or covered by another layer of material which drove the trees to the bottom of the sea. It is unlikely they simply became waterlogged because there does not seem to be enough time. If all the mountains were covered in less than forty days, then all the flood systems were all deposited in forty days or less. The Triassic system was likely formed only days or at the most weeks after the rains began. This hypothesis has the Carboniferous system forming no later than halfway through the forty days of rain, perhaps earlier. This does not seem to be enough time for the trees to waterlog.

Another possibility fits the evidence. The trees, probably almost all the trees on the planet, were stripped from the soil very early, perhaps in the initial blast which also triggered the Flood. The trees floated on the rising sea for some time. With this hypothesis, the trees likely sank because they accumulated material with each successive event (explosions and/or eruptions), and were eventually covered with so much material that in an additional layer of material drove the floating plant mass to the bottom. Whatever the mechanism, this took place before the larger Triassic and Jurassic organisms were entombed and fossilized, probably before the entire landmass was covered by water. This helps explain why even though coal beds cover much of the earth today, there were enough plants on the surface of the antediluvian world to account for the existing coal beds. It not only means that the entire antediluvian world was covered in vegetation, no deserts, but also that there was a greater landmass than we see today. The surface area of the antediluvian seas were smaller. This greater landmass was necessary to produce the vegetation we find in coal beds.[135]

The study of the dimensions of the ark gives us information about the conditions of the flood. The ark's design was most suitable for continuous winds from the same direction. So the amount of coal we find today tells us how much greater was the antediluvian land mass. It also tells us that this greater landmass was covered in vegetation. It also tells us that the conditions of the flood converted most of this vegetation into coal.

The larger animals of the antediluvian period were entombed in layers on top of the coal. These animals escaped the earlier catastrophes. As the Dr. Snelling quote pointed out, the pattern is consistent with animals attempting to escape flood waters. The plants in the various strata represented differences in various elevations or altitudes and ecological niches. Once again, the differences between the various strata are differences in location, ecological niches and some hydro-sorting of carcasses, not differences in time. "Index fossils" are being used by uniformitarians to date strata, but it is entirely possible that different strata systems were being deposited *at the same time* or at least only days apart, just in different places.

Unlike the Disney depiction in *Fantasia*, there was no drought. They drowned or were overwhelmed in a sudden catastrophe.

It is very likely that the strata were entombed in a very rapid series of volcanic eruptions combined with rapid flowing seawater in a matter of hours, days or at the most weeks. Some strata are comprised entirely of sand or other nonvolcanic material. Some strata are strictly volcanic material such as basalt. Much of the material in most strata, such as granite and shale, are a combination of materials. One or a series of these catastrophes ripped the trees out of the ground and the result was a floating mass of plant material larger than anything modern man has witnessed.

At some point, very likely no more than a few *weeks* later, as the Flood waters continued to rise, the final flood deposits entombed the remaining organisms. The important point is that these last organisms were able to escape the earlier waves of catastrophes by *where* they lived, not *when* they lived. The Cretaceous shells of saprophyte microbes which fed off of dead bodies of the antediluvian creatures are part of the Cretaceous strata. These organisms could have bloomed for years, perhaps decades or centuries (centuries is highly unlikely), until they completely devoured all remaining carcasses which were not entombed.

A brief summary; an explosive event stripped the land of vegetation, which floated on the surface of the water. The compressed biomass formed the coal we see today. A series of deposits buried organisms in different strata. The remains of unburied organisms were consumed by a saprophyte microbe bloom whose shells make up the world wide chalk strata named the Cretaceous system. There are possibly Ice Age strata on top of the flood strata.

"Some Paleocene ocean bottom sediments may be post-Flood, while some Pliocene sediments could be from the Flood, based on uncertainties in evolutionary microorganism classification." Michael Oard, *The Geologic Column Is a General Flood Order with Many Exceptions* (previously cited)

4) Residual (Post Flood)

While there is considerable disagreement as to which strata according to uniformitarian labels are preflood and which are post flood, the following describes a post flood world. It is interesting that the very term "Tertiary" is a creationist view of geology.

> "...the Italian[136] naturalist, Giovanni Arduino (1714-1795), divided the different types of rock strata into three categories: Primary rocks were the crystalline basement rocks present at creation. Secondary rocks were from the sediments laid down by the Genesis Flood and contained the fossil remains of pre-flood life. Tertiary rocks were those resulting from more recent local flood sediments, volcanoes and earthquakes."

The following is a typical uniformitarian description of the Tertiary climate.

> "The beginning[137] of the Tertiary Period was very warm and moist compared to today's climate. Much of the earth was tropical or sub-tropical. Palm trees grew as far north as Greenland! By the middle of the tertiary, during the Oligocene Epoch, the climate began to cool. This cooling trend continued and by the Pliocene Epoch at the end of the Tertiary Period, an ice age had begun."

When Noah stepped out of the Ark, the air was filled with volcanic ash and aerosols. The oceans were a thick soup of carcasses, ash, silt, and the beginning or in the midst of a saprophyte microbe bloom. Marine life, including immobile organisms such as corals survived. So either there were areas relatively free of pollutants, or the pollution was not so severe as destroy all sea life or both. Volcanic activity warmed the oceans and the vegetation which survived the Flood was likely tropical or subtropical, exactly what the uniformitarians describe.

We know that aquatic life survived, fresh water as well as marine. This tells us that the oceans either did not have the same level of contamination worldwide or that God in some fashion miraculously preserved these organisms. We can also assume that salinity levels were lower during the flood. Marine creatures can live in a reduced salt environment while fresh water organisms can tolerate some salt.

Immediately after flood the atmosphere was filled with volcanic ash and aerosols, especially the upper atmosphere, blocking sunlight. This contributed to snow in the higher altitudes, triggering an Ice Age. The sea levels dropped and mountains rose.

As the hot sea levels continued to slowly fall and mountains rose, the environment near the mountaintops turned colder. The heavy snowfall did not melt during the summers and turned into ice. As the sea levels fell, the temperate zone also fell. Mountains continued to rise, ice spread on the growing mountains, and this ice descended down the mountains, forming glaciers and followed the retreating sea levels. The temperature of the oceans likely remained fairly constant for hundreds of years. Over time, the volcanic ash and aerosols precipitated out of the atmosphere and settled to the sea floors.

Uniformitarians will, in the main agree with these statements because that is the evidence. Our disagreement with uniformitarians is that we believe the evidence shows that this took decades, years, or at the most centuries. The animals which left the ark had abundant food and at first few, if any predators. What followed was a population explosion. Once again, there was ecological separation, and very little chronological separation. We have the same conditions on earth today; polar regions, tropical regions, subtropical, deep ocean, reef regions, desert regions, high altitude regions, rain forest regions, prairies, central Asian steppes, African Savannas, swamps and thousands of other ecological niches.

While there was considerable adaptation to the new conditions after the Flood and organisms changed their physical appearance due to these adaptations, the majority of these creatures lived at the same time, just in different ecological niches. This is exactly what is observed today.

 5) Modern Strata:

This is the geologic[138] period when the earth stabilized into the ecology we know.

> The USGS sums up the fossils of the Modern Period (Quaternary System). "Fossils from the Holocene epoch are like the animals living today, whereas Pleistocene fossils are much like living animals but with some differences. Many observations show that Pleistocene time was characterized by long periods of arctic conditions that allowed ice and snow to cover vast areas of land and sea, and so it is sometimes called the Ice Age. Animals of that time, such as the mammoth and the saber-toothed cat, were equipped to deal with those conditions. Holocene time is the warmer epoch since the last time of widespread icy conditions."[138]

There is no way of knowing that these animals lived in different time periods. Perhaps they lived before the flood in the antediluvian period. The important point is that even uniformitarians admit that these adaptations are proof of a change in environment. Move an arctic animal such as a caribou, arctic fox, wolf, polar bear, etc., into a desert climate. It will lose its heavier fur and adapt. "The Gray Wolf has a larger natural distribution than any other mammal except humans. It once ranged through all of North America from the Arctic Circle to central Mexico."[139]

In the same manner, transport desert mammals such as jackrabbits and coyotes into an arctic environment and they will grow thicker fur to adapt to the climate. "The coyote's range has expanded and now reaches from Central America to the Arctic."[140]

These adaptations are observed today to be quite rapid, sometimes only taking only weeks, months or at the most a generation. Why is it *assumed* to take thousands of years when there is no observer?

3. Summary of the Fossil Record

This is easily the most lengthy and difficult material in any *Conflict of the Ages* module. It is an honest examination of facts which form the foundation for the religious belief in deep time and as such, is the bedrock foundation for the religion of secular humanism. So we need to carefully summarize the facts as a whole. These are the most significant points as to the fossil record.

a. The record of the Word of God is Authoritative.

The record of the Word of God should be read the same way we read Shakespeare, Julius Caesar, or Herodotus. The information is exact and accurate, but we might need to adjust our understanding. God created the universe and all that is in it in a period of six days (a day being a complete rotation of the earth, approximately twenty-four hours), evening and morning for each day. The earth and the universe were created perfect. Adam and Eve chose to join Satan in rebellion against our just, holy, perfect, and loving Creator. Unlike Satan, they repented of their sin. Before Adam and Eve left the garden, there was no death. Therefore, there were no fossils before the sin of Adam and Eve.

b. Antediluvian Geology

Like the Modern Mississippi/Missouri rivers system, land rose gradually from the sea to the garden of Eden. The river which watered the garden divided into 4 parts as it left the garden and watered the (entire?) earth. The modern Columbia/Snake river system originates in Alberta and Western Wyoming, then flows to the Pacific. The Modern Yellowstone/Missouri river system originates just in and North of Yellowstone and joins the Mississippi, then flows to the Gulf of Mexico. The modern Green River originates just south of Yellowstone, then joins the Colorado River and flows to the Gulf of California. The Snake, Yellowstone, Missouri, and Green rivers all originate in or near Yellowstone and flow in different directions, similar to the river which left the garden of Eden.

So the earth had one continent at creation. Perhaps there were islands. The entire climate was mild, the

seas were shallow compared to the oceans today,
winters were warmer, summers were cooler, organisms
lived longer, grew larger and there was great diversity
of the same kind. God had not given permission to eat
meat, so populations exploded, both plant and animals.
The abundance of organisms exceeds our
comprehension if we insist on thinking of the
antediluvian world in terms of what we observe today.
*All of the organisms in the fossil record from the
Cambrian system to at least the Jurassic system were
alive and co-existing at the beginning of the Flood.*

c. The Flood Begins

Volcanic activity began as the water began pouring
down (the sluice-gates of heaven were opened).
Geysers, steam eruptions and magma filled with steam
began flooding the depths of the seas. The eruptions
stripped the plant life, especially most of the trees,
from the land.

Any creature which could move fled from the
catastrophe. The entombing material came in waves
and consisted variously of sand, volcanic material,
conglomerate, and metamorphic material. The deepest
parts of the seas were entombed first. As we see by the
fish, microbes, algae, whales, sharks, corals, etc.
around us today, the waves of entombing deposits
never covered every place on earth and every creature
in the seas. Fresh water fish are capable of surviving in
salt water, especially when the salt content is diluted.
While vast numbers of corals, sea anemones, and other
slow-moving or fixed organisms perished, some
survived.

d. Geologic Strata Formed by the Flood

The similarities in creatures from one strata to the next
are best explained by creatures attempting to escape
the rising floodwaters. The strata from the Cambrian to
the Devonian are simple progression from deepest
seas. Those creatures who were the youngest, weakest
and otherwise least able to escape were entombed first.
The strongest and most able to escape were entombed
last. The Devonian system was also filled with fossils

such as corals which were fixed in place. This means that the catastrophic waves were growing in magnitude and covered more area.

The floating plant material was forced to the bottom and entombed in several strata of material, called by modern geologists the Carboniferous system. The Carboniferous system compressed with great heat and pressure. This was likely caused by the additional material, deposited later in the Flood. As these strata were pressured upward to form the present day mountains, after the floodwaters dropped, they formed coal from the plant material.

Up to this point many animals had survived the earlier waves of catastrophes. Though much of the earth's dry land was under water at this point, some of the land, maybe as much as a third of the land still was not covered by the seas yet. At least three more waves of catastrophes, which the USGS labels Permian, Triassic, and Jurassic, ended all air-breathing antediluvian life outside the ark (except for aquatic animals such as dolphins). A worldwide bloom of saprophyte microbes with calcium carbonate shells are part of the Cretaceous stratum.

Some creationists believe that the evidence concludes that the Cretaceous stratum is the last flood stratum. These scientists believe that all strata above the Cretaceous strata are from the Ice Age. Others disagree.

"Some Paleocene ocean bottom sediments may be post-Flood, while some Pliocene sediments could be from the Flood, based on uncertainties in evolutionary microorganism classification." Michael Oard *The Geologic Column Is a General Flood Order with Many Exceptions* (cited previously)

These strata and systems were not deposited in neat horizontal layers in perfect order. A simple cross-country trip in any country, but especially North America, where the highway system has exposed tens of thousands of folds and bends in every direction, causes any thoughtful person to realize that a catastrophic explanation is the only realistic explanation.

"When one realizes that there are hundreds of alleged overthrusts (they seem to occur in most mountain ranges of the world), and that mountains are usually among the few places to observe a thick vertical sequence, one is forced to conclude that out-of-order strata are common. A real overthrust should show abundant physical evidence; relying just on fossils is unreasonable. If these strata cannot be tied to a real overthrust, then the fossil distribution in the geological column is contrary to evolutionary predictions."[141] (Michael Oard)

G. The Ice Age

It might seem odd today, but it wasn't until around 1875 that more than a handful of people understood that an Ice Age, or a series of Ice Ages, ever existed. The primary evidences were the fossil moraines where ice had at one time pushed small stones, fossils, boulders and other material into piles. As the ice melted, the moraines puzzled later observers. A serious and worldwide examination of the evidence has come to many counterintuitive conclusions.

> "The causes of ice ages are not fully understood for both the large-scale ice age periods and the smaller ebb and flow of glacial/interglacial periods within an ice age. The consensus is that several factors are important..."[142]

On the subject of the Ice Age, these modules follow, in general, Michael Oard's *Frozen In Time*. The book is available as a paperback and free online from *Answers In Genesis*.

Michael Oard theorizes that there was a single Ice Age after the Flood which lasted about 700 years. Since this time period is well beyond the scope of this module, we will post several important points about the Ice Age here and begin the next module with the civilization of the Ice Age.

Here is a list of what we know about an Ice Age.

1. The Sea Levels Were Approximately 400 Feet Lower.

When Noah[143] and his family left the ark, the sea levels were very high.

> *But God remembered Noah and all the beasts and all the cattle that were with him in the*

*ark; and God caused a wind to pass over the
earth, and the water subsided. Also the
fountains of the deep and the floodgates of the
sky were closed, and the rain from the sky
was restrained; and the water receded
steadily from the earth, and at the end of one
hundred and fifty days the water decreased.
In the seventh month, on the seventeenth day
of the month, the ark rested upon the
mountains of Ararat. The water decreased
steadily until the tenth month; in the tenth
month, on the first day of the month, the tops
of the mountains became visible.* Genesis 8:1-
5 NASB

Note the phrases *the water subsided, the water
receded steadily from the earth, the water decreased,
the water decreased steadily*. This subsiding probably
continued for centuries, though at a lower rate.
Uniformitarians point out that at the lowest point, sea
level "was 120 m lower (394 feet) at the peak of the last
ice age"[144] than the current sea levels. That is the
evidence. The issue is when. It seems that this depth is
the edge of the continental shelves worldwide. The
continents had already moved to their existing
locations with this lower sea level. This was sometime
well after the flood, probably centuries after the flood.
It is very likely that the world's oceans remained at
these lower levels for some time.

Human towns, cities or villages existed in what is today
the English Channel. Not only were the sea levels
lower, but people lived in the lower elevations and were
able to walk from one continent to another.

2. The Ice Continuously Advanced and Retreated.

There are many guesses as to how far and how fast the
ice advanced and retreated. It seems that each article
states that "scientists *know*" there were five or eight or
three separate ice ages. The truth is no one "knows"
with certainty. It is very likely that there were
enormous differences just from one year to the next.

This is due to the Ice Age glaciers building up from "snowblitzes."

> (Note – The following sections all quote from the same article source noted here.)"The post-Flood Ice Age model reveals that the Ice Age developed over large areas all at once, immediately after Noah's flood."[145]

> "Most of the snow that fell during the Ice Age would have been associated with storms rather than appear as continuous snowfall. Understanding the location of the storm tracks is essential to predicting where the snow and ice first built up."

If the continents did not move to their current locations until near the end of Peleg's lifetime, 340 years after Noah left the ark, then the earlier storm tracks are completely unknowable. Storm tracks with the continents in their existing positions are knowable. They would be similar to the weather patterns we are familiar with today. Any differences can be calculated and accurate computer models can be developed.

3. The Arctic Ocean Was Free of Ice During the Ice Age.

> "There would be an interesting distribution of snow and ice over the northern areas of the ice sheets, those lands bordering the Arctic Ocean. Remember that, right after the Flood, the Arctic Ocean would have no sea ice, as the water temperature would be quite warm. During the first several years of the Ice Age, this warm water would often be subject to cool air masses overriding it. This would cause strong evaporation. At the same time, the air would be heated up by contact with the warm ocean and the release of latent heat from the water vapor when it condensed. The warm air would keep the areas bordering the Arctic Ocean ice free at the beginning of the Ice Age. But the heavy moisture in the area would greatly boost snow and ice accumulation

farther inland from the Arctic Ocean, a bit like
the Donn and Ewing Ice Age theory. This
explains why the Keewatin portion of the
Laurentide ice sheet, northwest of Hudson
Bay, was an ice dome during the Ice Age."[145]

The Ice Age oceans were warm, perhaps even hot by today's standards. High tides, such as the fifty-plus-foot tides in the Bay of Fundy, between New Brunswick and Nova Scotia, are capable of transporting this warm water far inland and keeping inland waterways free of ice.

4. Antarctica Was Tropical at One Time.

The frozen remains of tropical vegetation exist under the Antarctic ice caps.

The tropical vegetation found today under the existing Ice Caps might be post flood. According to this hypothesis, the vegetation we find today in Antarctica under the ice caps all grew in approximately 340 years after the flood. It might indicate how rapidly plants and likely plant eaters recovered after the flood.

5. Ice Was in the Higher Elevations.

The spring/summer thaws caused enormous annual changes in the size of the rivers, so that local and even regional floods were common. The warm seas attracted animals to a warm coastline. The warmer seas also prevented arctic ice.

"Southeast Canada and New England would
lie in a very favorable area for rapid
accumulation of snow and ice. That is
probably why Labrador was one of the ice
domes of the Laurentide ice sheet of central
and eastern Canada."

"The area just east of the Rocky Mountains in
North America would be unglaciated at this
time because of warm air from the Pacific
Ocean overriding the mountains and
descending as mild chinook winds. This is
called the ice-free corridor. The warm Arctic

and North Pacific Oceans would also have kept most of Siberia and Alaska unglaciated at this time. It was warm enough in the lowlands of Siberia and Alaska and the ice-free corridor to allow all the animal migrations into the Americas during the early and middle part of the Ice Age. By now you are getting an idea as to why the woolly mammoths would be able to live in Siberia and Alaska during the Ice Age and why the lowlands would remain unglaciated."[145]
(End of "Snowblitz"-sourced material)

6. There Are Remains[146] of Millions of Ice Age Animals.

From the Yukon through Siberia to Scandinavia there are millions of animal remains such as mammoths, saber-tooth tigers, woolly rhinoceros, bison, and wild horses. The year-round vegetation was plentiful and there was no ice near sea level, though the winters were cold. While most of these remains are now frozen in permafrost, few, if any, are actual fossils.

7. Humans were highly developed from the beginning.

Humans lived in cities, had writing skills, developed civilization and were adept sailors throughout this time period. The hunting parties which visited caves were not much different from hunting parties today.

8. Human artifacts are found in Glaciers.

Human[147] artifacts are constantly found in thawing glaciers; tools, weapons, clothing, jewelry, and items which are obviously man-made but we have no idea what they were.

Many of these items are less than two thousand years old. From these human artifacts, we understand that glaciers grow and retreat far more rapidly than textbooks teach us. The most scientific example of the rapid growth of glaciers is *Glacier Girl*. A squadron of WWII aircraft landed and were abandoned on a Greenland glacier during WWII. When they were found

more than 50 years later, one P38 was recovered under 268 feet of ice. The entire squadron, including a B17, had flowed three miles with the glacier. They were all found at the same depth in the ice. The borehole down to the planes went through thousands of layers of ice. Each one of those thousands of layers was deposited since the planes landed in WWII.
(Also see mention of this in our *Antidisestablishmentarianism* Ch. 14 Appendix)

9. Different groups of Ice Age organisms.

There are different organisms in different strata. However, there are multiple solutions to this. These answers are similar to the answers to how the geologic strata formed.

The first is separation by biological niche, not time. The catastrophes which entombed these creatures was neither worldwide nor are the creatures extinct. For example, though there are no woolly mammoths today, there are elephants. The catastrophe which killed millions of woolly mammoths, woolly rhinoceroses, bison and many other organisms was regional, not global.

The second solution is vastly different conditions in a very short period of time. Animals would adapt quickly to a rapidly changing environment. With this hypothesis, the changing environment brings about visible changes in organisms which are actually the same species, perhaps even parents and children. A modern example is transporting a pair of desert-bred shorthair dogs to an arctic climate. This has been documented many times. While the parents had thin short hair, usually the puppies have three coats of long hair suitable for arctic conditions. Adaptations do not need to take hundreds or thousands of years.

The third solution is that there are many kinds of animals found together in Siberian permafrost, tarpits and bone graveyards. The separation is not complete as the strata might indicate.

The standard creationist position is that both of these combine to make the most complete solution. The differences observed today in Ice Age organisms in geologic strata is separation by ecological niche and extremely rapid adaptation.

10. Summary

After Noah and his family left the ark, the seas were hot by today's standards. The sea level continued to fall for years until it was about 400 feet below what we know today as a normal sea level.

At some point, the highest mountain tops began to get snow. As the warm water evaporated large amounts of moisture, the storms became what modern meteorologists call snowblitzes. Instead of slow gradual ice buildup, the ice was deposited rapidly. The retreats and advances of the glaciers were rapid, perhaps many times per year. One reasonable theory proposes that the weight of the ice triggered the breakup of the continents.

The breakup of the continents might have taken place during an ice age. The change in the climate for many animals made it impossible for them to travel great distances. For some animals this meant an increase in food supply and a population explosion. Many other animals were unable to survive the changes.

This did not end the ice age, but likely changed the ice regions. It is easy to understand that some could interpret such a dramatic shift as an end to one ice age and the beginning of a new one.

The important point is that whatever happened, there was very little time from the single continent to the breakup and settling of the continents as we know them. Even if the single continent broke up during the Flood and not 340 years later during the lifetime of Peleg, the meteorological factors which caused the ice age were the same. The only factor we are not certain of is the exact placement of the mountains and the continents so we can know the patterns of the ice age snowblitzes. Whenever the continents settled into their current locations, the existing storm patterns became the rule.

How Much Is Enough?

H. How Much Is Enough?

Before examining the fossil evidence, every student with his teacher must decide how much detail is enough. The high priest of secular humanist physics said, "Today we still yearn to know why we are here and where we came from. Humanity's deepest desire for knowledge is justification enough for our continuing quest. And our goal is nothing less than a complete description of the universe we live in."[148] Stephen Hawking, *A Brief History of Time*.

Solomon correctly phrased the same idea 3000 years ago.

> [God]*"has made everything appropriate in its time. He has also set eternity in their heart, yet so that man will not find out the work which God has done from the beginning to the end."* (Ecclesiastes 3:11 NASB)

These questions, these issues, will never go away. If you, like Stephen Hawking, reject the information God gave us in His Word, then you will be searching without a final answer your entire life. However, even if you accept His Word as true and authoritative, you still need to know and understand how to answer questions. Other people will ask you questions. You will come across things you see your entire life that will cause you to question.

The answers to these questions are the foundation of our society. Politicians legalize and permit abortions because they accept the idea that we are the product of random chance. There never will be, according to uniformitarians, a final judgment before God. Survival of the fittest justifies gangs, wars, rapes, corporate raids on private property, concentration camps, and other nameless atrocities. Every action we take is because of what we believe. And uniformitarians believe that vast amounts of time explain a universe where God is not necessary.

There is easily enough material to spend the rest of your life studying geology in great detail. If you choose to dedicate your life to the study of geology, you will uncover more questions than answers and leave much work for your children, grandchildren and great-grandchildren.

1. Geology

A simple overview of God's overall plan, including the geology of the flood, is in David Bergsland's book *The Training Place of Mankind; God's Creation Explained For Normal Folk.* This book is reviewed on our blog. Whatever your level of experience and education, this inexpensive ebook should be read by everyone. Our review is included in the appendix of this work. While David Bergsland's work is an enjoyable and inexpensive read, it is not the work of a professional geologist. It is an excellent broad-ranging overview, quoting others correctly and in context.

Professionals wrote this next work, *A Pocket Guide To The Global Flood* by Ken Ham, Tim Lovett, Andrew A. Snelling, and John Whitmore. It is still a brief book written on the high school level, but it is longer and more detailed than David Bergsland's. It is also focused on the Flood. I have reviewed this book on our blog. We include that review in the appendix of this work. *A Pocket Guide* is published by AiG.

The Genesis Record by Henry M. Morris is a devotional commentary on the book of Genesis. Written in 1978, it includes a well-written scientific defense of Genesis as an historical record.

The Global Flood by Dr. John D. Morris covers the same material as *A Pocket Guide To The Global Flood* from a slightly more technical perspective. It is 176 pages, more than twice the size of *A Pocket Guide,* though less than 20% of the size of Dr. Andrew A. Snelling's *Earth's Catastrophic Past.* It is an introduction for people who are not familiar with the idea of a global flood. *The Global Flood* is published by ICR (2012).

Flood by Design (Design Series) by Michael Oard examines the geology of the earth after the cataclysm of the flood. 130 pages, Master books April 30, 2008

Geology By Design by Carl Freode Jr is a somewhat more technical work. This is an excellent refutation of secularist geology with their uniformitarian principles. Master Books October 4, 2007

The classic, *The Genesis Flood*, by Henry M. Morris and John C. Whitcomb is 518 pages in the softcover 50th anniversary edition. It was written in 1961. It is a detailed examination of the physical evidence and how it matches the historical record of the Word of God. Because this is an older technical work, there are places where the reading is difficult and the latest discoveries are not included. As with any scientific work over fifty years old, there is more information available today than at the time of publication. What is surprising for an older technical work is how much of the work is not only valid but also necessary for modern readers. While the authors are routinely attacked and vilified, the information contained in it has withstood the decades of attack. Its accuracy puts *The Genesis Flood* on the same level as Einstein's work on General Relativity.

The two volume *Earth's Catastrophic Past: Geology, Creation and the Flood* by Andrew A. Snelling is both an update and a massive rework of the classic *The Genesis Flood* by Whitcomb and Morris. The Institute For Creation Research published it in 2009. It has almost 1100 pages and 126 chapters. The language is technical, but not beyond the grasp of anyone willing to accept the challenge of understanding the material. The vocabulary is suitable for advanced homeschooled high school students. This is the most technical work on our recommended list. The table of contents is available online as a pdf file at icr.org.

There are also online sources such as biblicalgeology.net. We placed each of these books in order of progress in increasing difficulty and detail. While ICR and AiG publish most of these, they are not the only publishers presenting a biblical framework of history. Bob Jones University Press includes this perspective in all of their science and history textbooks. There are also many excellent books on individual subjects.

2. The Ark

Worldwide Flood is a website with considerable technical information on the ark.

http://www.worldwideflood.com/

Noah's Ark; Thinking Outside the Box by Tim Lovett is based on naval research of ancient ships. It does not come to the same conclusions I do, but the research is well worth reading. Master Books (March 18, 2008)

3. Apologetics

The Greatest Hoax on Earth? Refuting Dawkins on Evolution. by Jonathan Sarfati This is a point by point refutation of Richard Dawkins' book *The Greatest Show on Earth.* (Creation Book Publishers; First edition (March 1, 2010))

Ultimate Proof of Creation by Dr Jason Lisle

This is a little different. This book uses material evidence to support the teachings of Scripture about the original creation and the flood. It is a method of dealing with people. It also deals with evidence, but it is mostly about logical arguments. (Master Books, May 29, 2009)

4. Astronomy

Taking Back Astronomy by Jason Lisle

While this is primarily a book about light and astronomy, there is a small section on geology. Master Books (June 1, 2006)

Starlight and Time by Dr. Russell Humphreys:
This 1994 work deals with several leading theories on how a 6000 year old universe, earth time, can be billions of light years across. It also contains a

monograph on the original creation of the entire universe as water. It might just be the shortest book in this list.

Starlight, Time, and the New Physics by John Hartnett

Starting from the same thesis used by Dr. Russell Humphreys in Starlight and Time, that the world is 6000 years old and that the Bible is an accurate historical record of both the Cosmos and the Earth, Dr. Hartnett uses the latest information and combines that information with the best workable theories. (Creation Book Publishers, LLC; First edition (September 28, 2007)

5. Geology: Additional

These are not evaluated, nor are they in any particular order.

Rock Solid Answers: The Biblical Truth Behind 14 Geologic Questions by Mike Oard and John K. Reed
This is a more technical work. 272 pages. Master Books (November 17, 2009)

The Young Earth: The Real History of the Earth - Past, Present and Future by John Morris
This is mostly geology, but of some other areas to give an overview of evidence for a young earth. Master books (October 23, 2007)

Noah's Flood: Birth of the Ice Age by Robert L. Gielow
This book is included simply because the author believes in the authority of the Scriptures. It is safer than many who claim to believe in the authority of Scripture but put the findings of fallible men ahead of the Word of God by believing the earth to be millions of years old. I do not follow his reasoning and actually believe some of his thinking to be rather dangerous. However, this makes it clear that not everyone who holds to the accuracy of the Scriptures must come to the same conclusions. Simon and Schuster (January 25, 2000)

6. The Ice Age

Frozen In Time by Michael Oard
Not to be confused with many other works of the same
title, this looks at the evidence for an Ice Age, or Ice
Ages, after the Flood of Noah. Published October 1,
2004 by Master Books

An Ice Age Caused by the Genesis Flood by Michael J.
Oard
243 pages, it is the first book presenting the thesis of a
post-flood Ice Age. Institute for Creation Research
(December 1990)

Life in the Great Ice Age by Michael J. and Beverly
Oard
This is a brief (72 page paperback) fictional account of
Jabeth and his family living in the Ice Age. It includes
historical and accurate information written in an easy-
to-read and interesting style. It is a cartoon/comic book
style with a study guide. Master Books (October 1993)

The Ice Age and the Genesis Flood by Michael Oard
A brief article by the Institute of Creation Research
which includes the major pieces of evidence for a single
Ice Age. http://www.icr.org/article/272

Was There Really an Ice Age? by John D. Morris,
Ph.D.
This short article has a simple answer.
http://www.icr.org/article/1121/277/

7. Radiohalos

The work of the RATE team is included in the next
section, Radiometric Dating. However, several chapters
of each of their books are dedicated to radiohalos.

Mysterious Bullet Holes in Rocks Part One by Andrew
A. Snelling
http://www.answersingenesis.org/articles/am/v7/n2/
mysterious-bullet-holes

*Radiohalos: The Mysterious Vanishing Bullets Part
Two* by Andrew A. Snelling
http://www.answersingenesis.org/articles/am/v7/n3/r
adiohalos-vanishing-bullets

Radiohalos: the Mystery of the Missing Bullets Part Three by Andrew A. Snelling
http://www.answersingenesis.org/articles/am/v7/n4/radiohalos-part-three

Dr. Snelling's three-part series breaks a complex subject down into sections which are possible to understand. The tiny mystery of radiohalos has two parts; *How did they get where they are?* and *What processes are responsible for the unusual radiohalos we find worldwide?* The series concentrates on the second and more difficult question. His conclusion, "So unless the granites cooled quickly, no polonium radiohalos could be present. Thus, the existence of the polonium radiohalos implies that granites crystallized and cooled within just six to ten days, not millions of years!" is arrived at with thorough research. He also explains a very complex subject with skill and simplicity.

Implications of Polonium Radiohalos in Nested Plutons of the Tuolumne Intrusive Suite, Yosemite, California
Answers Research Journal 2 (2009) 53-78
by Andrew A. Snelling and Dallel Gates April 8, 2009
From the abstract "The biotite flakes must have formed and cooled below 150° C before the polonium supply was exhausted and the radiohalos could be preserved, so the U decay had to be grossly accelerated and the formation of the plutons had to be within 6-10 days. Furthermore, rapid cooling of the plutons was facilitated by the hydrothermal fluid convection that rapidly generated the Po radiohalos, challenging conventional thinking that cooling is a slow process by conduction. It is evident that there were greater volumes of hydrothermal fluids in the later central intrusions of the nested plutons of the Tuolumne Intrusive Suite. So as expected, more Po radiohalos were generated in these plutons as they were sequentially intruded, confirming the hydrothermal fluid transport model for Po radiohalo formation. Thus granite pluton formation is consistent with the timescale of a young earth, and accelerated

radioisotope decay renders the absolute ages for these granite plutons grossly in error."
http://www.answersingenesis.org/articles/arj/v2/n1/r adiohalos-in-yosemite-granites

Creation's Tiny Mystery by Robert V Gentry 1992
It is also available online
http://www.halos.com/book/ctm-toc.htm
Dr. Gentry wrote the first material on radiohalos and testified in behalf of creationists in 1981. There are a number of more recent discoveries, which I believe call for a fundamental change. Many of the events Dr. Gentry believes occurred during the Creation Week should be moved to the flood. But this foundational work has the best documentation of the history of scientific work done on radiohalos available. He was the only person with intellect and wisdom to understand the significance of Professor John Joly's 1918 paper (Dublin, Ireland) combined with the courage to publish the scientific conclusion the evidence led to in the face of ridicule and ostracism.

Also, this contains the only source I could find to the actual transcripts of the *McLean v Arkansas Board of Education* trial 1981, ruling 1982. In this trial the expert witness for the ACLU, Dr. G. Brent Dalrymple, testified under oath that radiohalos were *a very tiny mystery*. He used the term as a double meaning, very tiny in size (atomic particle) and very tiny in importance because the weight of the (never explained) other, opposing evidence, overruled it. It is a must read, but it is incomplete.

Polonium Radiohalos: Still "A Very Tiny Mystery"
by Dr. Andrew Snelling
http://www.icr.org/article/polonium-radiohalos-still-a-very-tiny-mystery/

This is a shorter, yet slightly more technical, version of the three-part article series at the top of the page. The different perspective is well worth reading.

New Record of Polonium Radiohalos, Stone Mountain Granite, Georgia (USA)
by Mark Armitage

Since many Secular Humanists complain that the primary samples of zircons and radiohalos are from a narrow geographic are, this is an expansion to a different area. The similarity in results is impressive.

http://creation.com/new-record-of-polonium-radiohalos-stone-mountain-granite-georgia-usa#top

http://www.answersingenesis.org/articles/tj/v15/n1/radiohalos

8. Radiometric Dating

From the very finite perspective of a human being, the available written material seems infinite. Perhaps that is just the desire of Secular Humanists deceive you into believing that a vast amount of written information on a subject automatically means the information is trustworthy, factual, correct, and valid. For that reason, no radiometric document is included in this recommended reading list. If you wish to examine something from the Secular Humanist perspective which teaches that the earth is millions of years old, begin with a *Wikipedia* article, go to the works the article references, and research them. Since these will constantly change, we do not provide a link.

Thousands not Billions: Challenging the Icon of Evolution, Questioning the Age of the Earth by Dr. Don DeYoung copyright 2005, published by Master Books It is available in both paperback and as an epub; there is also a DVD available
Dr. Don DeYoung is actually a general editor. Each chapter or section has a separate author. While the majority of the book is about radiometric dating, there is a section on radiohalos and zircons.
This book presents some of the major conclusions of the ICR RATE team in a very readable style. Though it is a technical work, it holds to very similar standards as the COA series you are reading. That is, the target reading level is High School for both grammar and vocabulary. More technical information is include in a reference section in the back and additional reading is recommended and included in the reference section. There is both a name and a subject index.

Additional authors are Dr. John Baumgardner, Dr. Russell Humphreys, Dr. Andrew Snelling, Dr. Steven Austin, Dr. Eugene Chaffin and Dr. Steven Boyd.

Radioisotopes and the Age of the Earth, Volumes I & II
Larry Vardiman author, editor, Andrew Snelling editor, Eugene Chaffin editor
From the description on the ICR page, "The RATE book is a definitive resource on radioactive dating for every scientist's library, whether evolutionist or creationist. It examines radioisotope theory, exposes its plaguing problems, and offers a better alternative."
These cover many of the same issues as the book *Thousands not Billions* but in more depth. The grammar is not any more difficult, but the subject of discussion and occasionally the vocabulary is more difficult. Anyone with a High School education should not have difficulty with either the content or the writing style.
It is available free online as a pdf file from ICR.

Any material produced by the RATE team or any member of the RATE team is well worth your time reading.

This *Answers In Genesis* page is a great page to start. It is a page of links to articles about radiometric dating arranged by subject.

http://www.answersingenesis.org/get-answers/topic/radiometric-dating

The following 1998 article by Dr. David Plaisted is a technical overview of Radiometric dating. As an overview, it might not satisfy every possible question, but it certainly raises the questions while introducing every possible topic. It is highly recommended.

The Radiometric Dating Game

tasc-creationscience.org/other/plaisted/www.cs.unc.edu/-plaisted/ce/indes.html

cs.unc.edu/~plaisted/ce/dating.html

9. Ancient Documents Outside of the Bible

Ancient Post-Flood History: Historical Documents That Point to Biblical Creation by Ken Johnson Th.D. 2010

This is an essential collection of ancient documents and only $6.99 as an ebook on Smashwords. If you are only going to acquire two or three of these reference resources, this should be in that small collection. CreateSpace Independent Publishing Platform (January 1, 2010)

The Text of the Ancient Seder Olam by Ken Johnson, Th.D. Seder Olam means "order of eternity" in Hebrew. The author is unknown. It is a Hebrew chronology of the world from creation to the destruction of the 2nd temple in AD 70. The introduction says "an ancient Jewish work dated approximately AD 169," making it almost as old as Josephus. It uses the AM calendar. "This proves, just like fundamentalist Christians believe today, the ancient Jews believed in a real, physical Messiah, his 1000 year reign, and in the person and work of the Holy Spirit." "The teaching of the *Seder* is based on Scripture and ancient Jewish tradition." One very interesting contrast with the *Talmud* is that the *Seder Olam* records erroneous teaching that Jews held and points out that those teachings are in error.

(The *Book of Jasher* (referenced from material in text. This is the "more information" section for additional study.) is referenced in the Bible in Joshua 10:13 and II Samuel 1:18. The LXX translates each of these references as "the Book of the Upright Ones" and the Latin Vulgate "the book of the Just Ones." There are several obviously spurious "Book[s] of Jasher," and one which contains Jewish traditions. It was printed in Hebrew in 1613 from a handwritten manuscript which was supposedly rescued from the second temple when the Roman Emperor Titus burned Jerusalem in 70 AD. It is recommended by Ken Johnson, Th.D., in *Ancient Post-Flood History; Historical Documents that Point to Biblical Creation* ©2012.

The © 1906 Jewish Encyclopedia traces the linage of

YASHAR, SEFER HA-: (What we call the *Book of Jasher*) Editions.

The "Yashar" has appeared in the following editions: Naples, 1552; Venice, 1625; Cracow, 1628; Prague, 1668; Frankfort-on-the-Main, 1706; Amsterdam, 1707; Constantinople, 1728; Fürth, 1768; Koretz, 1785; Frankfort-on-the-Oder, 1789; Grodno, 1795; Lemberg, 1816 and 1840; Warsaw, 1846; Wilna, 1848; Lemberg, 1850; Wilna, 1852; Warsaw, 1858. It was translated into Judæo-German by Jacob ha-Levi, and published with various annotations and Arabic glosses (Frankfort-on-the-Main, 1674; Sulzbach, 1783). A Latin version by Johann G. Abicht appeared in Leipsic in the middle of the eighteenth century under the title "Dissertatio de Libro Recti." The work was first translated into English by Thomas Ilive, as mentioned above, and later by M. M. Noah under the title "The Book of Yashar" (New York, 1840)." http://www.jewishencyclopedia.com/articles/15067-yashar-sefer-ha

Since the *Book of Jasher* is not inspired and contains errors, as far as we are concerned, the exact date of the original composition does not matter. It accurately records Jewish tradition in the same manner as the works of Josephus, Philo and the *Seder Olam.* You may either take Dr. Johnson's position that the existing *Book of Jasher* is older and that the *Babylonian Talmud* and other ancient sources quoted it, or you may take the position of the *Jewish Encyclopedia* that the *Book of Jasher* is younger and it quoted from the older *Babylonian Talmud* and other sources. Please see the appendix for a more detailed review of the *Book of Jasher*.

Antiquities of the Jews by Flavius Josephus

Josephus was the Jewish General of Northern Israel when the Jews revolted against Rome. Josephus surrendered to the Romans and was eventually transported to Rome. There he wrote a series of books explaining many Jewish positions for Roman readers. Josephus was an educated Pharisee and his writings present the positions and traditions of the Pharisees. *Antiquities of the Jews* is basically a commentary on the entire Old Testament and was written before the end of the first century AD. During the Middle Ages, Josephus was second only to the Bible in popular reading throughout Europe and England. While very helpful and overall very accurate, it has several well known and glaring errors, such as equating the Children of Israel in Egypt with the Hyksos. The most popular English translation is the 1737 William Whiston translation.

The Book of Jubilees or the "Little Genesis"

This work was virtually ignored by Christians until the discovery of the Dead Sea Scrolls. Only Psalms, Deuteronomy, 1 Enoch, Genesis, and Isaiah have more manuscripts among the Dead Sea Scrolls. *Jubilees* is a very detailed chronology, based on the time period of a Jubilee. It is considered part of the Canon by the Coptic Church. While there is very little information in the *Jubilees* not found in Genesis, it is a very reliable and ancient source.

V. Conclusion

In all things, charity.

For those unfamiliar with the King James Bible and Elizabethan English, charity is *agape* love, the highest form of love. We are very much aware that the information we present here puts us in the minority.

Jesus never defended the historical records of the Old Testament. Jesus simply expects you to accept the reliable historical record of the Old Testament as a reliable historical record.

> *"Do not think that I will accuse you to the Father: there is one that accuseth you, even Moses, in whom ye trust. For had ye believed Moses, ye would have believed me: for he wrote of me. But if ye believe not his writings, how shall ye believe my words?"* John 5:45-47

The Word of God is both historically accurate and authoritative. Other ancient writings have errors, but also contain much valid information. These other ancient writings vary greatly in quality. The *Book of Jubilees* is considered to be Scriptures by the Coptic Church. At the other extreme are the massive number of copies of the *Epic of Gilgamesh* and other tales written to deceive people and bolster the authority of tyrants. Yet contained within these hero tales or epics are some tiny yet valuable gems of historical information. Finally, the most likely to be misinterpreted is the material world around us. In rebelling against God humanity reverses this order and "overlooks" the interpretation errors of the geological record.

God gave the information about Noah to Moses to write down for us. Moses was raised in the highest civilization in the world, so he had access to "all the learning of the Egyptians."

The antediluvian world was judged by God for their wickedness. That judgment took the form of a worldwide flood that killed all air-breathing life outside of the Ark (except for aquatic animals). The ark was built by Noah in obedience to the directions God gave to Noah.

The Flood and the time after the Flood which we call the Ice Age formed the strata we observe today. Except for the strata from the original creation week and the most recent stratum, most likely all geologic strata were formed by the flood/Ice Age. The earth has impact craters formed during the flood/Ice Age time period. There were massive volcanic eruptions throughout the earth and massive uplifts. Billions of tons of sand and other material were created and moved. Ice sheets formed and caused continental movement. Plate tectonics rapidly moved continents. These cataclysms bent, folded, and upthrust most of the strata on earth.

Fitting these known geological events together into their proper order is difficult. It is doubtful we will ever fit them together with complete accuracy. The important point is; do we examine the evidence and glorify God or do we ignore the evidence and deliberately forget the God of glory?

1. What verse explains why evidence and information is unlikely to persuade Secular Humanists to give up belief in deep time.

2. What is the order of classical science based on?

3. What is the only ancient record describing history in chronological order beginning with Creation?

4. According to Jesus Christ, what does rejection of the accuracy and truth of the Old Testament Scriptures lead to?

5. In a paragraph, explain the hypocrisy of Secular Humanists, (including the example of Dr. Larry Vardiman meeting Carl Sagan, if desired) in your own words.

6. How can mathematical formulas, archaeological evidence, or physics, however correct they may be in themselves, merely conceal something that is incorrect?

7. Write a short essay explaining the contrasting conclusions based on the opposing assumptions (Secularist and biblically based) about conditions shortly after the flood.

8. Study the bullet points under II. B. describing the normal historical and literary aspects of the Scriptures and summarize them in your own words.

9. *[Optional longer writing project]* Choose three of the five areas of study under II. C. (Astronomy,

Geologic Column, Radiometric Dating, Dendrochronology, and the Ice Age) that do not prove deep time and write an essay to explain why they are not proof of it.

10. What does the Hebrew word *toldot,* translated "generations", mean?

11. How could the Earth be 6000 years old but the stars be billions of years old, with both still being created on the same day? *[Note that this is just a theory and there is no known method of proving it.]*

12. What is the one thing that seems certain about the Earth after Creation?

13. Explain two viewpoints on the theory that the Earth may not have been tilted on its axis.

14. Give at least two evidences of a possible change in Earth's gravitation field after the flood.

15. During the continental breakup, volcanic activity like that during the flood occurred. Scientists are uncertain about what concerning this activity?

16. What are two theories about the formation and preservation of the canyons of Kaibab plateau and Colorado River channel?

17. What two claims to people make about God based on the phrase *"for it repenteth (me) that (I) have made"* man? What makes these claims erroneous?

18. List the three sources of scientific information.

19. What is another term for the examination of material evidence?

20. What is the most reasonable explanation for both the presence of intact marine fossils on high mountains and the earth being covered by water to a depth of 15 cubits?

21. What is the approximate dimensional ratio of both the ark and of many barges and ships even today?

22. Briefly restate in your own words the discussion about coating the bottom of the ark with pitch/asphalt, as well as the issue of closing the door.

23. Give the two possible explanations for how Noah might know the 15 cubit measurement of the height of the water.

24. Explain in your own words the Japanese concept of a "harbor wave" and how it explains the need for the ark to be built on a high mountain.

25. What is one explanation for how so many animals could have been taken aboard the ark and cared for there?

26. What does the Bible say about water storage and waste removal aboard the ark?

27. Briefly summarize the discussion about kinds of animals likely to have been brought on the ark.

28. Besides the fact that the time had arrived for the end of the flood, what is the meaning of the phrase "*God*

29. Briefly describe the two ways in which water receded off the earth.

30. Optional timeline project

Create a chart or graphic illustration based on the book of Genesis and also, if desired, on the *Book of Jubilees* showing the timeline of the flood.

31. What does the *Book of Jasher* say about people who may have tried to force their way onto the ark?

32. List the theories of the origin of the rain from the flood.

33. What occurred in the upper atmosphere to aid in the evaporation of flood waters?

34. What was the second cause of the receding of floodwaters?

35. What was probably the most dangerous time for the ark?

36. What caused the Ice Age?

37. Write a short essay about the probable conditions and lifestyles of the postdiluvians.

38. Optional research projects: a. Write a paper using outside sources on what James Hutton and/or Charles Lyell wrote on the subject of uniformitarianism. Find out information about people who disagreed with their findings in the same time period (such as Richard Kirwan) and present their viewpoints as well.

b. Research the Catastrophic Position of geologic history: The belief that catastrophes, rather than millions of years, shaped the earth as we know it today. Note that it was the majority position among geologists before Hutton.

39. Both secularists and Creationists concede that catastrophes helped shape geologic features like the Columbia/Snake River Gorge. On what point do they differ?

40. What percentage of the earth's geology is available for study?

41. Optional research project: Find background material on the Walker/Klevberg model. Who created it? What does it teach? Are there ways it could be improved? How is it different from studies of the Geologic Column, and what does it have in common with them? If desired, make comparative charts or graphics to illustrate the findings of your study.

42. Define phreatic eruptions and explain why they are important when studying evidence for a worldwide flood.

43. Briefly summarize the conditions in the Missouri-Mississippi River system that may be similar to what existed in the area around Eden, and what may have been different.

For Eden to be the highest point, yet have had such a mild climate, it likely had a much lower elevation than the highest point of the modern Missouri-Mississippi river system (8626 feet). Otherwise similar conditions likely existed, a gentle, shallow slope with a few waterfalls and steeper rises.

45. What is the real problem with the concept of geologic "periods" as opposed to "systems"?

46. How could "the floodgates of heaven open" if no extraterrestrial water caused the rain in the Flood?

47. Briefly summarize the explanation for why there could be vastly different strata formed in relatively short periods of time, even at the same time.

48. Optional Research Assignment: Chose one or more of these catastrophist scientists and write on their lives and work. Adam Sedgewick, Roderick Murchison, William Coneybeare. Include information on the Catastrophist position and how the geologic column originated with them and what use they made of it.

49. What is the observable truth about the geologic column and why is it important?

50. Instead of drawing conclusions from the data, the relativistic form of "science" practiced by secularist begins with _________________ and attempts to
____from the data.

51. Diamonds, petroleum, petrified wood, coal, stone, and fossils are all important to uniformitarians because of what assumptions?

52. What is the truth about these substances?

53. Optional Research project: Write about the 1981 trial *McLean v Arkansas Board of Education*. Include brief backgrounds on D. Brent Dalrymple, Mr. Robert Gentry, and other scientists mentioned in the trial. Find out the reason for the case coming to court and the implications of the trial, evidence presented, and decision.

54. Why is the radioactive decay rate of polonium important in the discussion of radiohalos?

55. Uniformitarians first published what information to discredit Robert Gentry's contention that radiohalos were formed at Creation?

56. Concerning the question of whether volcanic activity was the cause or a result of another cause at the time of the flood, what is the other possible cause and, briefly, what is the evidence for it?

57. Summarize in one sentence what conditions accurate radiometric dating depends on from a secularist point of view. What does it mean, at the very least, if any of these conditions vary?

58. What are the assumptions made by uniformitarians to excuse widely inconsistent and varying ages of tested samples in the examples presented by the RATE researchers? Are these arguments valid? Why or why not?

57. Briefly explain the significance of the radiohalo testing from the Los Alamos borehole sample.

58. What are the two basic assumptions of uniformitarians about the fossil record?

59. Summarize the three reasons for believing that fossil deposit rates were much greater in the past.

60. In what respect are microorganism blooms beneficial, and how would this apply to conditions during the flood?

61. Write a short essay explaining T° assemblages and their significance in layer formation. Also include an explanation of the term Polystrate.

62. [Optional longer essay assignment] Write an essay on simple scientific observations about fossils. Include mass fossil beds, the realities of our ability to find and study fossils, and what the evidence about fossils seems to show.

63. What is the observable evidence about the lowest sea level during the Ice Age?

64. The majority of the ice and snow came from what source?

65. What was true about the Arctic and Antarctic
regions (and other areas today known for being
extremely cold)?

66. What do we learn from the fact that human artifacts
are found in glaciers, and also that mammals with
undigested vegetation in their stomachs are found in
permafrost?

67. What is the simple explanation for the "extinction"
of Ice Age organisms and their differences from
animals today?

1. inexplicable

"Yet for some inexplicable reason, this understanding of education is completely ignored by the true believers in the

new religion of "science.""

2. eyewitness

"These scientific eyewitnesses are providing us with an education."

3. straightforward

"The Exodus of the children of Israel from Egypt is told in the Bible as a straightforward, factual, historical event ... "

4. indoctrinate

"People are indoctrinated to accept this as science."

5. acceptance

"Mockers require acceptance of their religious mockery to obtain a PhD, to be offered a job, to hold any position of authority, and in many cases, to even earn enough money to make a living."

6. Pharisee

"Like the first century Jew facing the Pharisees of his day, people today fear to challenge this establishment of religion because they love the glory of men more than the glory of God."

7. engage

"We are engaged in a spiritual warfare; a war we didn't choose."

8. opposition

"Mockers dishonestly proclaim that refusal to believe in their religion is opposition to science."

9. oversimplify

"To give an oversimplified explanation, science is *how* things work, while religion is *why* things work."

10. all-encompassing

"Modern science has completely rejected this basic definition of science and elevated 'Science' to an all-encompassing religion."

11. professing

"Newton's laws of physics (Note that Newton wrote more defending his beliefs in Christianity than he did about physics) and monk Gregor Mendel's laws of genetics are examples of people professing faith in God who laid the foundation for entire branches of science (physics and genetics)."

12. special revelation (context sentence follows number 13 below)

13. general revelation

"Geology compares the information from special revelation (the Word of God) with general revelation (the material universe)." [Note that student should explain how these are types of revelation, not just repeat the brief definitions in parentheses]

14. compare

"This 'general revelation' can be compared to the historical record.

15. chronological

"When compared to *any* other ancient religious document, the Word of God is the *only* historical document having a record in chronological order beginning with the creation of the universe."

16. interspersed

"Other ancient documents, such as the *Qur'an,* describe the Creation and Flood in pieces interspersed throughout these writings."

17. massive

"We are simply not capable of distinguishing the difference between a global Flood and massive local floods in many writings outside the Bible."

18. cataclysmic

"Neither do they have labels saying they were formed cataclysmically less than five thousand years ago."

19. reject

"Jesus meant that rejection of the Old Testament Scriptures as historically and scientifically accurate and true leads to rejection of Him."

20. complex

"They almost always justify their positions with highly complex circular reasoning."

21. confidence

"He immediately began asking me a series of leading questions about how a well-trained scientist such as myself could have confidence in a book written by a bunch of ignorant sheep herders thousands of years before any real science had been discovered."

22. decision

"Whatever decisions you make, you make because of assumptions."

23. archaeological

"archaeological evidence"

24. deludes

"But they also might be nothing more than a ploy that deludes some people into thinking that they are intellectually superior."

25. statistically

"Though men likely died from accidents or murders during this time period, the natural death rate from old age for three hundred forty years after the Flood was, statistically, zero."

26. Abundant

"The scientific evidence shows abundant vegetation at the end of the Ice Age."

27. permafrost

"This evidence is preserved in much of the permafrost of Siberia and the Yukon."

28. subsistence

"The hunter/gatherer culture, popularly depicted as a primitive, bare subsistence struggle for life, would more likely be a lifestyle based on extreme abundance and laziness."

29. contradiction

"If these artificially contrived "contradictions" in the Bible concern you, Answers In Genesis has two very good books answering these mythical contradictions, *Demolishing Supposed Bible Contradictions Volumes 1 & 2* by Ken Ham, Bodie Hodge and Tim Chaffey."

30. synonym

"In this COA series, the word *assumption* is a synonym for belief."

31. Integrate

"His series on civilization, *How Should We Then Live? The Rise and Decline of Western Thought and Culture* integrates art, literature and languages, as we intend to do."

32. axiomatic

"When the plain sense of Scripture makes common sense, seek no other sense; therefore, take every word at its primary, ordinary, usual, literal meaning unless the facts of the immediate context, studies in the light of related passages and axiomatic and fundamental truths, indicate clearly otherwise."

33. progressive creation

"It can also be some form of theistic evolution or it can be progressive creation, which believes that God directed evolution."

34. foundational

"So the foundational assumption or belief of Secular Humanism, deep time, has two key parts."

35. radiometric dating

"The assumptions underpinning radiometric dating are more complicated, so the details of these assumptions are explained in section VI. Material Results of the Flood."

36. stellar parallax

"Stellar parallax carefully measures the position of stars and their relationship to one another."

37. Measurement

"Six months later, when the earth is on the opposite side of the sun and as great a distance as possible separating the two measurements, a second set of measurements is taken. Extremely careful measurements are taken of the differences, which allow calculations to determine the exact position of the stars and other interstellar objects being measured."

38. precise (context sentence follows number 39 below)

39. sensitive

"However, there is no way of verifying those distances and the measurements must be extremely precise with very sensitive instruments."

40. confirmation

"In this case confirmation does not mean other astronomers examining the same information with the same assumptions. Confirmation means examining astronomical distances using a different technique."

41. verification

"The term "death" of astronomical objects is also frequently given as some form of verification."

42. connection (context sentence follows number 43 below)

43. geologic column

"The phrase deep time is probably misused even more in connection with the 'geologic column' than it is with astronomy."

44. strata

"Very few places on earth have as many exposed strata as the Grand Canyon, so it is frequently referenced for strata of the "geologic column."

45. isotope (context sentence follows number 48 below)

46. parent isotope

47. daughter isotope

48. decay chain

Daughter material is the result of the decay of a radioactive isotope from parent material. In a decay chain, the original parent material decays into a daughter isotope. The original daughter isotope now becomes a parent isotope which will decay into yet another different isotope.

49. inviolate (context sentence follows number 50 below)

50. radioactive decay

"The third assumption used to be considered inviolate, that nothing can alter the rate of radioactive decay."

51. approximation

"So dendrochronology, even under ideal conditions, is only an approximation, though it can be a very good approximation."

52. calibrate

"When the tree rings are calibrated against another known standard, dendrochronology can be very useful."

53. fossilization

"Scientifically, volcanic eruptions are the only known method of large-scale fossilization, including petrifying wood."

54. ultimately (context sentence follows number 55 below)

55. catastrophically

"As the water rose, the pressure against the ice dam increased, ultimately, causing the dam to fail catastrophically."

56. buoyant (context sentence follows number 58 below)

57. sub-glacial

58. exponential

"The water pressure caused the glacier to become buoyant, and water began to escape beneath the ice dam by carving sub-glacial tunnels at an exponential rate."

59. immense

"The floodwater carved an immense channel system across eastern Washington."

60. eruption (context sentence follows number 61 below)

61. petrify

"During the Ice Age, perhaps at the very beginning as the sea level dropped, volcanic eruptions petrified the trees."

62. uplift

"It is also very likely the uplifting occurred in stages over hundreds or even thousands of years."

63. parable (context sentence follows number 64 below)

64. allegory

"This sets it apart from parables and allegories."

65. bramble bush

"When Gideon's son Jotham told the parable of the trees and the bramble bush in Judges 9, he also gave the interpretation, and named the men that the plants in his parable represented."

66. coalesce

"The stars were put in place and were visible on earth soon after they coalesced."

67. Instantaneous

"Perhaps this was instantaneous."

68. constant

"This points out that even though the speed of light is a constant, time is not a constant."

69. nomenclature (context sentence follows number 70 below)

70. co-ordinate

"Everything in the Bible is, to use Einstein's nomenclature, from the co-ordinate system of earth."

71. hypothesis

"For this hypothesis to be valid, every hour on earth equals thousands of years on distant stars."

72. consistent (context sentence follows number 73 below)

73. temperate

"What is certain is the overall consistent, mild, temperate climate was very different from ours."

"Volcanic activity keeps areas of modern Yellowstone warm and comfortable throughout the bitter Wyoming, Idaho, and Montana winters."

75. antediluvian (context sentence follows number 77 below)

76. moderating

"While this is an *assumption,* it is quite reasonable to assume similar moderating influences in the antediluvian world."

77. genealogical

"After the Fall, there were 1,656 years of steady, mild climate, according to the genealogical record of Genesis Chapter Five."

78. disaster

"Any disasters or catastrophes during the antediluvian period were not global."

79. continuous

"The single river which flowed through Eden then split into four rivers, continuously putting silt into shallow seas."

80. landmass

"Though we do not know with certainty, there was likely a landmass much larger than all the dry land today."

81. vegetation

"The vast majority of that landmass was either covered in lush vegetation or farmed by mankind."

82. silt (context sentence follows number 84 below)

83. annual (context sentence follows number 84 below)

84. harvest

"Silt strata would not be annual, but would depend on currents, tides and perhaps even planting and harvest cycles."

85. explanation

"Others point out that a lack of an axis tilt would produce a colder, not a milder climate so they look for other explanations for the milder climate ..."

86. entombed

"Flying insects are found entombed in amber with wingspans of 75 cm (over 29.5 inches)."

87. sauropod

"A 60 ton, 50 foot sauropod would almost certainly be unable to walk on land today."

88. propose (context sentence follows number 92 below)

89. canopy

90. magnetic

91. metabolize

92. efficient

"Again, some of the proposed differences between the antediluvian world and today's world are: lower gravity in the past; a water canopy protecting the earth; the earth with a different tilt to its axis (perhaps not tilted at all); some type of change in the earth's magnetic field; much lower nitrogen content in atmosphere (resulting in higher levels of oxygen and carbon dioxide); greater air pressure so that organism could metabolize the oxygen more efficiently; greater humidity and a much higher quality diet."

93. Uniformitarian

"Even uniformitarian evolutionists are forced by the evidence to recognize these vastly different conditions in the past."

94. Devonian

"Articles about the Devonian Period always begin with their timeline mythology."

95. admission

"However, this is followed by some very significant admissions."

96. relatively

"Devonian was a relatively warm period."

97. reconstruction (context sentence follows number 97 below)

98. tropical

"Reconstruction of tropical sea surface temperatures shows an average temperature of 86° F."

99. geological

"It gives few details which might help us understand the geological causes."

100. plate tectonics (context sentence follows number 100 below)

101. geyser

"As the single continent rapidly broke apart, eventually becoming the continents we are familiar with, plate tectonics (not the slow continental drift we see today) caused multiple geysers and super-volcanoes down fault lines."

102. Sediment

"These repeatedly stirred the floodwaters, creating multiple new layers of sediment, moving existing layers, for years."

103. Inhabit

"There were some also who passed over the sea in ships, and inhabited the islands."

104. Himalayas

"Sometime after the Flood, perhaps soon after the Flood or perhaps thousands of years later, a sudden uplift or series of uplifts put the Americas, the Alps, the Himalayas, and every other mountain range, as well as the Grand Canyon, into approximately their present positions."

105. vertical

"To keep the vertical walls from collapsing, extreme heat had to rapidly turn the newly exposed undersea sediment to stone."

106. destructive

"An air blast is far more destructive than a ground blast."

107. generate

"An air blast of this size could easily have generated enough heat to turn most of the southwest to stone."

108. random

"The Flood was not a random event."

109. translate

"They are translated correctly."

110. concrete

"How do we communicate when words, especially the words in the Word of God, have lost all concrete meaning?"

111. deluge

"Before the deluge of waters upon the whole wicked world,"

112. preserved

"When Josephus wrote about the Flood itself he said, "the water poured down forty entire days, till it became fifteen cubits higher than the earth; which was the reason why there was no greater number preserved, [than those in the ark] since they had no place to fly to."

113. community

"Even sources outside of the Jewish and Christian communities indicate that the Flood was universal."

114. category (context sentence follows number 114 below)

115. perform

"The third category includes geology and tests performed on models of the ark."

"It contains thousands of uncrushed fossils of marine creatures known as Ammonites."

117. mechanism

"If this were true, then this was the mechanism God used to cause the sea level to fall."

118. feasibility

"The book *Noah's Ark: A Feasibility Study* by John Woodmorappe starts with the above information, then, with reasonable assumptions comes to reasonable conclusions."

119. navigate (context sentence follows number 119 below)

120. propulsion

"The ark was never intended either to navigate or to move under its own propulsion."

121. structural integrity

It seems odd that the structural integrity of the ark is questioned.

122. structure

The *Ex Nihilo* study also assumes that some unusual structures on ancient ships were based on the design of the ark.

123. commence

"In his five hundred and ninety-fifth year Noah commenced to make the ark, and he made the ark in five years, as the Lord had commanded."

124. reproduction

"An important point missed by many modern ark studies or reproductions is that the ark was covered, inside and out, with pitch."

125. asphalt (context sentence follows number 125 below)

126. Syriac Peshitta

Syriac Peshitta: the Bible in the Syriac or Aramaic language (the language spoken by Jews around the time of Christ), possibly translated in the 2nd Century AD. 127. scaffold

"The only possible way for this, the bottom of the ark, to be completely covered in asphalt, would be to put the ark on some type of scaffold, like a modern dry dock."

128. draft

"If the ark was built on top of a high mountain, perhaps the highest mountain, then the fifteen cubits are probably the draft of the ark."

129. aground

"Another reasonable assumption is that the fifteen cubit measurement was made after the ark ran aground."

130. recede (context sentence follows number 141 below)

131. constantly

"Since the Scriptures record that the waters receded very slowly and God sent a wind to remove the water, this wind blew the ark about constantly."

132. evaporate

"This was a wind Noah could see as it evaporated the water."

133. circumnavigate

"A very strong wind would likely cause the ark to circumnavigate the globe in less than a month."

134. waterline

"If the draft of the ark was fifteen cubits (probably a little over 26 feet) and it was either built on the highest mountain before the Flood or rested on the highest mountain after the Flood, then all that Noah had to do was measure the waterline on ark after leaving the ark to know that *fifteen cubits upward did the waters prevails; and the mountains were covered.*"

135. devastate

"The reason for the Japanese name 'harbor wave' is that sometimes a village's fishermen would sail out, and encounter no unusual waves while out at sea fishing, and come back to land to find their village devastated by a huge wave"

136. shoreline

"But as they approach shoreline and enter shallower water they slow down and begin to grow in energy and height."

137. crest

"The greatest danger from a tsunami is the crest as the wave approaches land."

138. protection (context sentence follows number 138 below)

139. shore breakers

Building the ark on top of a mountain provided protection "against shore breakers."

140. minimal

"There would be a minimal amount of land to form waves."

141. micro-evolution (context sentence follows number 141 below)

142. macro-evolution

"The last piece of information we can know for certain is that all of their genetic information adapted (not evolved, either micro or macro) into what we see today."

143. representation

"Then the only genetic representation of the dog needed on the ark was one pair of gray wolves."

144. juvenile

"The animals would be the smallest juveniles that no longer needed special attention."

young, immature creatures

145. hibernation (context sentence follows number 145 below)

146. estivation

"Many, perhaps most, would either go into hibernation or estivation, requiring even less attention."

147. whelp (context sentence follows number 147 below)

148. crouch

"And a lioness came, with her two whelps, male and female, and the three crouched before Noah, and the two whelps rose up against the lioness and smote her, and made her flee from her place, and she went away, and they returned to their places, and crouched upon the earth before Noah."

149. organism

"We do not know the total number of organisms on the ark, but we know that there were seven pairs of clean animals and birds and a single pair of each kind of unclean animals."

150. preparation

"The insects or microbes on the ark required neither human care, space, nor food preparation by Noah."

151. fertile

"Animals which do not interbreed naturally and produce fertile offspring are different kinds."

152. approximate (context sentence follows number 153 below)

153. genetic viability

"Though we do not know for certain the exact limits, it is not difficult to know the approximate limits of genetic viability, or 'kinds'."

154. classification (context sentence follows number 155 below)

155. taxonomy

"The classification system originally developed by Carl Linnaeus is still the basic system used in taxonomy today."

Classification: not exact; close but not perfectly accurate

156. equivalent

"This system makes 'kind' roughly equivalent to the genus, perhaps in some cases the family level."

157. kind (context sentence follows number 166 below)

158. kingdom

159. Phylum

160. class

161. order

162. family

163. genus

164. observe

165. similarity

166. common ancestry

Above the level of "kind" (genus, perhaps family in certain cases), family, order, class, phylum and kingdom, the observed similarities do not indicate common ancestry.

167. unwarranted

"A common, and completely unwarranted, criticism of the ark is the difficulty of only eight people taking care of that many animals."

168. estimate

"Estimates for the number of animals on the ark range from 10,000 to 16,000."

169. provision

"Trains and ships carrying animals to slaughter routinely transport many times that number with minimal provision for their survival."

170. accredited

"The average number of animals in accredited zoos is more than 5000 animals per zoo."

171. subterranean

"Even so, the conditions on the ark for the first forty days were extremely difficult, while the "fountains of the great deep" were breaking up and adding subterranean water to the rainwater."

172. pottage (context sentence follows number 172 below)

173. cauldron

"And the ark floated upon the face of the waters, and it was tossed upon the waters so that all the living creatures within were turned about like pottage in a cauldron."

174. anxiety

"And great anxiety seized all the living creatures that were in the ark, and the ark was like to be broken."

175. veterinarian

"This phrase does not mean that Noah had no veterinarian responsibilities."

176. insurmountable

"It means that God miraculously took care of the health of the animals on the ark so that the health of the animals was not an insurmountably difficult task."

177. saturate (context sentence follows number 177 below)

178. consistency

"The wind evaporated the water from above and the water from below filtered back to where it came from, but the earth was still saturated and had the consistency of thick soup."

178. visualization

"For a good visualization of the beginning of this catastrophe, see Disney's 1940 original *Fantasia, Rite of Spring, Dance of the Adolescents.*"

179. Propaganda (context sentence follows number 181 below)

180. depict

181. accurate

"Though Disney produced this as a propaganda piece for millions of years of evolution, it accurately depicts the catastrophic upheaval of the beginning of the Flood."

182. expanse

"The Hebrew means the face of the expanse and the LXX means the foundation of heaven."

183. boundary (context sentence follows number 184 below)

184. Oort Cloud

"The remaining water, if there is any, would either be in the Oort Cloud at the boundary of our solar system or it could be a boundary at the edge of the universe."

185. monograph

"Dr. Russell Humphreys has written monographs on the boundary conditions of the universe, which include defining the canopy God created in Genesis One."

186. dissolve

"Some volcanic material would remain unmixed; some would dissolve partially and some would dissolve completely in seawater."

187. turbidity

"Then once again the turbidity slows, allowing this different material to settle and form a different type of stratum."

188. hydrologic cycle

"This great wind initiated the current hydrologic cycle, with the atmosphere absorbing some of the water."

189. dissipate

"This permitted the hydrogen atoms to dissipate into space."

190. sounding (context sentence follows number 191 below)

191. subside

"It is also possible that Noah took soundings, which let him know that the water was subsiding."

192. radiate

"These winds at the end of the Flood were powerful enough to transport considerably more water into the upper atmosphere to allow for the water molecules to break down and the hydrogen atoms to radiate into space."

193. basin

"The other mechanism to lower the water level is for continents to rise while creating deeper ocean basins."

194. plate tectonics

"So continuous plate tectonics were moving the continents after the major volcanic and geyser activity stopped."

195. circumnavigate

"With a constant speed of just over 35 miles per hour (30.5 knots approximately), the ark would circumnavigate the globe about every 28 days."

196. aground

"It likely ran aground on the highest mountain."

197. Pretentious

"This is pretentious because the information necessary for understanding the origin of the earth is not to be found in the 'structure of the earth'."

198. concise

"Though there are many other definitions, that is a concise and popular definition of uniformitarianism."

199. vestige

"James Hutton's paper concluded with 'The result, therefore, of our present enquiry is, that we find no vestige of a beginning: no prospect of an end'."

[Note that this use of the word enquiry is a British form. Americans would say "inquiry".]

200. realization

"An important geologic point is the realization that over 99% of all geologic evidence is buried, most of it deep beneath the sea."

201. aligning

"The Walker/Klevberg model is superior for aligning the known strata into understandable categories."

Setting up in a useful or understandable order; organizing by related

202. primordial (context sentence follows number 203 below)

203. ensuing

"The Foundational Stage is further divided into the Primordial and Ensuing Phases, covering the first two days of creation."

204. formative (context sentence follows number 206 below)

205. derivative

206. biotic

"The Formative Stage is subdivided into the Derivative and Biotic Phases for the rest of the Creation Week."

207. inundatory (context sentence follows number 210 below)

208. eruptive

209. ascending

210. zenethic

"The Inundatory Stage is further subdivided into Eruptive, Ascending, and Zenethic Phases."

211. recessive (context sentence follows number 213 below)

212. abative

213. dispersive

"The Recessive Stage is further subdivided into Abative and Dispersive Phases."

214. residual

"The Postdiluvial Era is not broken down into stages, but it is further subdivided into Residual and Modern Phases."

215. eradicated

"Or they might have changed so little that the later cataclysmic changes have eradicated all evidence of any antediluvial catastrophes."

216. anaerobic

"an anaerobic environment, that is, the absence of oxygen."

217. pyroclastic (context sentence follows number 218 below)

218. phreatic

"Pyroclastic surges originating from secondary phreatic explosions at Mount St. Helens in 1980 produced these cross-bedded layers."

219. tephra

"(for example, tephra and pyroclastic-flow deposits)"

220. basaltic lava

"The intense heat of such material (as high as 1,170° C for basaltic lava) may cause water to boil and flash to steam, thereby generating an explosion of steam, water, ash, blocks, and bombs."

221. predominant

"Geysers and phreatic eruptions were predominant during the period that the *fountains of the great deep were broken up*, that is, were venting water."

222. theorizes

"Dr. Andrew Snelling theorizes that there was no additional extraterrestrial water."

223. precipitate

"He believes that the Phreatic eruptions and geysers put water into the upper atmosphere, where it cooled and precipitated as 'the sluice gates of heaven'."

224. restrain

After forty days the flood-gates of heaven were restrained and the fountains of the great deep were closed.

225. magma

"At this time it is likely that the volcanic activity changed over from geysers and phreatic eruptions to magma eruptions."

226. abyss

"And (on the new moon) in the fourth month the fountains of the great deep were closed and the flood-gates of heaven were restrained; and on the new moon of the seventh month all the mouths of the abysses of the earth were opened, and the water began to descend into the deep below."

227. unconformities (context sentence follows number 228 below)

228. discontinuities

These "unconformities" or "discontinuities" are expected in a catastrophic formation, but do not easily fit into uniformitarian assumptions.

229. eliminate

"Any type of erosion, volcanic activity, uplift or any other drastic geologic activity would hide or eliminate earlier evidence."

230. unintentional

"This type of deception is common with geologic strata and much of the deception is unintentional because the person making the statement sincerely believes the falsehood he is putting forth."

231. discernment

"Understanding Geology calls for great skill and discernment."

232. transformation (geology)

"Third, there are strata formed by transformation."

233. preconceptions

"It ignores any knowledge or observations which contradict its preconceptions."

234. preponderance

"But I don't think you can take one little fact for which we now have no answer, and try to balance, say that equals a preponderance of evidence on the other side."

235. translucent

"It is so thin that each individual slice is translucent."

236. concentric

"This allows examination of the same set of concentric circles, in different layered slices."

237. subatomic (context sentence follows number 238 below)

238. emit

"Each stage of radioactive decay emits different subatomic particles and each kind of particle travels a different distance."

239. polonium

"So unless the granites cooled quickly, no polonium radiohalos could be present."

240. subsequent

"Subsequent erosion has exposed at the Earth's surface the cooled granite bodies intruded into those fossiliferous sediments."

241. outcrops

"In the field it is possible to literally walk over the outcrops from fossiliferous sedimentary rocks through zones of metamorphosed sedimentary rocks ..."

242. constituents

" ... whose mineral constituents reflect the increasing temperatures and pressures of regional metamorphism ... "

243. metamorphic

"One classic example is the Cooma Granodiorite in the centre of the Cooma metamorphic complex in southeastern Australia."

244. intrusion (geology)

"In the field, and in three dimensions within mines (both open cast and underground), the effects on the host rocks of the intrusion of hot granitic magmas can be observed, including veining, stoping and contact metamorphism."

245. crystallize

"Thus, 'the existence of the polonium radiohalos implies that granites crystallized and cooled within just six to ten days, not millions of years!'"

246. erode (context sentence follows number 247 below)

247. deposit

"... sediments were eroded and deposited catastrophically on a global scale."

248. reference

"While the referenced articles explain in detail, this means that while the rocks we see were forming (a process which required great heat), water carried the core of the decaying radioisotope, which began as uranium, a tiny distance while it was radon gas."

249. postmagmatic (context sentence follows number 250 below)

250. hydrothermal

"The geology of the sites shows that the uranium, and most likely the polonium, were deposited via postmagmatic hydrothermal fluids."

251. discoloration (context sentence follows number 252 below)

252. nuclei

"The most widely accepted explanation is that the discolouration is caused by alpha particles emitted by the nuclei; the radius of the concentric shells are proportional to the particle's energy."

253. juxtapositioned

254. conclusion

"The sentences are juxtapositioned to imply that creationists either do not believe the Henderson & Bateson paper or that creationists arrive at different conclusions from the Henderson & Bateson paper."

255. gratuitous assertion

"Wakefield simply makes a lengthy series of gratuitous assertions."

256. legitimate (context sentence follows number 257 below)

257. refereed journal

"'And if there were articles in the open scientific literature: Excuse me: in refereed journals which supported the Creation Science model, would that not be something you would want to look at in trying to review the Creation Science literature?'"

258. intermediate

"Now, polonium-218 is one of the isotopes intermediate in the decay chain between uranium and lead."

259. decay

"Uranium doesn't decay directly from [sic, to] lead."

260. primordial

"And then he says that the only way it could have gotten there unsupported by radon-222 decay is to have been primordial polonium, that is polonium that was created at the time the solar system was created, or the universe."

261. infrasonic

"Twenty infrasonic monitors were triggered, including a station in Alaska, after the shock waves had circled the globe three times."

262. Submitted

"According to Buhl and Wimmer, the combined mass of the submitted finds is just 117 pounds (53 kg)."

263. seismic

"The seismic activity measured on the Richter scale was 5.0; and the air compression wave went twice around the world, according to recordings at meteorological stations."

264. deform

"Some storage huts in the nearby vicinity of the focus were found devastated by fire and the silverware and tin utensils within were deformed by intense heat."

265. precede

"Preceding the front of the shock wave there arises a heated zone whose radiating surface area is far larger than that of the shock wave itself."

266. substantiate

"This is substantiated by Semedec who first felt the heat wave, then was thrown to the ground by the air shock wave."

267. taiga

"Eighty million trees in the taiga (coniferous forest) were uprooted and blown down for a radius of 30-40 km."

268. ravage (context sentence follows number 252 below)

269. unnatural

"After the impact, forest fires broke out and ravaged an area of 10-15 km in radius describes these forest fires as being unnatural."

270. scorch (context sentence follows number 252 below)

271. sear

272. conventional

"Apparently a searing heat wave caused the scorching, yet a conventional forest fire was not present."

273. epicenter

"Some trees were entirely scorched in standing position, but were bent away from the epicenter. In normal fires in the Vadecara area, trees remained vertical with fire damage occurring at the lower sections while the tree tops remained untouched."

274. unique (context sentence follows number 252 below)

275. mysterious

"The Tunguska explosion is indeed unique and mysterious."

276. consensus (context sentence follows number 277 below)

277. tenuous

"However, suggesting a consensus is quite tenuous."

288. plausible

"Though the other theories have plausibility, they have difficulty explaining the observed event and the resulting physical evidence."

289. preserve

"Near Winslow, Arizona is the most well-known and best-preserved impact crater in the world."

290. extinction

"If these were nearly simultaneous, the impacts and the resulting volcanic activity would almost certainly trigger a continental breakup, flood, massive volcanic activity, and would certainly be an extinction level event (ELE)."

291. fraught

"There are many of types of radiometric dating. Carbon-14 is fraught with potential pitfalls, but is still very usable."

292. contaminate

" ... samples are rarely, or never, contaminated ... "

293. neutrinos

"Neutrinos from the sun seem to be slightly altering decay rates on earth."

294. noticeable

"The decay rate change noticed by the Stanford/Purdue study is very small, yet quite noticeable."

295. seasonable (context sentence follows number 296 below)

296. coincide

"The variations are seasonable and coincide with variations in recorded neutrino output from the sun."

297. abstract

"The *Answers In Genesis* article is a semi-technical, detailed "abstract" of the technical ICR article."

298. progressively

"The samples were sent progressively in batches to Geochron Laboratories in Cambridge, Boston (USA)..."

299. analyze

"There is a table at the end of each article which details samples, how they were prepared and analyzed, and the results."

300. irrevocable

"There may, in fact, be some pattern or systematic way in which 'excess 40 Ar' has been trapped in rocks and occluded in minerals at different levels (depths and relative ages) in the geological record. If so, then K-Ar and 40 Ar/ 39 Ar "dating" would irrevocably be discredited."

301. particular

"... some might mistakenly *assume* that there is either problem with incorrect reading from one particular laboratory or just one particular method.

302. professional

The 'whole rock', rock powder, and four-mineral concentrates were submitted for potassium-argon analysis to Geochron Laboratories of Cambridge, MA: a high-quality, professional radioisotope-dating laboratory."

303. commercial (context sentence follows number 304 below)

304. laboratory

"All the samples were sent to two well-respected commercial laboratories for radioisotope testing."

305. discrepancy (context sentence follows number 306 below)

306. illustrate

"The discrepancies are far greater than these few examples can begin to illustrate."

307. tremendous

"The problem of vastly different dates from the same sample using different radiometric methods is usually not noticed because of the tremendous cost of radiometric testing."

308. committee (context sentence follows number 309 below)

309. timetable

"As the Committee on the Measurement of Geological Time said in 1950, 'These figures are, as railway timetables say, subject to change without notice'."

310. diffusion

"3. Compared to Helium diffusion rates"

311. zircon (context sentence follows number 313 below)

312. crystal

313. microscopic

"Zircon crystals usually vary in size from microscopic to grains of sand."

314. anomaly

"Since the original tests were performed, other zircons from other locations were tested with similar results, proving these were not anomalies."

315. indication

"These issues have been examined repeatedly for over a decade and there is no indication that there was any contamination, misreading of the data, or any other type of human error."

316. alter

"The zircons are less than 6000 years old and something altered the decay rate of the Uranium."

317. recover

"Robert Gentry and his colleagues at Oak Ridge National Laboratory reported surprisingly high amounts of nuclear-decay-generated helium in tiny radioactive zircons recovered from Precambrian crystalline rock, the Jemez Granodiorite on the west flank of the volcanic Valles Caldera near Los Alamos, New Mexico (Gentry, Glish, & McBay, 1982)."

318. retain

"Yet the zircons were so small that they should not have retained the helium for even a tiny fraction of that time."

319. retention (context sentence follows number 320 below)

320. accelerate

"The high helium retention levels suggested to us and many other creationists that the helium simply had not had enough time to diffuse out of the zircons, and that *recent accelerated nuclear decay had produced over a billion years' worth of helium within only the last few thousand years*, during Creation and/or the Flood."

321. intermediary

"We used an existing mining company as an intermediary, and we asked it to not tell the experimenter about us or our goals."

322. prediction

"The experimenter, being a uniformitarian (believer in long ages) and not having read our prediction, had no idea what results we were hoping for."

323. alignment (context sentence follows number 325 below)

324. validate

325. probability

"This alignment validates the young-age model even for readers who are not experts in this field, because the probability of such a lineup by accident is small."

326. resounding

"The data resoundingly reject the '1.5 billion year' model."

327. sequence (context sentence follows number 328 below)

328. burden of (dis)proof

"This sequence of events places the burden of disproof on the critics, because they must explain how, if there is no truth to our model, the data 'accidentally by sheer coincidence just happened by blind chance' to fall right on the predictions of our model."

329. indicator

"There are other indicators of altered radioactive decay rates, but these two examples were chosen because: ..."

330. peripheral

"The second thing to notice is how peripheral they are."

331. inconsequential

"One of my challenges in answering those charges was to find different words describing their basic character: 'molehill, not a mountain ... distinction without a difference ... haggling ... ridiculous quibble ... inconsequential ... majoring on minors ... irrelevant'."

332. scarce

"But despite his scarcity of significant issues, Henke chose to puff them up to enormous proportions with a torrent of hot air: fifty single-spaced pages using up my printer supplies."

333. monograph

"Unless the reader is technically well-informed in this specialty and wants to take the time to examine Henke's monograph carefully ..."

334. previous (context sentence follows number 335 below)

335. response

"All the previous material is from the Humphreys response."

336. fallacy

"The basic fallacies of radiometric dating apply to all forms of radiometric dating."

337. bedrock

"These two beliefs are the bedrock foundations of uniformitarianism and evolution in general."

338. overall (context sentence follows number 339 below)

339. dependable

"But the overall rate of deposits is still an overall accurate and dependable rate of deposits in the fossil record."

340. recent

"There is a progression of fossils from simple organisms in 'older' strata to increasingly complex, or at least more 'modern' organisms in more 'recent' strata."

341. correspond

"Those he corresponded with confirmed this belief."

342. calcium carbonate

"One example: he simply *assumed* a continuous and constant death rate and rate of deposit for the calcium carbonate of the billions of dead bodies of microorganisms he observed whose shells made up the White Cliffs of Dover."

343. torrential (context sentence follows number 344 below)

344. bloom

"With catastrophic volcanic activity warming the oceans and releasing large amounts of CO_2, and with the torrential rains and the churning and mixing of fresh and salt waters, the Flood of Noah's day produced the right conditions for a 'blooming' production of microorganisms and the chalk's rapid accumulation.

345. formation

"The same chalk formation in the Netherlands has yielded a very large Mosasaurus skull."

346. saprophyte

"This is especially true of marine saprophyte microbes, even today."

347. predator

"For a brief period of time, the natural predators of the saprophyte microbes nearly died off and their food supply exploded."

348. accommodation

"To be preserved, not only must T° assemblages be buried rapidly, they must also occur in settings subject to high rates of accommodation that permit a longer-term escape from exposure by post-burial erosion."

349. preservation

"Following burial, their preservation follows a pathway similar to that of any other deposit containing terrestrial organic matter."

350. tectonically

"First, in the shorter term, the entombed plants must be removed from the effects of aerobic decay in the vadose zone (Gastaldo & Demko 2010); this may occur rapidly following sea-level rise, tectonically driven earth movements, or even compaction,, in the case of a substrate such as peat."

351. immobilize

"The individual stratum which immobilized the upright tree is evidence that the stratum was deposited almost instantaneously."

352. *In situ*

"Of the fossils viewed by humans, less than one percent of these fossils are viewed *in situ*, literally "in position" fossils."

353. concentration

"The Shandong quarry is described as 'one of the largest concentrations of dinosaur bones in the world".

354. concede

"Uniformitarians concede these dinosaurs were swept into the bed by a flood, but how big of a flood would be necessary to overcome a dinosaur of that size, and such a huge number of others as well?"

355. intruded (geology)

"Uniformitarians are quick to dismiss these out-of sequence fossils, explaining them away as somehow intruded rather than admitting they might actually belong there."

356. interpretative (context sentence follows number 358 below)

357. synonymous

358. manipulative

"Interpretative in this case is synonymous with manipulative and indoctrinating."

359. descended

"But all organisms alive today are descended from organisms from the past."

360. susceptible

"There are even different temperaments, athletic abilities, susceptibility to illnesses, etc."

361. gestation

"They also have slightly longer gestation periods ..."

362. sacrosanct

"To a uniformitarian, fossil progression is sacrosanct."

363. resin

"Either a volcanic eruption or explosion from a comet/meteor can easily cause a tree to release the resin, capturing an organism inside."

364. amber

"A tiny sample list of a few of the organisms trapped in amber that appear to be identical to the same organism today, except for size …"

365. essentially

"… (genus Penaeus) is essentially the same as the fossil shrimp (Antrimpos)"

366. morphological

"Despite its Bathonian age, the new cryptobranchid [salamander] shows extraordinary morphological similarity to its living relatives.

367. underscore

"This similarity underscores the stasis [no change] within salamander anatomical evolution."

368. dissertation

"In another study, James W. Valentine, in his PhD dissertation, found that 76.8% of the marine mollusk species currently living along the southern California and Baja California coast are also found in the fossil record."

369. encounter

"In other words, as the Flood waters rose, they would tend to bury organisms in the order that they were encountered, so the major groups should appear in the fossil record according to *where* they lived, and not *when* they lived."

370. accumulate

"You would expect many larger animals to survive the Flood waters initially, leaving their tracks in the accumulating sediment layers as they tried to escape the rising waters."

380. exhausted

"But eventually they would become exhausted, die, and get buried."

381. recognizable

"They contain fossils in a recognizable order, too, reflecting the order in which the organisms were buried during the Flood."

382. initial

"Furthermore, even the pattern of finding tracks before bodies is consistent with creatures surviving in the initial flood waters before eventually perishing."

383. analysis

"In keeping with the above analysis of Dr. Snelling, let us examine the actual fossil record."

384. arrangement

"In a very general arrangement, the Precambrian system is the Creation Week, before there was life in the soil."

386. Minute (size)

A minute number of organisms, usually microbes, can be found in the Precambrian system.

387. various

"These massive volcanic eruptions in turn entombed organisms in various strata."

388. identical

"There are similar, often identical organisms in each of these systems."

389. circumstances

"The difference was location and circumstances, not vast amounts of time."

390. cataclysm

"Most organisms survived the cataclysm which deposited the Ordovician system."

391. successive

"With this hypothesis, the trees likely sank because they accumulated material with each successive event (explosions or eruptions), and were eventually covered with so much volcanic material that in an additional layer of material drove the floating plant mass to the bottom."

392. elevation

"The plants in the various strata represented differences in various elevations or altitudes and ecological niches."

393. flora

"Once again, the differences in flora between the various strata prior the Paleocene system are differences in location, ecological niches and some hydro-sorting of carcasses, not differences in time."

394. comprise

"Some strata are comprised entirely of sand or other nonvolcanic material."

395. resourceful

"The final flood stratum of antediluvian organisms, Jurassic, entombed the dinosaurs and the most resourceful of the antediluvian organisms on top of the Triassic."

396. devour

"These organisms could have grown for years, perhaps decades or centuries, until they completely devoured all remaining carcasses which were not entombed."

397. exaggerate

"The total number of fossils not represented by living organisms is massively exaggerated."

398. specimen

"What was once thought to be distinct animals were in fact juvenile and nearly sexually mature specimens from the same species."

399. identify

"... as many as a third of named dinosaur species could be cleared from the record books as they might simply be juvenile versions of another identified dinosaur."

400. invertebrate (context sentence follows number 406 below)

401. majority

402. skeletal

403. accumulation

404. excellent

405. ordinary

406. episodic

"The bulk of the marine invertebrate fossil record [which is the majority of the fossil record] does not represent a series of unusual skeletal accumulations, but rather the preserved remnants of an excellent original record formed through ordinary though episodic processes."

407. durable

"According to Valentine's article, "At least 85% of durably skeletonized living species …"

408. erosion (context sentence follows number 409 below)

409. decomposition

"He admits that not all are represented in the fossil record but explains that some were lost because of erosion, decomposition before fossilizing, etc."

410. antiquity

"…based on his assumptions that the 200-year observed extinction rate continued back into antiquity at the same rate."

411. naturalist

"…the Italian naturalist, Giovanni Arduino (1714-1795), divided the different types of rock strata into three categories:…"

412. mineralize

"Unlike fossils in all lower strata, that is, strata deposited by the Flood, Tertiary strata are frequently not mineralized and the organisms are usually not completely fossilized."

413. assessment

"It might stun uniformitarians to learn that we agree completely with their assessment of the climate of the Tertiary system, except for their timeline."

414. carcass

"When Noah stepped out of the Ark, the air was filled with volcanic ash and the oceans were a thick soup of carcasses, ash, silt, and the beginning or in the midst of a saprophyte microbe bloom."

415. steppe (context sentence follows number 416 below)

416. savanna

"We have the same conditions on earth today; polar regions, tropical regions, subtropical, deep ocean, reef regions, desert regions, high altitude regions, rain forest regions, prairies, central Asian steppes, African Savannas, swamps and thousands of other ecological niches."

417. stabilize

"This is the geologic period when the earth stabilized into the ecology we know."

418. characterize

"Many observations show that Pleistocene time was characterized by long periods of arctic conditions that allowed ice and snow to cover vast areas of land and sea, and so it is sometimes called the Ice Age."

419. modification

"The Walker/Klevberg model might need some "tweaking" modifications, but it fits the evidence."

420. module

"One serious question many creationists ask, and these modules have no answer for: 'Did the strata of the Creation Event include minerals or stones near the surface where men would see/use them or was the original surface of the earth entirely or almost entirely clay/soil?'"

421. hydrodynamic

"The sorting according to strata are best explained by hydrodynamic sorting, ecological niches and attempts by various organisms to escape the rising floodwaters."

422. originate

"The modern Columbia/Snake river system originates in Alberta and Western Wyoming, then flows to the Pacific."

423. comprehension

"The abundance of organisms exceeds our comprehension if we insist on thinking of the antediluvian world in terms of what we observe today."

424. dilute

"Fresh water fish are capable of surviving in salt water, especially when the salt content is diluted."

425. magnitude

"This means that the catastrophic waves were growing in magnitude and covered more area."

426. realistic

"...the highway system has exposed tens of thousands of folds and bends in every direction, causes any thoughtful person to realize that a catastrophic explanation is the only realistic explanation."

427. alleged (context sentence follows number 428 below)

428. overthrust

"When one realizes that there are hundreds of alleged overthrusts..."

429. distribution

"If these strata cannot be tied to a real overthrust, then the fossil distribution in the geological column is contrary to evolutionary predictions."

430. moraines

"As the ice melted, the moraines puzzled later observers.

431. counterintuitive

"A serious and worldwide examination of the evidence has come to many counterintuitive conclusions."

432. civilization

"... we will post several important points about the Ice Age here and begin the next module with the civilization of the Ice Age."

433. enormous

"It is very likely that there were enormous differences just from one year to the next."

434. necessitate

"Clicking the link to the appendix each time will necessitate linking back to this point and scrolling down to the next sections."

435. evaporation

"This would cause strong evaporation."

436. latent (context sentence follows number 437 below)

437. condense

"At the same time, the air would be heated up by contact with the warm ocean and the release of latent heat from the water vapor when it condensed."

438. attract

"The warm seas attracted animals to a warm coastline."

439. prevent

"The warmer seas also prevented arctic ice."

440. glaciate

"The area just east of the Rocky Mountains in North America would be unglaciated at this time because of warm air from the Pacific Ocean overriding the mountains and descending as mild chinook winds."

441. interpret

"It is easy to understand that some could interpret such a dramatic shift as an end to one ice age and the beginning of a new one."

442. placement

"The only factor we are not certain of is the exact placement of the mountains and the continents so we can know the patterns of the ice age snowblitzes."

III. References, Footnotes, Expanded Study, and Appendix Materials

References to Outside Sources

1 *The Orthodox Jewish Bible*, completed by Phillip Goble in 2002, is an English language version that applies Yiddish and Hasidic cultural expressions to the Messianic Bible. Copyright Information: The Orthodox Jewish Bible fourth edition, OJB. Copyright 2002,2003,2008,2010, 2011 by Artists for Israel International. All rights reserved.
http://www.biblegateway.com/versions/Orthodox-Jewish-Bible-OJB/

2 A New Creationist Cosmology: In No Time at All
Parts One, Two and Three
Larry Vardiman, Ph.D., & D. Russell Humphreys, Ph.D.
http://www.icr.org/article/5686/
http://www.icr.org/article/5830/
http://www.icr.org/article/5870/

3 Flavius Josephus, The Antiquities of the Jews, 93 AD, Translator: William Whiston, 1737.
http://sacred-texts.com/jud/josephus/index.htm#aoj

4 "How Did The Dinosaurs Grow So Big?"
http://creation.com/how-did-dinosaurs-grow-so-big

5 General theories about pre-flood and flood conditions:
http://creation.com/flood-models-biblical-realism

6 Devonian Period
"The Devonian was a relatively warm period and is thought to have been glacier free. Reconstruction of tropical sea surface temperature from conodant apatite shows an average temperature

247

of 86° F in the Early Devonian. CO2 levels dropped steeply throughout the Devonian period…"
http://www.universetoday.com/60172/devonian-period/#ixzz2RLX8OVI9

"The warm temperatures made life on land particularly good for the plants.

The plant-covered lands made a good home for the (first) [propaganda word, not true] wingless insects and spiders.

The Devonian Period is known as the Age of Fishes. It is famous for the thousands of species of fish that (developed) [propaganda word, not true] in Devonian seas.

The work of the sponges and corals went on through the Devonian Period. They built some of the largest reefs in the world. Invertebrates grew well in Devonian seas too…."
http://www.fossils-facts-and-finds.com/devonian_period.html

"Near the end of the Devonian, a mass extinction event occurred."
http://www.ucmp.berkeley.edu/devonian/devonian.php

7 *The Book of Jasher* Copyright Ken Johnson 2013 Biblefacts Edition http://biblefacts.org/creation/Jasher_intro.pdf
Also; Salt Lake City, J.H. Parry and Company, 1887.
http://www.sacred-texts.com/chr/apo/jasher/

8 Flavius Josephus *Antiquities of the Jews , Book I,* Translated by William Whiston, 1737

9 *Seder Olam* or *Seder Olam Rabbah* (The Hebrew words mean "The Great Order of the World") Tradition says that rabi Yose ben Halafta wrote the *Seder Olam* approximately 160 AD. Written in Hebrew, it begins with Creation and ends with Alexander the Great. The exact dates are not certain.
English Translation of the *Seder Olam*
http://www.betemunah.org/sederolam.html

10 Volcanic Cones
http://www.answersingenesis.org/articles/am/v1/n1/radioactive-dating

11 The Annals of the World "The Origin of Time, and Continued to the Beginning of the Emperor Vespasian's Reign and the Total Destruction and Abolition of the Temple and Commonwealth of the Jews." by James Ussher 1650.

12 The *Book of Jubilees* from "The Apocrypha and Pseudepigrapha of the Old Testament" R.H. Charles Oxford: Clarendon Press, 1913.

13 Quran

From Quransearch.com

http://www.quransearch.com/cgi-bin/quran/quran_search1.cgi?search_text=11:42-47&B1=Search

14 *The History of al-Tabari* is an English translation of *The History of the Prophets and Kings.* It is an historical and religious chronicle written by the Muslim historian Ibn Jarir al-Tabari (838-923), beginning with the Islamic Creation to the year 915 AD.

15 *The Book of Jasher* Copyright Ken Johnson 2013 Biblefacts Edition http://biblefacts.org/creation/Jasher_intro.pdf
Also; Salt Lake City, J.H. Parry and Company, 1887.
http://www.sacred-texts.com/chr/apo/jasher/

16 Clark's Foreign Theological Library Keil and Delitszch (Multivolume Series) 1867ff Edinburgh T and T Clark, George Street Keil & Delitzsch Commentary on the Old Testament Johann (C.F.) Keil (1807-1888) & Franz Delitzsch (1813-1890)

17 *Noah's Ark: A Feasibility Study*, John Woodmorappe, Inst for Creation Research, Dallas, TX, July 1996. (Currently out of print.)

18 Ark Information
http://www.worldwideflood.com/ark/hull_form/hull_optimizatio
n.Grahamhancock.com/forumhtm
Two sites with more information on worldwide measurement standards.
http://www.grahamhancock.com/forum/nealJohn_ancientMeasur
es.php
http://www.worldwideflood.com/ark/noahs_cubit/cubit_reference
s.htm

19 In 1994 The *Journal of Creation* published *Safety Investigation of Noah's Ark in a Seaway,* an English version of a 1992 Korean study by S.W. Hong and others on the seaworthiness of the ark. They were supported by the Korea Association of Creation Research.
Hong, S.W. et al., Safety investigation of Noah's Ark in a seaway, *Journal of Creation* 8(1):26-36, 1994; http://creation.com/safety-investigation-of-noahs-ark-in-a-seaway
Safety Investigation of Noah's Ark in a Seaway, Proceedings of the International Conference on Creation Research, Korea Association of Creation Research, Taejon, 1993, pp. 105-137

20 Comments on Noah's Ark
http://worldwideflood.org/ark/safety_aig/safety_aig_comments.h
tm

21 Possible meanings of Gopher Wood

The Hebrew word translated into English as *gopher wood* has many interpretations. The *LXX* translates it *wood* (general Greek word for wood) *four-cornered* followed by the word *nested compartments.* There is considerable disagreement as to whether the word *four-cornered* belongs to the word *wood* and means *square beams* or if it goes with *nested compartments* and means that the overall ark was box-shaped. The *Latin Vulgate* translates the word *timber planks.*

The *Qu'ran* calls *gopher wood* cedar and says that Noah had to plant the trees. Other sources translate the word as teak, laminated and sawed. Keil and Deilitzch believe the word means *cypress wood*.

22 Tsunami Information
http://en.m.wikipedia.org/wiki/Tsunami
http://environment.nationalgeographic.com/environment/natural-disasters/tsunami-profiles/

23 *The Book of Jasher* Copyright Ken Johnson 2013 Biblefacts Edition http://biblefacts.org/creation/Jasher_intro.pdf
Also; Salt Lake City, J.H. Parry and Company, 1887.
http://www.sacred-texts.com/chr/apo/jasher/

24 Zoo statistics
http://www.statisticbrain.com/zoo-statistics/

25 Noah caring for the animals
http://creation.com/how-could-noah-care-for-the-animals#endRef1

26 *The Book of Jasher* Copyright Ken Johnson 2013 Biblefacts Edition http://biblefacts.org/creation/Jasher_intro.pdf
Also; Salt Lake City, J.H. Parry and Company, 1887.
http://www.sacred-texts.com/chr/apo/jasher/

27 Vegetarian diets
Catchpoole, David. "Lea, the spaghetti lioness." *Creation* 29(4):44–45, 2007.
http://creation.com/lea-the-spaghetti-lioness
______. "The Lion that wouldn't eat meat." *Creation* 22(2):22–23, 2000.
http://creation.com/the-lion-that-wouldnt-eat-meat

28 Elephants in captivity
"Impressive Elephants." Sandiego Zoo Website. (No author, no date.) March 2000.
http://animals.sandiegozoo.org/animals/elephant

29 African Elephant weight
http://animals.nationalgeographic.com/animals/mammals/african-elephant/

30 The *Book of Jubilees* from "The Apocrypha and Pseudepigrapha of the Old Testament" R.H. Charles Oxford: Clarendon Press, 1913.

31 *Seder Olam* or *Seder Olam Rabbah* (The Hebrew words mean "The Great Order of the World") Tradition says that rabi Yose ben Halafta wrote the *Seder Olam* approximately 160 AD. Written in Hebrew, it begins with Creation and ends with Alexander the Great. The exact dates are not certain.
English Translation of the *Seder Olam*
http://www.betemunah.org/sederolam.html

32 Underground Water
http://news.nationalgeographic.com/news/2002/03/0307_0307_
waterworld.html
http://www.livescience.com/1312-huge-ocean-discovered-
earth.html

33 *The Book of Jasher* Copyright Ken Johnson 2013 Biblefacts
Edition http://biblefacts.org/creation/Jasher_intro.pdf
Also; Salt Lake City, J.H. Parry and Company, 1887.
http://www.sacred-texts.com/chr/apo/jasher/

34 Dr. Russell Humphreys, *Starlight and Time: Solving the Puzzle
of Distant Starlight in a Young Universe*, Master Books, Green
Forest, AR, 1996.

35 References on comet theories Dr. Kent Hovind DVD seminar #6
No author. "Comets and the Great Flood of Noah." Creationism.org
http://www.creationism.org/articles/CometsHovindTheory.htm
Faulkner, Danny, "A biblically-based cratering theory," *Journal of
Creation* 13(1):100-104 April 1999.
http://creation.com/a-biblically-based-cratering-theory
Doyle, Shaun, "Noah's comet? Was Noah's Flood a tsunami caused
by a comet imact?" 2 January 2008. Creation.com
http://creation.com/noahs-comet
"Burckle Crater: Dating the Flood." No author no date
Geocreationism.com
http://www.geocreationism.com/science/dating-the-flood-burckle-
crater.html
Scott Carney, Did A Comet Cause The Great Flood?
Discover Magazine, November 15, 2007 posted in Free Republic
Website.
http://www.freerepublic.com/focus/news/1929074/posts

36 Hydrogen Loss
Charlotte McDonald, "Who, What, Why: Is the Earth getting
lighter?" BBC News Magazine, 31 January, 2012.
http://www.bbc.co.uk/news/magazine-16787636

37 Ice Age conditions
http://www.answersingenesis.org/articles/nab/where-does-ice-
age-fit
Michael J. Oard November 22, 2007
The New Answers Book Where Does The Ice Age Fit?

38 *Seder Olam* or *Seder Olam Rabbah* (The Hebrew words mean
"The Great Order of the World") Tradition says that rabi Yose ben
Halafta wrote the *Seder Olam* approximately 160 AD. Written in
Hebrew, it begins with Creation and ends with Alexander the Great.
The exact dates are not certain.
English Translation of the *Seder Olam*
http://www.betemunah.org/sederolam.html

39 Flavius Josephus *Antiquities of the Jews , Book I,* Translated by
William Whiston, 1737

40 Missoula Glacial Lake Information
No author, "Glacial Lake Missouri and the Ice Age Floods," Website
for the Montana Natural History Center, Missoula, MT, (No date.).
http://glaciallakemissoula.org/story.html
41 The information and chart in the text is based on Walker's
biblical geological model, modified by Klevberg, from Tas Walker's
Biblical Geology site.
http://biblicalgeology.net/General/geologic-column.html
Chart of relative eras and events in geologic/biblical history

42 *The Book of Jasher* Copyright Ken Johnson 2013 Biblefacts
Edition http://biblefacts.org/creation/Jasher_intro.pdf
Also; Salt Lake City, J.H. Parry and Company, 1887.
http://www.sacred-texts.com/chr/apo/jasher/

43 River lengths and elevations
http://www.livescience.com/29558-the-worlds-longest-rivers.html
Melina,Remy (*Our Amazing Planet* staff writer.) "The World's
Longest Rivers". June 23, 2010. Livescience.com
After clicking the following link, click on the "Transcript of Untitled
Prezi" text for Missouri River figures.
Richard Murray, "Missouri Watershed Profile," 14 November 2013.
Prezi.com (A site for creating and sharing presentations.)
http://prezi.com/dnywzascnp6k/untitled-prezi/

44 Dr. Gary Parker, *How Fast?* January 1, 1994 *Creation Facts of
Life*
http://www.answersingenesis.org/articles/cfl/how-fast

45 Underground Water sources
Dr. Vincent Post,, et al, News and Media Media release: "Scientists
find vast new freshwater sources under the sea." 05 Dec 2013 The
National Centre for Groundwater Research and Training is an
Australian Government initiative, supported by the Australian
Research Council and the National Water Commission.
http://www.groundwater.com.au/news_items/media-release-
scientists-find-vast-new-freshwater-sources-under-the-sea
Vincent Post et. al., Offshore fresh groundwater reserves as global
phenomenon. Nature 504, 71-78 (05 Dec 2013). International
weekly journal of science. Nature.com
http://www.nature.com/nature/journal/v504/n7478/full/nature12
858.html
Ker Than, "Huge Ocean Discovered Inside Earth," February 28,
2007. *Livescience.com*
http://www.livescience.com/1312-huge-ocean-discovered-
earth.html

46 Volcanic Properties
James St. John, "Replacement," (Fossil preservation involving
change in crystal structure and mineralogy of an organism's hard
parts.) (No date) Ohio State University at Newark Website.
http://www.newark.osu.edu/facultystaff/personal/jstjohn/Docume
nts/Cool-fossils/Replacement.htm

47 Type/Process: Pyroclastic Flow
Volcanic Status: Historical
Image Number: 029-008
Photographer: Norm Banks, 1980 (U.S. Geological Survey)
Summit Elevation: 2549 meters
Latitude/Longitude: 46.20 N / 122.18 W
Timeframe: Last known eruption 1964 or later
Region: Canada and Western USA

"Pyroclastic surges originating from secondary phreatic explosions at Mount St. Helens in 1980 produced these cross-bedded layers. They were deposited from successive, rapidly moving horizontal clouds of gas, ash, and rock fragments that resulted from the interaction of still-hot pyroclastic-flow deposits from the May 18 eruption with groundwater and fragments of Mount St. Helens glaciers carried down by the collapse of the summit." Paint brush shows scale.

48 Sources for volcanic activity, Mt. St. Helens and Underground Oceans (Below link is same as for note 171)
http://www.livescience.com/1312-huge-ocean-discovered-earth.html
Barry, Sharon, et. al. The Dynamic Earth Geogallery Smithsonian Website. (No Date)
http://www.mnh.si.edu/earth/text/dynamicearth/6_0_0_GeoGall ery/geogallery_specimen.cfm?SpecimenID=220&categoryID=5&ca tegoryName=Volcanoes&browseType=volcanoname&volcanoName =St.%20Helens
Swanson, D.A., (photographer). Phreatic Eruption, Mount St. Helens 18 May 1980.
http://volcanoes.usgs.gov/images/pglossary/HydroVolcEruption.p hp

49 The *Book of Jubilees* from "The Apocrypha and Pseudepigrapha of the Old Testament" R.H. Charles Oxford: Clarendon Press, 1913

50 *Seder Olam* or *Seder Olam Rabbah* (The Hebrew words mean "The Great Order of the World") Tradition says that rabi Yose ben Halafta wrote the *Seder Olam* approximately 160 AD. Written in Hebrew, it begins with Creation and ends with Alexander the Great. The exact dates are not certain.
English Translation of the *Seder Olam*
http://www.betemunah.org/sederolam.html

51 Austin, S.A., Ten misconceptions about the geologic column. ICR *Impact*, No. 137, 1984.
(Though we have just a few quotes, it is worth reading in its entirety on their website icr.org.)

52 Divisions of Geologic Time explanation
U.S. Geological Survey Geologic Names Committee, 2010, Divisions of geologic time—major chronostratigraphic and geochronologic units: U.S. Geological Survey Fact Sheet 2010–3059, 2 p.
http://pubs.usgs.gov/fs/2010/3059/

53 ICR "Ten Misconceptions about the Geologic Column" by Steven A. Austin, Ph.D. 1984
http://www.icr.org/article/ten-misconceptions-about-geologic-column/

54 *'Millions of years' are missing*
Jonathan Sarfati interviews biologist and geologist Ariel Roth
http://creation.com/ariel-roth-interview-flat-gaps

55 *The Geological Column Is a General Flood Order with Many Exceptions.* Michael J. Oard, "The Geological Column Is a General Flood Order with Many Exceptions," *The Geologic Column: Perspectives Within Diluvial Geology.* Reed, J.K and M.J. Oard (editors). Creation Research Society.
biblicalgeology.net/General/geologic-column.html

56 Synthetic Diamonds No author, "Education: How are Gemesis lab-created diamonds made?" (No date.)
http://gemesis.com/education/faqs/

57 Radiocarbons in Diamonds
Dr. Andrew Snelling, Radiocarbons in Diamonds Confirmed. November 7, 2007. AiG-U.S.
http://www.answersingenesis.org/articles/aid/v2/n1/radiocarbon-in-diamonds

58 Petroleum Information
"Oilgae: Glossary. Synthetic petroleum Definition." Website promoting Algae-based biofuels. (no date) Oilgae.com
http://www.oilgae.com/ref/glos/synthetic_petroleum.html

59 Artificial Petrified Wood
Brandon Miller, "Presto! Instant Petrified Wood Created in Lab," Tech,. January 27, 2005, LiveScience website.
http://www.livescience.com/110-presto-instant-petrified-wood-created-lab.html

60 Artificial Coal Anonymous. Artificial coal made from wood substance. Journal of Chemical Education (J.Chem. Educ. January 1929.
http://pubs.acs.org/doi/abs/10.1021/ed006p64

61 Detectable [14]Carbon in coal (Same source as 183)
http://www.answersingenesis.org/articles/aid/v2/n1/radiocarbon-in-diamonds

62 Artificial Fossils Anonymous. "Fake Chinese Fossils: Their Proliferation in Today's Market." Paleodirect website. (No date.)
http://www.paleodirect.com/fakechinesefossils1.htm

63 *Creation's Tiny Mystery, Dr. Robert Gentry, "Creation's Tiny Mystery." Earth Science Associates 3rd edition (May 1992)* (also available online @http://www.halos.com/book/ctm-toc.htm)

64 "Radiohalos: Solving the Mystery of the Missing Bullets" Part Three

Snelling, Andrew. Radiohalos: The Flood's Smoking Gun. (Three-Part series)
1. Mysterious Bullet Holes in Rocks March 5, 2012
2. Radiohalos: The Mysterious Vanishing Bullets June 6, 2012
3. Solving the Mystery of the Missing Bullets. Sept. 11, 2012
Answers in Genesis Website.
http://www.answersingenesis.org/articles/am/v7/n4/radiohalos-part-three

65 "Mysterious Bullet Holes In Rocks", by Dr. Andrew A. Snelling, March 5, 2012 (Same source as 64)
http://www.answersingenesis.org/articles/am/v7/n2/mysterious-bullet-holes

66 Open Letter Andrew Snelling, "Snelling's Reply to Gentry." Nov 17, 2002. Earth Science Associates website.
http://www.halos.com/faq-replies/snelling-to-gentry-11-17-2002.htm

67 *Radiohalos*: Solving the Mystery of the Missing Bullets by Dr. Andrew Snelling (Same source as 64)
http://www.answersingenesis.org/articles/am/v7/n4/radiohalos-part-three

68 (Image) "Fingerprints of Creation" video. Earth Science Associates Knoxville, TN, 1996.
http://www.halos.us/fingerprints.htm

69 Radiohalo article (Same source as 64)
http://www.answersingenesis.org/articles/am/v7/n3/radiohalos-vanishing-bullets

70 Tiny Mystery Article
Andrew A. Snelling, Ph.D. 2000. Polonium Radiohalos: Still "A Very Tiny Mystery". Acts & Facts. 29 (8).
http://www.icr.org/article/polonium-radiohalos-still-a-very-tiny-mystery/

71 "They Are Not Rare". (Same source as 64)
http://www.answersingenesis.org/articles/am/v7/n4/radiohalos-part-three

72 Wikipedia article on Radiohalos
"Radiohalos." Wikipedia. (No author, no date.) Wikimedia Foundation Created by Jimmy Wales, Larry Sanger, Launched January 15, 2001.
http://en.wikipedia.org/wiki/Radiohalo

73 Chelyabinsk article
Beatty, Kelly. "Chelyabinsk Mega-meteor: Status Report" June 25, 2013. Sky & Telescope The Essential Guide to Astronomy website.
http://www.skyandtelescope.com/astronomy-news/chelyabinsk-mega-meteor-status-report/

74 Meteor fragment Olga Zenkova, "Libra did not survive the severity of Chelyabinsk meteorite." (Translation provided on the

site page. It is in Russian). Novosti website 10/16/2013
http://www.ntv.ru/novosti/677303/
David M. Herzenhorn,"Lifted From a Russian Lake, a Big, if Fragile,
Space Rock," October 16, 2013, New York Times website.
http://www.nytimes.com/2013/10/17/world/europe/meteorite-
pulled-from-russian-lake-breaks-into-3-pieces.html

75 Tunguska Article
Brazo, Mark W. and Steven A. Austin. The Tunguska Explosion of
1908. Institute for Creation Research, Origins 9(2):82-93 (1982).
http://www.icr.org/research/index/researchp_sa_r05/

76 Meteor Crater
Meteor Crater official website.
http://www.meteorcrater.com/
Wikipedia article on the crater.
https://en.wikipedia.org/wiki/Meteor_Crater
"Meteor Crater Sample Collection" US Geological Service
Astrogeology Science Center. (No author, no date.)
http://astrogeology.usgs.gov/facilities/meteor-crater-sample-
collection

77 *Impact mechanics at Meteor Crater, Arizona*
1959, Shoemaker, Eugene Merle
Shoemaker, Eugene M. Impact Mechanics at Meteor Crater,
Arizona. Prepared on behalf of the U.S. Atomic Energy
Commission. US Geological service Publications.
USGS Open-File Report: 59-108
http://pubs.usgs.gov/of/1959/0108/report.pdf

78 Meteor Impacts
Dr. Andrew Snelling *Did Meteors Trigger Noah's Flood? December
6, 2011,*
http://www.answersingenesis.org/articles/am/v7/n1/meteors-
trigger-flood

79 Other Meteor Impacts
http://en.wikipedia.org/wiki/List_of_impact_craters_on_Earth

80 Foundational Assumptions of Radiometric Dating
Riddle, Mike, "Does Radiometric Dating Prove the Earth Is Old?"
October 4, 2007 Excerpted from The New Answers Book, Answers
in Genesis Master Books New Leaf Press, Green Forest, AR. 2006.
http://www.answersingenesis.org/articles/nab/does-radiometric-
dating-prove

81 Radioactive Decay Rates
Alex Knapp, "Radioactive Decay Rates May Not Be Constant After
All," *Forbes* Tech, May 3, 2011.
http://www.forbes.com/sites/alexknapp/2011/05/03/radioactive-
decay-rates-may-not-be-constant-after-all/

82 Detecting neutrinos
Larson, Kirsten. "Neutrinos!" IceCube South Pole Neutrino
Observatory. National Science Foundation. University of

Wisconson-Madison. (No date.)
http://www.astro.wisc.edu/~larson/Webpage/neutrinos.html

83 Definition of Cherenkov light (radiation) "is electromagnetic
radiation emitted when a charged particle (such as an electron)
passes through a dielectric medium at a speed greater than the
phase velocity of light in that medium."
http://en.wikipedia.org/wiki/Cherenkov_radiation]

84 Altered Decay Rates John Woodmorappe. "Billion-Fold
Acceleration of Radioactivity Demonstrated in Laboratory." Journal
of Creation Answers in Genesis. August 1, 2001.
http://www.answersingenesis.org/articles/tj/v15/n2/acceleration#
r6
Bosch, F. et al., Observation of bound-state b: decay of fully ionized
187Re, Physical Review Letters 77(26)5190-5193, 1996. For further
discussion of this experiment, see: Kienle, P., Beta-decay
experiments and astrophysical implications, in: Prantzos, N. and
Harissopulus, S., Proceedings, Nuclei in the Cosmos, pp. 181-186,
1999.
Andrew A. Snelling, PhD, The Cause of Anomalous Potassium-
Argon "Ages" for Recent Andesite Flows at Mt. Ngauruhoe, New
Zealand, and the Implications for Potassium-Argon "Dating"
Answers in Genesis Presented at the Fourth International
Conference on Creationism, Pittsburgh, Pennsylvania, August 3–8,
1998. Published in: Proceedings of the Fourth International
Conference on Creationism, R. E. Walsh (editor), pp. 503–525.
http://static.icr.org/i/pdf/technical/The-Cause-of-Anomalous-
Potassium-Argon-Ages.pdf

85 New Zealand dating samples (same source as 210)
http://www.answersingenesis.org/articles/cm/v22/n1/dating

86 Flaws in radioactive Dating (same source as 210)
http://static.icr.org/i/pdf/technical/The-Cause-of-Anomalous-
Potassium-Argon-Ages.pdf

87 Dacite Lava Dome
"*National Geographic* Plays the Dating Game" By John
Woodmorappe April 1, 2002, Answers in Genesis website.
http://www.answersingenesis.org/articles/tj/v16/n1/dating-game

88 Radio-Dating in Rubble by Keith Swenson Creation Magazine
June 1, 2001
http://www.answersingenesis.org/articles/cm/v23/n3/radiodating

89 *The Fallacies of Radioactive Dating of Rocks*
Basalt Lave Flows in Grand Canyon by Dr. Andrew Snelling 2005
http://www.answersingenesis.org/articles/am/v1/n1/radioactive-
dating

90 Dating of Radioisotope samples. Andrew A. Snelling,
"Radioisotope Dating of Rocks in the Grand Canyon," June 1, 2005,
Creation, Answers in Genesis website.

http://www.answersingenesis.org/articles/cm/v27/n3/canyon#fnList_1_7

91 D.G.A. Whitten and J.R.V. Brooks, The Penguin Dictionary of Geology (Middlesex, England: Penguin Books, (1972).

92 *Helium Diffusion Rates Support Accelerated Nuclear Decay* by Dr. Russell Humphreys, 2003
Abstract [in part] The entire paper is available for download as a .pdf file.
http://logosresearchassociates.org/Documents/Baumgardner/Helium-Diffusion-Rates-Support-Accelerated-Nuclear-Decay.pdf

93 Helium Evidence Russell Humphreys, "Helium Evidence For A Young World Remains Crystal-Clear" Institute for Creation Research April 27, 2005. The True Origin Archive.
http://www.trueorigin.org/helium01.asp

94 Fallacies in dating (No author), "Fallacies in Dating: Reason 8: Radioactivity," June 1, 2007,
http://www.answersingenesis.org/articles/2007/06/01/reason-eight-radioactivity

95 The Chalk Formations quote was from an *Answers In Genesis* article with no author given. "Wonders of Geology: White Cliffs of Dover." August 21, 2008, Answers in Genesis.
http://www.answersingenesis.org/articles/wog/white-cliffs-dover

96 Oil Spill cleanup Todd Woody, "Gulf oil spill methane bloom disappears, Grist: A Beacon in the Smog, January 7, 2011.
http://grist.org/article/2011-01-06-gulf-oil-spill-methane-bloom-disappears/

97 After the Flood White Cliffs of Dover Image.
http://www.answersingenesis.org/assets/images/articles/2008/05/geology-brochures/white-cliffs-top.jpg
Kansas chalk formation image.
http://www.oceansofkansas.com/images2/!monrks2.jpg

98 Paramecium
Eric Russell, "The Biology Classics: Paramecium Reproduction," Biomedia Associates: Learning Programs for Biology Education. (No Date.)
https://www.ebiomedia.com/the-biology-classics-paramecium-reproduction.html

99 Fossil Forests
William A. Dimichele and Howard J. Falcoln-Lang, "Pennsylvania: 'fossil forests' in growth position (T° assemblages): origin, taphonomic bias and palaeoecological insights," Journal of the Geological Society, London, Vol. 168, 2011, pp. 585-605.

100 Photo courtesy of Ian Juby and Creation Evidence.
http://ianjuby.org/polydisplay.html. creationevidence.org
Team from Creation Evidence Museum: David Lines (photographer), (left to right) Neil Owens, with Shauna and Matt

Carrie, Dr. Don Patton and Dr. Carl Baugh. A preliminary survey of the mine and the polystrates was undertaken in the winter.

101 Extinction events
Anthony Barnosky, et. Al, "Has the Earth's sixth mass extinction already arrived?" *Nature* (International Weekly Journal of Science), 471, 51-57 (03 March 2011)
http://www.nature.com/nature/journal/v471/n7336/fig_tab/natur e09678_T1.html
Anonymous. "Big Five Mass Extinction Events." Nature/Prehistoric Life. (No Date) BBC.co.uk
http://www.bbc.co.uk/nature/extinction_events

102 The World's a Graveyard by Andrew Snelling, February 12, 2008
http://www.answersingenesis.org/articles/am/v3/n2/world-graveyard

103 Dinosaur Fossil Brian Thomas,, M.S., Dinosaur Fossil "Wasn't Supposed to Be There." April 14, 2011. Institute for Creation Research. icr.org
http://www.icr.org/article/dinosaur-fossil-wasnt-supposed-be-there/

104 "Chinese Dinosaurs Were Fossilized by Flood," Brian Thomas, M.S. Chinese Dinosaurs Were Fossilized by Flood April 8, 2011. Institute for Creation Research.
http://www.icr.org/article/6052/

105 "Canadian 'Mega' Dinosaur Bonebed Formed by Watery Catastrophe," Brian Thomas, M.S., July 13, 2010,Institute for Creation Research.
http://www.icr.org/article/5521/

106 Out of Sequence Fossils Dr. Walt Brown, "24. Missing Trunk," *In the Beginning: Compelling Evidence for Creation and the Flood,* Center for Scientific Creation, 2008
http://www.creationscience.com/onlinebook/ReferencesandNotes 23.html#wp1013046

107 Example of uniformitarian manipulation of the fossil evidence and those who view it. Dr. Dennis O'Neil, "Interpreting the Fossil Record." RECORD OF TIME: An Introduction to the Nature of Fossils and Paleoanthropological Dating Methods. Website created and maintained by , Behavioral Sciences Department, Palomar College, San Marcos, California Copyright © 1998-2012 by Dennis O'Neil. All rights reserved.
http://anthro.palomar.edu/time/Default.htm

108 *Answers in Genesis* The World's A Graveyard Flood Evidence number two by Dr. Snelling (same source as 228)
http://www.answersingenesis.org/articles/am/v3/n2/world-graveyard

109 Michael Oard *The Geological Column Is a General Flood Order with Many Exceptions.* biblicalgeology.net/General/geologic-column.html

110 Index fossils Graphic by USGS.
http://pubs.usgs.gov/gip/geotime/fossils.html

111 Real fossil record John Morris, 2010, "The Real Nature of the Fossil Record," *Acts & Facts.* 39 (2): 12-14. Institute for Creation Research.
http://www.icr.org/article/real-nature-fossil-record/

112 Two Articles about fossils in Amber
European Synchrotron Radiation Facility. "Scientists Discover 356 Animal Inclusions Trapped In Opaque Amber 100 Million Years Old." ScienceDaily.
www.sciencedaily.com/releases/2008/04/080401120513.htm (accessed April 14, 2014).
Sherwin, F. 2006. Amber: A Window to the Recent Past. Acts & Facts. 35 (7). Institute for Creation Research.
http://www.icr.org/index.php?module=articles&action=view&ID=2824

113 "Dinosaur Tree"
'Dinosaur Tree' Behind Bars. June 1, 2001. No Author.
http://www.answersingenesis.org/articles/cm/v23/n3/wollemi

114 Folded fern
Folded Ferns Simple, Logical Observation Shows How 'Slow and Gradual' Belief Systems Fail. September 1, 1996 Creation (no author).
http://www.answersingenesis.org/articles/cm/v18/n4/folded-ferns

115 Plants in the fossil record
Parker, Gary, Dr. "Fossil Plants." Creation Facts of Life. January 1, 1994. Answers in Genesis.
http://www.answersingenesis.org/articles/cfl/fossil-plants

116 Living fossils
Scheven, Joachim. "Living Fossils." Creation. September 1, 1993. Answers in Genesis.Sherwin, F. 2006. Amber: A Window to the Recent Past. *Acts & Facts.* 35 (7). Institute for Creation Research.
http://www.answersingenesis.org/articles/cm/v15/n4/living-fossils

117 Ferns (same source as 242)
http://www.answersingenesis.org/articles/cm/v16/n1/living-fossils

119 Flying Fish
"Fish that 'Fly'. December 1. 1997. Creation (no author) Answers in Genesis.
http://www.answersingenesis.org/articles/cm/v20/n1/fish-fly

120 Tadpole Shrimp "'Ghostly' Shrimp Update. September 1, 1994. Creation. Answers in Genesis. (No Author)
http://www.answersingenesis.org/articles/cm/v16/n4/shrimp

121 Horseshoe crab (same source as 242)
http://www.answersingenesis.org/articles/cm/v16/n1/living-fossils

122 Fossil shrimp (same source as 242)
http://www.answersingenesis.org/articles/cm/v16/n2/fossil

123 Identical Seashell and fossil (same source as 242)
http://www.answersingenesis.org/articles/cm/v17/n4/fossils

124 English and Japanese shells (same source as 242)
http://www.answersingenesis.org/articles/cm/v17/n2/fossils

125 Polistes wasp images (same source as 242)
http://www.answersingenesis.org/articles/cm/v17/n1/wasp-living-fossil

126 Ke-Qin Gao & Neil H. Shubin, Earliest known crown-group salamanders, Nature 422:428, March 27, 2003
Mortenson, Terry, Dr. "Fossil Turtles Confound Evolutionists" April 18, 2005 Answers in Genesis.
http://www.answersingenesis.org/articles/2005/04/18/fossil-turtles-evolutionists

127 Laotian Rock Rat
"Rodent Resurrected." Anonymous. May 2, 2006. Answers in Genesis.
http://www.answersingenesis.org/articles/am/v1/n1/rodent-resurrected
Inman, Mason. "New Asian Rodent Found as Food Is 'Living Fossil,' Gene Study Confirms." National Geographic News. April 24, 2007.
http://news.nationalgeographic.com/news/2007/04/070424-fossil-rodent.html

128 K. Wise, "The Fossil Record: The Ultimate Test Case for Young-Earth Creationism," Opus: A Journal for Interdisciplinary Studies (1991-92): 17-29. (sources used in this article follow, and then a link to the AiG reprint)
B. Kurtén, Pleistocene Mammals of Europe (Chicago: Aldine, 1968).
J. W. Valentine, "How Good Was the Fossil Record? Clues from the California Pleistocene," Paleobiology 15 no. 2 (1989): 83 -94.
Completeness of the Fossil Record by Kurt Wise
http://www.answersingenesis.org/articles/am/v5/n1/completeness-fossil-record

129 By Dr. Snelling Order in the Fossil Record November 23, 2009 *Answers.* Answers in Genesis.
http://www.answersingenesis.org/articles/am/v5/n1/order-fossil-record

130 Correction of Precambrian Label Froede, Carl R. Jr.
"Precambrian Plant Fossils and the Hakatai Shale Controversy." Volume 36(3):106-113 December 1999. Creation Research Society Quarterly Journal.
http://www.creationresearch.org/crsq/articles/36/36_3/plantfossils.html

131 Walker/Klevberg chart
"Time/Rock Transformation" chart based on the Walker system
modifed by Klevberg. Tas Walker's Biblical Geology.
http://biblicalgeology.net/images/stories/model/figure1.jpg

132 Flood Timeline
http://www.answersingenesis.org/articles/2010/08/23/overview-
flood-timeline

133 Dino do-overs: Fixes to paleontology
By Talal Al-Khatib, Published August 14, 2013, *Discovery News*
http://www.foxnews.com/science/2013/08/14/dino-do-overs-
fixes-to-paleontology/#ixzz2bzsAxp4U
http://www.foxnews.com/science/2013/08/14/dino-do-overs-
fixes-to-paleontology/

134 Valentine, J. W. (1989). "How good was the fossil record? Clues
from the Californian Pleistocene." Paleobiology 15(2): 83-94.

135 Vegetation before the Flood Andrew Snelling, PhD. "Coal Beds
and Noah's Flood." June 1, 1986. Creation Ex Nihilo; Answers in
Genesis.
http://www.answersingenesis.org/articles/cm/v8/n3/noah
http://www.answersingenesis.org/articles/am/v8/n2/how-did-we-
get-coal
Woolley, Joanna F. "The origin of the Carboniferous coal measures
part 1: Lessons from history" Journal of Creation 24(3):76–81
December 2010
http://creation.com/carboniferous-floating-forest-1
http://creation.com/carboniferous-floating-forest-2
http://creation.com/Carboniferous-floating-forest-3

136 Primary, Secondary, Tertiary Rocks
http://www.creationmoments.com/content/geology-and-genesis

137 "The Tertiary Period: The Age of Mammals Begins."
http://www.fossils-facts-and-finds.com/tertiary_period.html

138 *What is the Quaternary?*
http://geomaps.wr.usgs.gov/sfgeo/quaternary/stories/what_is.ht
ml

139 Wolf varieties
http://www.desertusa.com/mag98/mar/papr/du_mexwolf.html

140 Coyotes
http://www3.ag.purdue.edu/entm/wildlifehotline/pages/coyotes.a
spx

141 "The Geological Column Is a General Flood Order with Many
Exceptions" by Michael Oard
http://biblicalgeology.net/General/geologic-column.html

142 While Wikipedia is not an authoritative source by itself, this is a
very clear and accurate statement.
http://en.wikipedia.org/wiki/Ice_age

143 Earthguide team members and Scripps Institution of
Oceanography. Climate Change Past and Future: The Ice Ages.
"General Overview of the Ice Ages." University of California, San
Diego. Earthguide A part of the Geosciences Research Division at
Scripps Institution of Oceanography.
http://earthguide.ucsd.edu/virtualmuseum/climatechange2/01_1.s
html

144 NASA information about sea level Vivien Gornitz, "Sea Level
Rise, After the Ice Melted and Today," *Science Briefs,* National
Aeronautics and Space Administration Goddard Institute for Space
Studies, January 2007.
http://www.giss.nasa.gov/research/briefs/gornitz_09/

145 Snowblitz Michael Oard, Chapter 8: The Snowblitz, October 1,
2004. From the book Frozen in Time, Masterbooks, a division of
New Leaf Press (Green Forest, Arkansas) 2004.
http://www.answersingenesis.org/articles/fit/snowblitz#fnMark_1
_1_1 (Note that this source applies to several quoted sections.)

146 Ice Age Remains Michael J. Oard, How did 90% of large
Australian Ice Age animals go extinct? *Journal of Creation*
22(1):17–19 April 2008.
http://creation.com/australian-ice-age-animal-extinction
http://www.answersingenesis.org/articles/fit/mammoth-
carcasses-siberia

147 Human artifacts in glaciers Climate Change: "Melting Glaciers
Expose Ancient Artifacts In Northern Europe Faster Than
Archaeologists Can Collect Them." Huff Post Green September 16,
2010. video from Reuters, with Archaeologist Lars Piloe.
http://www.huffingtonpost.com/2010/09/16/climate-change-
melting-gl_n_717860.html
James Brooke, Lost Worlds Rediscovered as Canadian Glaciers
Melt, New York Times on the Web Learning Network, October 5,
1999.
http://www.nytimes.com/learning/teachers/featured_articles/199
91005tuesday.html
"CU-Boulder researchers hunt for artifact-rich glaciers." INSTAAR
(Institute of Arctic and Alpine Research) University of Colorado
Boulder June 26 2002 (No author.)
http://instaar.colorado.edu/news-events/instaar-news/cu-boulder-
researchers-hunt-for-artifact-rich-glaciers/
Freed from the ice: around the world, glaciers are melting--
revealing human remains and artifacts that have been trapped in
ice for thousands of years. The Free Library by Scholastic.

Freed from the ice: around the world, glaciers are melting--
revealing human remains and artifacts that have been trapped in
ice for thousands of years. The Free Library by Scholastic.
http://www.thefreelibrary.com/Freed+from+the+ice%3A+around
+the+world,+glaciers+are+melting--revealing...-a0195324757
http://www.trussel.com/prehist/news310.htm

148 Hawking, Stephen. *The Illustrated A Brief History of Time.*
New York, NY: Bantam Dell, a division of Random House, 1996.
(Although the text refers to the better-known original *A Brief
History of Time,* we cite from this illustrated version of the book
because it is the one we own.)

Bibliography

Note that sources for all the first three modules in this series are included here. For links to most of the sources we used, as well as why and how we use certain references, and background and further information on sources, please consult the appendix.)

Adam of Bremen. *Gesta Hammaburgensis Ecclesiae Pontificum.* Berlin. (translated and edited by G. Waitz, 1876).

Adams, Donald A. Pastor of Trinity Baptist Church, Weatherly PA. In the text of this work are emailed comments on the position that the Sons of God in Genesis 6 refers to descendants of Seth corrupting the godly line by intermarrying with female descendants of Cain. 11/18/2011.

Anonymous. "Antimony Poisoning" article from *Encyclopaedia Britannica* online.

_______. Artificial coal made from wood substance. *Journal of Chemical Education* (J. Chem. Educ.), January 1929.

_______. Australian Aborigine "Dreaming" or "Dreamtime" Creation Story. Fulbright Foundation. The Australian American Educational Foundation, T/A the Australian American Fulbright Commission

_______. "Big Five Mass Extinction Events." Nature/Prehistoric Life. (No Date) *BBC.co.uk*

________. Bluecloud Dakota Creation Legend from the Black Hills of Western South Dakota. (No date.)

________. British Museum website. 'Adam and Eve' cylinder seal. Acquired from the John Robert Stewart Collection in 1846. T.C. Mitchell, *The Bible in the British Museum* (London, The British Museum Press, 1988) D. Collon, Catalogue of the Western Asi-1 (London, 1982). (References quoted in the description.)

________. "Burckle Crater: Dating the Flood." (No date.) *Geocreationism.com*

________. Climate Change: "Melting Glaciers Expose Ancient Artifacts In Northern Europe Faster Than Archaeologists Can Collect Them." *Huff Post Green* September 16, 2010. Video from Reuters, with Archaeologist Lars Piloe.

________. Climate Change Past and Future: The Ice Ages. "General Overview of the Ice Ages." University of California, San Diego. Earthguide A part of the Geosciences Research Division at Scripps Institution of Oceanography.

________. "Comets and the Great Flood of Noah." (No Date) *Creationism.org*

________. "CU-Boulder researchers hunt for artifact-rich glaciers." INSTAAR (Institute of Arctic and Alpine Research) University of Colorado Boulder June 26 2002.

________. "'Dinosaur Tree' Behind Bars." *Creation*. June 1, 2001. Answers in Genesis.

________. "Education: How are Gemesis lab-created diamonds made?" (No date.) Gemesis Website. http://gemesis.com (laboratory-produced diamonds)

________. "Entheogen." Dictionary.com. Dictionary.com's 21st Century Lexicon. Dictionary.com LLC.http://dictionary.reference.com/browse/enth eogen

________. "Fake Chinese Fossils: Their Proliferation in Today's Market." Paleodirect website. (No date.)

________. "Fallacies in Dating: Reason 8: Radioactivity," June 1, 2007, Answers in Genesis website.

________. "Fish that 'Fly'." December 1. 1997. *Creation* Answers in Genesis website.

________. "Folded Ferns: Simple, Logical Observation Shows How 'Slow and Gradual' Belief Systems Fail." September 1, 1996. Creation. Answers in Genesis.

________. "'Ghostly' Shrimp Update." September 1, 1994. *Creation*. Answers in Genesis.

________. "Glacial Lake Missouri and the Ice Age Floods." (No date.) Website for the Montana Natural History Center, Missoula, MT.

________. "Ice Ages." BBC Science/The Earth/Water&Ice (No Date.)

________. "Impressive Elephants." (No Date) SanDiegoZoo.org

________. "A majestic landscape reflecting a history of extremes. Ancient Bristlecone Pine Forest, Inyo National Forest." (No Date)The Sierra Web, Your complete guide to the eastern Sierra.

________. "Meteor Crater Sample Collection" US Geological Service Astrogeology Science Center. (No date.)

________. "Oilgae: Glossary. Synthetic petroleum Definition." Website promoting Algae-based biofuels. (no date) Oilgae.com

________. "Radiohalos." Wikipedia. Wikimedia Foundation Created by Jimmy Wales, Larry Sanger, Launched January 15, 2001.

________. "Rodent Resurrected." May 2, 2006. Answers in Genesis.

________. "Scientists Discover 356 Animal Inclusions Trapped In Opaque Amber 100 Million Years Old."

European Synchrotron Radiation Facility. *ScienceDaily*. April 2008.

________. "Wonders of Geology: White Cliffs of Dover." August 21, 2008, Answers in Genesis.

Augustine. *City of God and Christian Doctrine,* Chapter 6, Book XI Translator, Schaff, Philip (1819-1893) Print Basis: New York: *The Christian Literature Publishing Co.*, 1890. (Electronic version from the Internet Sacred Text Archive, managed by John Bruno Hare.)

________ *Confessions* Book 11 Chapter XXX paragraph 41 . (Electronic version from the Internet Sacred Text Archive, managed by John Bruno Hare.)

Austin, S.A. *Ten misconceptions about the geologic column.* ICR *Impact,* No. 137, 1984.

Banks, Norm, photographer. "Pyroclastic Flow." 1980 photograph. U.S. Geological Survey

Barnosky, Anthony, et. al. "Has the Earth's sixth mass extinction already arrived?" *Nature* (International Weekly Journal of Science), 471, 51-57 (03 March 2011)

Barry, Sharon, et. al. "The Dynamic Earth: Geogallery." Smithsonian Website. (No Date)

Beatty, Kelly. "Chelyabinsk Mega-meteor: Status Report" June 25, 2013. Sky & Telescope The Essential Guide to Astronomy website.

Bellows, Henry Adams, translator. *The Poetic Edda* Princeton University Press and American Scandinavian Foundation, Princeton, NJ: 1936. From the Internet Sacred Text Archive, managed by John Bruno Hare.

Bosch, F. et al., "Observation of bound-state b: decay of fully ionized 187Re," Physical Review Letters 77(26)5190-5193, 1996. For further discussion of this experiment, see: Kienle, P., Beta-decay experiments and astrophysical implications, in:

Prantzos, N. and Harissopulus, S., Proceedings, Nuclei in the Cosmos, pp. 181-186, 1999.

Brazo, Mark W. and Steven A. Austin. The Tunguska Explosion of 1908. Institute for Creation Research, Origins 9(2):82-93 (1982).

Brodeur, Arthur Gilchrist, translator. *The Prose Edda of Snorri Sturlson* New York: The American-Scandinavian Foundation, 1916. From the Internet Sacred Text Archive, managed by John Bruno Hare.

James Brooke. "Lost Worlds Rediscovered as Canadian Glaciers Melt." *New York Times on the Web Learning Network,* October 5, 1999.

Brown, Walt, Dr. "24. Missing Trunk." *In the Beginning: Compelling Evidence for Creation and the Flood.* Center for Scientific Creation 2008

Budge, E.A. Wallis, translator. *The Babylonian Legends of Creation.* 1921. "The Legend of the Creation According to Berosus and Damascius, written in Greek by Berosus, a priest of Bel-Marduk about 250 BC at Babylon from Alexander Polyhistor." from the Internet Sacred Text Archive, managed by John Bruno Hare.

______. *The Book of the Cave of Treasures,* Part One (Brit. Mus. MS. Add. 25875.) [The Title of the Work: *The Scribe's Prayer* Translated from the Syriac by [London, The Religious Tract Society] [1927] {scanned and edited by Christopher M. Weimer, June 2002}
from the *Internet Sacred Text Archive* managed by John Bruno Hare.

______. A History of Creation. "The Book of knowing the Evolutions of Ra and of the overthrowing of Apep (Egyptian)". *Legends of the Gods, The Egyptian Texts.* London: Kegan Paul, Trench and Trübner & Co. Ltd., 1912. Scanned at sacred-texts.com 1999 and 2003. J.B. Hare, redactor.

Carney, Scott. "Did A Comet Cause The Great Flood?" *Discover Magazine,* November 15, 2007 re-posted in Free Republic Website.

Catchpoole, David. "Lea, the spaghetti lioness." *Creation* 29(4):44–45, September, 2007.

______. "The Lion that wouldn't eat meat." *Creation* 22(2):22–23 March, 2000.

Catholic Catechism, English translation of the Catechism of the Catholic Church for the United States of America copyright © 1994, United States Catholic Conference, Inc.—Libreria Editrice Vaticana. English translation of the Catechism of the Catholic Church: Modifications from the Editio Typica copyright © 1997, United States Catholic Conference, Inc.—Libreria Editrice Vaticana.

Charles, R. H., translator. The *Book of Enoch* I. *The Apocrypha and Pseudepigrapha of the Old Testament.* Oxford: The Clarendon Press, 1913. From the Internet Sacred Text Archive, managed by John Bruno Hare.

______. *Book of Jubilees,* The. The Society for Promoting Christian Knowledge, London, 1917. (Electronic version from the Internet Sacred Text Archive, managed by John Bruno Hare.)

______. Zadokite or Damascus Document in *The Apocrypha and Pseudepigrapha of the Old Testament in English,* vol. 2: Pseudepigrapha (Oxford: Clarendon Press, 1913) http://fam-faerch.dk/pseudigrapher/dsea/zadok01.html, (Webpage of Rolf Ivan Faerch)

Cooper, David L, Dr. *Rules for Interpretation.* Biblical Research Monthly, 1947, 1949.

Cory, I. P. *Ancient Fragments* [1832 ed.] The Theology of the Phoenicians: From Sanchoniatho (reduced to HTML by Christopher M. Weimer, Dec. 2002) From the Internet Sacred Text Archive, managed by John Bruno Hare.

Dalley, Stephanie, translator. *Epic of Atrahasis --
     Myths from Mesopotamia: Creation, the Flood,
     Gilgamesh, and Others* Oxford World's Classics.
     Oxford University Press, 1998.

Von Däniken, Erich. *Chariots of the Gods?* Penguin
     Group (USA) New York, NY January 1999.

Dawkins, Richard. *The Greatest Show on Earth: The
     Evidence for Evolution.* Free Press, Simon and
     Schuster, New York, NY, 2009.

Dimichele, William A. and Howard J. Falcoln-Lang.
     "Pennsylvania: 'fossil forests' in growth position
     (T° assemblages): origin, taphonomic bias and
     palaeoecological insights." Journal of the
     Geological Society, London, Vol. 168, 2011, pp.
     585-605.

Dixon, Roland B. *Oceanic Mythology* Part I. "Polynesia
     Myths of Origins and the Deluge New Zealand,"
     1916(Electronic version from the Internet Sacred
     Text Archive, managed by John Bruno Hare.)

Doyle, Shaun, "Noah's comet? Was Noah's Flood a
     tsunami caused by a comet impact?" 2 January
     2008. Creation.com

Edmonds, Molly. "How the Ice Age Worked" 13 May
     2008. HowStuffWorks.com.
     http://geography.howstuffworks.com/terms-and-
     associations/ice-age.htm 12 April 2014.

Eldredge, Sandy and Bob Biek. "Ice Ages: What Are
     they and what causes them?" *Glad You Asked*
     article, Survey Notes, v. 42 no. 3, September 2010.
     Utah Geological Survey, Salt Lake City, UT.

Elias, Scott. Homepage. "Welcome to the World of Ice
     Age Paleoecology." University of Colorado at
     Boulder website.

Faulkner, Danny. "A biblically-based cratering theory."
     Journal of Creation 13(1):100-104 April 1999.

Felgenhauer, Joseph (Grand Canyon Park Ranger).
     "Inside Grand Canyon: How the Grand Canyon
     Was Shaped Over Time" (Transcript of oral

presentation). National Park Service, U.S. Department of the Interior. Grand Canyon National Park, Arizona. (No Date.) National Park Service Website.

Ferdowsi, Hakim Abol-Ghasem (Toosi). *The Epic of Shahnameh Ferdowsi* (940-1020) Helen Zimmern translator. (*The Epic of Kings: Hero Tales of Ancient Persia* Chapter 1: The Shahs of Old (Zoroastrian). http://www.enel.ucalgary.ca/People/far/hobbies/iran/shahnameh.html

Findley, Michael J. *Rightly Dividing the Word of Truth. Elk Jerky for the Soul blog, August 6, 2012.*

Froede, Carl R. Jr. "Precambrian Plant Fossils and the Hakatai Shale Controversy." Volume 36(3):106-113 December 1999. Creation Research Society Quarterly Journal.

Gao, Ke-Qin & Neil H. Shubin. "Earliest known crown-group salamanders." *Nature* 422:428, March 27, 2003.

Gentry, Robert, Dr. "Creation's Tiny Mystery." Earth Science Associates 3rd edition (May 1992).

_______ , et. al. "Fingerprints of Creation" video. Earth Science Associates Knoxville, TN, 1996.

Gish, Duane, Ph.D. "Origin of Life: Critique of Early Stage Chemical Evolution Theories." *Impact.* Institute for Creation Research, Jan 1, 1976

Goble, Phillip. *The Orthodox Jewish Bible.* English language version that applies Yiddish and Hasidic cultural expressions to the Messianic Bible. fourth edition. Copyright 2002,2003,2008,2010, 2011 by Artists for Israel International. All rights reserved.

Goetz, Delia and Sylvanus G. Morley, English translators. (Spanish translation by Adrián Recinos.) *Popol Vuh* ("Written Leaves") Book of the Mayas. The Book of the Community Book 1, copyright 1950 by the University of Oklahoma

Press. (Electronic version from the Internet Sacred Text Archive, managed by John Bruno Hare.)

Gornitz, Vivien. "Sea Level Rise, After the Ice Melted and Today." *Science Briefs*. National Aeronautics and Space Administration Goddard Institute for Space Studies, January 2007.

Gould, Stephen Jay. "Nonoverlapping Magisteria," *Natural History* 106 (March 1997): 16-22. http://www.stephenjaygould.org/library/gould_noma.html

Halafta, Yose ben, rabi. *Seder Olam* or *Seder Olam Rabbah* (The Hebrew words mean "The Great Order of the World"). approximately 160 AD. English Translation of the *Seder Olam* http://www.betemunah.org/sederolam.html

Ham, Ken, Bodie Hodge, and Tim Chaffey. *Demolishing Supposed Bible Contradictions. Volumes 1, II. Master Books, Green Forest, AR, 2010.*

Hancock, Graham. *Fingerprints of the Gods*. Three Rivers Press. New York, NY, 1996.

______. *Supernatural: Meetings with the Ancient Teachers of Mankind*. Disinformation Books. New York, NY, Revised edition 2006.

Hardy, Julia. "Afterlife and Salvation." Religion Library: Buddhism. *Patheos Library: Hosting the Conversation on Faith*. (No Date.)

Hawking, Stephen. *The Illustrated A Brief History of Time*. New York, NY: Bantam Dell, a division of Random House, 1996.

Heinlein, Robert A. *Time for the Stars*. Tor Books, New York, NY, 1956.

Herzenhorn, David M. "Lifted From a Russian Lake, a Big, if Fragile, Space Rock." October 16, 2013. New York Times website.

Hesiod. *The Theogony*. (ll. 116-138) Hugh G. Evelyn-White.translator. 1914. From the Internet Sacred Text Archive, managed by John Bruno Hare.

Hinduism http://marbaniang.wordpress.com/2010/08/22/hinduism-4-stages-of-life-and-3-ways-of-salvation-parallels-with-christianity/

Hitler, Adolph. *Mein Kampf*. Franz Eher Verlag (Publisher), Munich, Germany, 1925.

Hodge, Bodie. "Biblical Overview of the Flood Timeline." August 23, 2010 Answers in Genesis.

Hong, S.W. et al. Safety investigation of Noah's Ark in a seaway, *Journal of Creation* 8(1):26-36, 1994. (English version of a 1992 Korean study by on the seaworthiness of the ark supported by the Korea Association of Creation Research.) Proceedings of the International Conference on Creation Research, Korea Association of Creation Research, Taejon, 1993

Houdmann, S. Michael. Question: "How to get to heaven - what are the ideas from the different religions?" Answer concerning Confucianism. From the website *Got Question.org? The Bible has answers! We'll help you find them!*

Humphreys,D. Russell. *Earth's Magnetic Field is Decaying Steadily —with a Little Rhythm,* CRSQ (Creation Research Society Quarterly) July 1, 2010.

______. *Helium Diffusion Rates Support Accelerated Nuclear Decay* 2003 Abstract [in part] The entire paper is available for download as a .pdf file. http://logosresearchassociates.org/Documents/Baumgardner/Helium-Diffusion-Rates-Support-Accelerated-Nuclear-Decay.pdf

______. "Helium Evidence For A Young World Remains Crystal-Clear." Institute for Creation Research. April 27, 2005. The True Origin Archive.

______. "New time dilation helps creation cosmology." *Journal of Creation* 22(3):84–92 December 2008.

______. *Starlight and Time: Solving the Puzzle of Distant Starlight in a Young Universe*. Master Books, Green Forest, AR, 1996.

Ilive, Thomas and M. M. Noah, translators (based on the Jewish Encyclopedia article). *Book of Jasher*, The. Also called *Sepher HaYasher*. Copyright Ken Johnson, 2013. Biblefacts Edition. also; Salt Lake City, J.H. Parry and Company, 1887.

Inman, Mason. "New Asian Rodent Found as Food Is 'Living Fossil,' Gene Study Confirms." *National Geographic News*. April 24, 2007.

Jewish Encyclopedia
http://www.jewishencyclopedia.com/
The unedited full-text of the 1906 Jewish Encyclopedia

Josephus, Flavius. *Antiquities of the Jews , Book I*. William Whiston, translator. 1737. From the Internet Sacred Text Archive managed by John Bruno Hare.

Kelsen, Hans. *The Flood Myth*. Alan Dundes, editor. University of California Press: Berkely and Los Angeles, California, University of California Press, Ltd., London, England, The Regents of the University of California, 1988.

Al-Khatib, Talal. "Dino do-overs: Fixes to paleontology" Published August 14, 2013, *Discovery News*. *Foxnews.com*/Science

Kurtén, B. Pleistocene Mammals of Europe (Chicago: Aldine, 1968).

King, Leonard William. *The Seven Tablets of Creation*. Another Version of the Creation of the World by Marduk. Luzac's Semitic text and translation series. vol. xii-xiii Luzac and Co. London, 1902. From the Internet Sacred Text Archive, managed by John Bruno Hare.

______. *Enuma Elish* ("When on High") (Babylonian/Assyrian/Sumerian/ Chaldean/

Akkadian), Narration 1. London, 1902. From the Internet Sacred Text Archive, managed by John Bruno Hare.

Knapp, Alex. "Radioactive Decay Rates May Not Be Constant After All." *Forbes* Tech. May 3, 2011.

Larson, Kirsten. "Neutrinos!" IceCube South Pole Neutrino Observatory. National Science Foundation. University of Wisconson-Madison. (No date.)

Livingston, David, Jr., PhD. *Correlating the Texts of Ancient Literature with the Old Testament* © 2003 David Livingston http://davelivingston.com/corancienttexts.htm From the site "Ancient Days"

López, Raúl Erlando. "The Antediluvian Patriarch and the Sumerian King List." *Journal of Creation* 12(3):347-357, 1998.

McDonald, Charlotte. "Who, What, Why: Is the Earth getting lighter?" BBC News Magazine, 31 January, 2012.

McDowell, Josh. *New Evidence That Demands a Verdict*. Thomas Nelson; Nashville, TN. 1st edition, 1999.

Meyer, T. and J. Martin. *Clark's Foreign Theological Library* 1854-1858. Keil and Delitszch (Multivolume Series) 1867ff Edinburgh T and T Clark, George Street Keil & Delitzsch Commentary on the Old Testament Johann (C.F.) Keil (1807-1888) & Franz Delitzsch (1813-1890).

Miller, Brandon. "Presto! Instant Petrified Wood Created in Lab." Tech. January 27, 2005. LiveScience website.

Morris, J. 2010. "The Real Nature of the Fossil Record." *Acts & Facts*. 39 (2): 12-14. Institute for Creation Research.

Mortenson, Terry, Dr. "Fossil Turtles Confound Evolutionists." April 18, 2005. Answers in Genesis.

Munro IR, Guyuron B "Split-Rib Cranioplasty". *Annals of Plastic Surgery* 7 (5): 341-346, November 1981.

Murray, Richard. "Missouri Watershed Profile." 14 November 2013. Prezi.com (A site for creating and sharing presentations.)

Naso, Publius Ovidius. (Ovid) The *Metamorphoses*, Book 1. John Dryden, et al, translators, 1717. From the Internet Sacred Text Archive, managed by John Bruno Hare.

Oard, Michael J. "Chapter 8: The Snowblitz, October 1, 2004." From the book *Frozen in Time,* Masterbooks, a division of New Leaf Press (Green Forest, Arkansas) 2004.

______. "The Geological Column Is a General Flood Order with Many Exceptions." *The Geologic Column: Perspectives Within Diluvial Geology.* Reed, J.K and M.J. Oard (editors). Creation Research Society.

______. "How did 90% of large Australian Ice Age animals go extinct?" *Journal of Creation* 22(1):17–19, April 2008.

______. *The New Answers Book Where Does The Ice Age Fit?* Master Books, Green Forest, AR, 2007.

O'Neil, Dennis, Dr. "Interpreting the Fossil Record." RECORD OF TIME: An Introduction to the Nature of Fossils and Paleoanthropological Dating Methods. Website created and maintained by , Behavioral Sciences Department, Palomar College, San Marcos, California Copyright © 1998-2012 by Dennis O'Neil. All rights reserved.

Orr, James, editor. *ISBE* (*International Standard Bible Encyclopedia*) originally published in 1939 by Wm. B. Eerdmans Publishing Co. Website HTML copyright 2011.

Parker, Gary. Dr. "Fossil Plants." *Creation Facts of Life, Answers in Genesis website,* January 1, 1994.

______. "How Fast?" *Creation Facts of Life, Answers in Genesis website,* January 1, 1994.

Plato. *Cratylus*. 360 B.C.E Benjamin Jowett, translator.

Post, Vincent, Dr. et al. News and Media Media release: "Scientists find vast new freshwater sources under the sea." 05 Dec 2013 The National Centre for Groundwater Research and Training is an Australian Government initiative, supported by the Australian Research Council and the National Water Commission.

________ "Offshore fresh groundwater reserves as global phenomenon." *Nature* 504, 71-78 (05 Dec 2013). International weekly journal of science. Nature.com

Quran and Islam http://www.truthnet.org/islam/Quran/Rodwell/50/

Reedy, Anaru, *Ngā Kōrero a Mohi Ruatapu, tohunga rongonui o Ngāti Porou: The Writings of Mohi Ruatapu*. Canterbury University Press: Christchurch, 1993.

Remy, Melina. ("Our Amazing Planet" staff writer.) "The World's Longest Rivers." June 23, 2010. Livescience.com

Riddle, Mike, "Does Radiometric Dating Prove the Earth Is Old?" October 4, 2007 Excerpted from *The New Answers Book*, Answers in Genesis. Master Books/New Leaf Press: Green Forest, AR, 2006.

Roys, Ralph L. *The Book of Chilam Balam of Chumayel* (Mayan), XIII ("The Creation of the Uinal")Washington, D.C.:Carnagie Institution, 1933. From the Internet Sacred Text Archive, managed by John Bruno Hare.

Ruse, M. "Leading anti-creationist philosopher admits that evolution is a religion. How Evolution Became a Religion: Creationists Correct?" *National Post*, pp. B1, B3, B7 May 13, 2000.

Russell, Eric. "The Biology Classics: Paramecium Reproduction." Biomedia Associates: Learning

Programs for Biology Education. (No Date.) Beaufort, SC.

Sachs, Mendel, Dr. from his website.

St. John, James. "Replacement." (Fossil preservation involving change in crystal structure and mineralogy of an organism's hard parts.) (No date) Ohio State University at Newark Website.

Sarfati, Jonathan. "Flood models and biblical realism." Journal of Creation 24(3):46–53 December 2010.

______. "How did dinosaurs grow so big?" Creation 28(1):44–47 December 2005

______. *'Millions of years' are missing.* (Interview with biologist and geologist Ariel Roth.) Creation.com

Sawyer, Diane. "Stephen Hawking on Religion: 'Science Will Win,'" Interview with Diane Sawyer, as quoted on ABC World News (07 June 2010).

Scheven, Joachim. "Living Fossils." Creation. September 1, 1993. Answers in Genesis.

Shakespeare, William. *Romeo and Juliet.* Act 3, Scene 1.

Sherwin, F. 2006. Amber: A Window to the Recent Past. *Acts & Facts.* 35 (7). Institute for Creation Research.

Shoemaker, Eugene M. "Impact Mechanics at Meteor Crater, Arizona." Prepared on behalf of the U.S. Atomic Energy Commission. US Geological service Publications.

Smith, George. *The Chaldean Account of Genesis.* London: Thomas Scott, 1876. From the Internet Sacred Text Archive, managed by John Bruno Hare.

Snelling, Andrew A., PhD. The Cause of Anomalous Potassium-Argon "Ages" for Recent Andesite Flows at Mt. Ngauruhoe, New Zealand, and the Implications for Potassium-Argon "Dating" Answers in Genesis Presented at the Fourth International Conference on Creationism,

Pittsburgh, Pennsylvania, August 3–8, 1998. Published in: Proceedings of the Fourth International Conference on Creationism, R. E. Walsh (editor), pp. 503–525.

______. "Coal Beds and Noah's Flood." June 1, 1986. Creation Ex Nihilo; Answers in Genesis.

______. "Did Meteors Trigger Noah's Flood?" December 6, 2011, Answers in Genesis website.

______. "The Earth's magnetic field and the age of the Earth," first published: *Creation (Creation Ministries International)*, 13(4):44-48 September 1991.

______. "The Fallacies of Radioactive Dating of Rocks: Basalt Lava Flows in Grand Canyon. *Answers*. Sept. 5, 2006.

______. "Order in the Fossil Record." November 23, 2009. *Answers*. Answers in Genesis.

______. "Polonium Radiohalos: Still 'A Very Tiny Mystery'." *Acts & Facts*. 29 (8). 2000.

______. Radioactive "Dating" Failure: Recent New Zealand Lava Flows Yield "Ages" of Millions of Years. December 1, 1999. Creation Answers in Genesis website.

______. "Radiocarbons in Diamonds Confirmed." November 7, 2007. AiG-U.S. (Answers in Genesis website).

______. Radiohalos: The Flood's Smoking Gun. (Three-Part series) Answers in Genesis Website.
1. Mysterious Bullet Holes in Rocks March 5, 2012
2. Radiohalos: The Mysterious Vanishing Bullets June 6, 2012
3. Solving the Mystery of the Missing Bullets. Sept. 11, 2012

______. "Radioisotope Dating of Rocks in the Grand Canyon." June 1, 2005. Creation Answers in Genesis website.

________. "Snelling's Reply to Gentry." Nov 17, 2002. Earth Science Associates website.

________. "The World's a Graveyard: Flood Evidence Number Two." Answers in Genesis. February 12, 2008

Solomon, S., et. al., (eds.). "Changes Before the Industrial Era?" IPCC, 2007: Climate Change 2007: The Physical Science Basis. Contribution of Working Group I to the Fourth Assessment Report of the Intergovernmental Panel on Climate Change. Cambridge University Press, Cambridge, United Kingdom and New York, NY, USA.

Spence, Lewis. *The Myths of Mexico and Peru,* 1913. Garcia's *Origin de los Indias* (Translation of Mixtec picture-manuscript) quoted in this work.

Swanson, D.A., (photographer). Phreatic Eruption, Mount St. Helens 18 May 1980.

Swenson, Keith. "Radio-Dating in Rubble: The Lava Dome at Mount St Helens Debunks Dating Methods." Creation Magazine June 1, 2001 Answers in Genesis Website.

al-Tabari, Ibn Jarir. (Muslim historian 838-923.) *The History of al-Tabari*. English translation of *The History of the Prophets and Kings*.

Than, Ker. "Huge Ocean Discovered Inside Earth." February 28, 2007. Livescience.comTharpar, Romila. *Frontline* magazine Volume 18, Issue 19, Sep. 15-28, 2001.

Theoi Classical E-Texts Library, New Zealand.

Thom, Harrie. "How could Noah care for the animals?" Creation 30(1):50–51, December 2007.

Thomas, Brian, M.S. "Canadian 'Mega' Dinosaur Bonebed Formed by Watery Catastrophe." July 13, 2010. Institute for Creation Research.

________. "Chinese Dinosaurs Were Fossilized by Flood." April 8. 2011. Institute for Creation Research.

________. Dinosaur Fossil "Wasn't Supposed to Be There." April 14, 2011. Institute for Creation Research. icr.org

Ussher, James. The Annals of the World "The Origin of Time, and Continued to the Beginning of the Emperor Vespasian's Reign and the Total Destruction and Abolition of the Temple and Commonwealth of the Jews." London: Printed by E. Tyler for F. Crook and B. Bedell, 1658. From the Internet Sacred Text Archive, managed by John Bruno Hare.

U.S. Geological Survey. Geologic Names Committee, 2010, Divisions of geologic time—major chronostratigraphic and geochronologic units: U.S. Geological Survey Fact Sheet 2010–3059, 2 p.

________. Graphic of Index Fossils. http://pubs.usgs.gov/gip/geotime/fossils.html

Valentine, J. W. "How Good Was the Fossil Record? Clues from the California Pleistocene," *Paleobiology* 15 no. 2 (1989): 83 -94.

Vardiman, Larry, Ph.D. Scientific Naturalism as Science. *Acts & Facts* (Institute for Creation Research), 26 (11). 1997.

________. and D. R. Humphreys. 2010. *A New Creationist Cosmology: In No Time at All* Part 1. Acts & Facts. 39 (11): 12-15, 40 (1): 12-14, 40(2): 12-14.

Velikovsky, Immanuel. *Ages in Chaos*. Harper, New York, NY, 1950.

________. *Worlds in Collison*. Harper, New York, NY, 1950.

Voth. H.R. Hurúing Wuhti and the Sun. From Field Columbian Museum Publication 96 Anthropological Series Volume VIII, The Traditions of the Hopi. The Stanley McCormick Hopi Expedition George A Dorsey, Curator, Department of Anthropology, Chicago, IL March, 1905 Scanned, proofed and formatted at sacred-texts.com, February 2001, by John Bruno Hare. Reformatted, August 2003. From the Internet Sacred Text Archive, managed by John Bruno Hare.

Walker, Tas. Walker/Klevberg chart. "Time/Rock Transformation" Chart based on the Walker system modifed by Klevberg. Tas Walker's Biblical Geology website.

WELLINGTON. *"THE SAMOAN STORY OF CREATION-A 'Tala.' " JOURNAL OF THE POLYNESIAN SOCIETY CONTAINING THE TRANSACTIONS AND PROCEEDINGS OF THE SOCIETY. VOL. I.* [Wellington, 1892] {Reduced to HTML by Christopher M. Weimer, November 2002

West, E.W., translator. Narration 28 Bundahis, Chapter I, "In the name of the creator Aûharmazd." (Persian*) Sacred Books of the East,* Volume 5, Oxford: the Clarendon Press, 1880. From the Internet Sacred Text Archive, managed by John Bruno Hare.

______. *Pahlavi Texts.* Part V "Marvels of Zoroastrianism." *Sacred Books of the East,* Volume 47 Oxford: the Clarendon Press, 1897. From the Internet Sacred Text Archive, managed by John Bruno Hare.

Whitten, D.G.A. and J.R.V. Brooks. The Penguin Dictionary of Geology. Middlesex, England: Penguin Books, 1972.

Wilkins, W. J. *Hindu Mythology, Vedic and Puranic.* Calcutta: Thacker, Spink & Co.; London: W. Thacker & Co. 1900. Kamadeva/Madana. From the Internet Sacred Text Archive, managed by John Bruno Hare.

Wise, K. "The Fossil Record: The Ultimate Test Case for Young-Earth Creationism," Opus: A Journal for Interdisciplinary Studies (1991-92): 17-29. Answers in Genesis.

Woodmorappe, John. "Billion-Fold Acceleration of
     Radioactivity Demonstrated in Laboratory."
     Journal of Creation. Answers in Genesis. August 1,
     2001.

________. "Caring for the Animals on the Ark." March 29,
     2007. *Answers*. Answers in Genesis. (This may be
     a valuable source, given that the author's
     Feasibility Study book is out of print. See entry
     below.)

________. *"National Geographic* Plays the Dating Game."
     April 1, 2002. Answers in Genesis website.

________. *Noah's Ark: A Feasibility Study*. Institute for
     Creation Research, Dallas, TX, July 1996.

Woody, Todd. "Gulf oil spill methane bloom
     disappears." *Grist: A Beacon in the Smog*. January
     7, 2011.

Woolley, Joanna F. "The Origin of the Carboniferous
     Coal Measures Part 1: Lessons from History"
     Journal of Creation 24(3):76–81.

Xocipilli information:
     http://www.biroz.net/visions2012/xochipilli.htm

Zenkova, Olga. "Libra did not survive the severity of
     Chelyabinsk meteorite." (Translation provided on
     the site page. It is in Russian). Novosti website,
     10/16/2013.

Uniformitarian Answer Appendix

This material contains uniformitarian responses and beliefs in greater detail than can be contained in the main text. It is included to be fair and honest.

Mclean v Arkansas Board of Education

The following is testimony of Dr. G. Brent Dalrymple under oath in December 1981 representing the ACLU. The text of the trial transcript is from *Creation's Tiny Mystery* by Dr. Robert V Gentry, p. 122 and following.

Q I think you stated earlier that you reviewed quite a bit of creation-science literature in preparation for your testimony in this case and also a case in California, is that correct?

A Yes. I think I've read either in whole or in part about two dozen books and articles.

Q But on the list of books that you made or articles that you have reviewed, you did not include any of Robert Gentry's work as having been reviewed, did you?

A That's right. I did not.

Q Although you consider Gentry to be a creation scientist?

A Well, yes. But, you know, the scientific literature and even the Creation Science literature, which I do not consider scientific literature. It's outside the traditional literature: there is an enormously complex business. There is a lot of it. And we can't review it all. Every time I review even a short paper, it takes me several hours to read it, I have to think about the logic involved in the data, I have to reread it several times to be sure I understand what the author has said; I have to go back through the author's references and sometimes read [p. 122] as many as twenty or thirty papers that the author has referenced to find out whether what has been referenced is true or makes any sense; I have to check the calculations to find out if they are correct. It's an enormous job. And given the limited amount

of time that I have to put in on this, reviewing the
Creation Science literature is not a terribly
productive thing for a scientist to do.

Q How many articles or books have you reviewed,
approximately?

A You mean in Creation Science literature?

Q Creation Science literature.

A I think it was approximately twenty-four or twenty-
five, something like that, as best I can remember. I
gave you a complete list, which is as accurate as I
can recall.

Q And if there were articles in the open scientific
literature: Excuse me; in refereed journals which
supported the Creation Science model, would that
not be something you would want to look at in
trying to review the Creation Science literature? A
Yes, and I did look at a number of those. And I still
found no evidence.

Q But you didn't look at any from Mr. Gentry?

A No, I did not. That's one I didn't get around to.
There's quite a few others I haven't gotten around
to. I probably never will look into all the creationists'
literature. I can't even look into all the legitimate
scientific literature. But I can go so far as to say that
every case that I have looked into in detail has had
very, very serious flaws. And I think I've looked at a
representative sample.

And also in Gentry's work, he's proposed *a very tiny
mystery* which is balanced on the other side by an
enormous amount of evidence. And I think it's
important to know what the answer to that little
mystery is. But I don't think you can take one little
fact for which we now have no answer, and try to
balance, say that equals a preponderance of
evidence on the other side. That's just not quite the
way the scales tip.

Answer (Continuing) Okay, sir. The experiment that
Doctor Gentry proposed ...

THE COURT: Let me ask you a question. As I understand it, that's his conclusion. I still don't understand what his theory is.

THE WITNESS: [Dalrymple]: He [Gentry] has proposed that it is either a theory or a hypothesis that he says can be falsified.

THE COURT: What's the basis for the proposal? How does he come up with that?

THE WITNESS: Well, basically what he has found is there is a series of radioactive haloes within minerals in the rocks. Many minerals like mica include very tiny particles of other minerals that are radioactive, little crystals of zircon and things like that, that have a lot of uranium in them.

And as the uranium decays, the alpha particles will not decay, but travel outward through the mica. And they cause radiation damage in the mica around the radioactive particle. And the distance that those particles travel is indicated by these radioactive haloes. And that distance is related directly to the energy of the decay. And from the energy of the decay, it is thought that we can identify the isotopes.

That's the kind of work that Gentry has been doing.

And what he has found is that he has identified certain haloes which he claims are from Pollonium-212 [sic, polonium-218; correct form of the chemical elements used hereafter]. Now, polonium-218 is one of the isotopes intermediate in the decay chain between uranium and lead.

Uranium doesn't decay directly from [sic, to] lead. It goes through a whole series of intermediate products, each of which is radioactive and in turn decays.

Polonium-218 is derived in this occasion from radon-222. And what he has found is that the polonium haloes, and this is what he claims to have found, are the polonium-218 haloes, but not radon-222 haloes. And therefore, he says that the polonium could not have come from the decay of radium, therefore it could not have come from the normal decay change [sic, chains].

And he says, how did it get there? And then he says that the only way it could have gotten there unsupported by radon-222 decay is to have been primordial polonium, that is polonium that was created at the time the solar system was created, or the universe.

Well, the problem with that is polonium-218 has a half-life of only about three minutes, I believe it is. So that if you have a granitic body, a rock that comes from the melt, that contains this mica, and it cools down, it takes millions of years for a body like that to cool.

[p. 126]

So that by the time the body cooled, all the polonium would have decayed, since it has an extremely short half-life. Therefore, there would be no polonium in the body to cause the polonium haloes.

So what he is saying, this is primordial polonium; therefore, the granite mass in which it occurs could not have cooled slowly; therefore, it must have been created by fiat, instantly.

And the experiment he has proposed to falsify this is that he says he will accept this hypothesis as false when somebody can synthesize a piece of granite in the laboratory.

And I'm claiming that that would be a meaningless experiment.

Does that ... know this is a rather complicated subject.

THE COURT: I am not sure I understand all of this process. Obviously I don't understand all of this process, but why don't you go ahead, Mr. Ennis?

Wikipedia is more straightforward, but takes the same position using the same reasoning. In a 2013 article they say, "The most widely accepted explanation is that the discolouration is caused by alpha particles emitted by the nuclei; the radius of the concentric shells are proportional to the particle's energy (Henderson & Bateson 1934) The phenomenon of radiohalos has been known to geologists since the early part of the 20th century, but wider interest was prompted by the claims of creationist Robert V. Gentry that radiohalos in biotite are evidence for a young earth (Gentry 1992). These claims are rejected by the scientific community as an example of creationist pseudoscience (Wakefield 1988)."

http://en.wikipedia.org/wiki/Radiohalo

The sentences are juxtapositioned to say that Creationists do not believe the Henderson & Bateson paper. That is not true.

The Geology of Gentry's "Tiny Mystery." 1988 by J.R. Wakefield is the source cited by Wikipedia as "proof" of "creationist pseudoscience." The opening abstract says, "The unusual polonium halos described by Robert Gentry have been a problem for some years now. Gentry claimed that the polonium halos show that the Precambrian granite they are hosted in were 'instantly created.'

Some research on the halos has been carried out by other scientists, but most of it has been aimed at solving the problems of the peculiar configuration of these halos. Fortunately, Gentry provided two specific site locations in the Canadian Shield where his samples came from. The geological setting of these sites shows conclusively that Gentry's notion of an 'instantly created' earth composed of granite is false. Specifically the samples came from crystallized rocks which can be shown to crosscut several sedimentary and other plutonic rocks. Some of the sedimentary rocks contain stromatolites. The geology of the sites shows that the uranium, and most likely the polonium, were deposited via postmagmatic hydrothermal fluids. Besides ignoring the geology at his collection areas, Gentry also makes numerous grossly erroneous generalizations about the origin of plutonic rocks."

His introduction includes "The polonium halos constitute a case of misinterpretation because Gentry's preconceived ideas blinded him to some very important facts. His work has been devoted solely to the physics of the halos, and he has completely neglected the geological setting of the samples in which the halos are found. The result is the same though, a false conclusion reached because of an unjustified expectation of what the data should show.

"In both cases conclusions vindicating preconceived religious convictions were desired so badly that often scientific integrity was compromised, intentionally or inadvertently" (Hastings. 1982, p. 51-52)

Because of his apparent ignorance of geology, Gentry makes numerous unwarranted generalizations about the nature of the world's Precambrian rocks. The purpose of this paper is to explain the geological setting of three of Gentry's sample sites. The geology at each of these sites clearly shows that the samples came from uranium-rich dikes that crosscut many other pre-existing rocks, including sedimentary rocks. Thus, Gentry's claims are disproven and provide a clear example of a creationist researcher (Gentry) misinterpreting his data."

The first page of the body of his paper, after three pages of attacks on creationists, finally states his thesis. "I do not intend to discuss the physics of halos in this paper. What I will describe here is the geology of three of the locations where some of Gentry's biotite samples came from - the Fission Mine, the Silver Crater Mine and the Faraday Mine, all near Bancroft in southern Ontario (see Figure 1). On the basis of the geology of the sample sites. I will hypothesize that the uranium, and hence the polonium, were deposited by precipitation from circulating fluids."

All of J.R. Wakefield boils down to 1) He is not going to "discuss the physics of halos" and 2) "the uranium, and hence the polonium, were deposited by precipitation from circulating fluids."

The rest of this paper is immaterial because his second point is exactly the position of the majority of creationists. The mechanism of *how* that happened, which determines *when* it happened is the issue, but that is not discussed in this paper. So nothing in the cited source supports *Wikipedia's* false assertion that Creationism is Pseudoscience.

TalkOrigins is a website devoted to promoting uniformitarianism and evolution, but aimed at creationists. It is designed to sound "unbiased" and "impartial." It is frequently a good reference to cite when dealing with uniformitarians because they will accept the information on this site more readily. They frequently obfuscate, so if you go to their site, read very, very carefully.
http://www.talkorigins.org/faqs/po-halos/gentry.html
"Igneous rocks form from molten material, and are further subdivided into two main categories, the volcanic rocks which form from lava extruded at or near the surface; and plutonic rocks which form from magma, deep within the crust."
"Plutonic rocks on the other hand cool very slowly, on the order of a million years or more for some deeply buried and insulated magmas."
[This information is near the top of the first page. Notice that "million of years" is a dogmatic assertion. Remember the earlier warnings to look for their assumptions. Their assertions are based on their assumptions.]
"Granite is a well-known type of plutonic igneous rock..." [Building on the assertion that plutonic rock is millions of years old, their meaning here is that granite is therefore "well-known" to be millions of years old.]

"Radiation damage haloes around mineral inclusions are well known from the geological literature. Discoloration haloes in younger rocks tend to be smaller and less intense than in older rocks, indicating that the zone of crystal damage increases with time. From these observations early attempts were made to

use the dimensions of haloes as an age dating technique. This was never fully successful as the size/intensity of an observed damage halo was also a function of the abundance of radionuclides present in the inclusion, and the crystalline structure of the host mineral."
[The most important point is in the last sentence. "Age dating" [is]"never fully successful as...observed damage halo was also a function of...the crystalline structure of the host mineral." This is the same argument used earlier. The "crystalline structure of the host mineral" is assumed to be millions of years old, therefore the radiohalos are millions of years old because they are found in the "crystalline structure of the host mineral." Please note the very devious form of circular reasoning.]

"Gentry's thesis has several components. [?] First is his contention that the granitic rocks from which samples reportedly came constitute the 'primordial' crust of the Earth. Within these rocks are biotite (an iron-bearing form of mica) and fluorite crystals which bear a relatively uncommon class of tiny, concentric discoloration 'haloes'." [Biotite and fluorite crystals in granite containing radiohaloes is an observable fact. The phrase "from which samples reportedly came" is a slanderous attack on the reliability of the scientist performing the test. This is especially egregious since the tests have been repeated multiple times by several organizations with identical results.]

"Gentry utilized microscope thin sections of rocks from samples sent to him by others from various places around the world. [Very true] Thus, he is unable to say how his samples fit in with the local or regional geological setting(s). He also does not provide descriptive information about the individual rock samples that make up his studies - i.e., the abundance and distribution of major, accessory, or trace minerals; the texture, crystal size and alteration features of the rocks; and the presence or absence of fractures and discontinuities." [This statement places a burden of proof on *TalkOrigins* to prove how and why any of the listed variables would alter Dr. Gentry's published results.]

"Gentry does not acknowledge that the Precambrian time period represents fully 7/8 of the history of the Earth [another very true statement, but still not fulfilling their requirement of burden of proof] as determined by decades of intensive field and laboratory investigations by thousands of geologists. [This is their "proof." For centuries, it was necessary to believe in bloodletting to become an M.D. Just simply being in the majority and working hard does not mean that you are correct.] Consequently, he does not recognize the wide diversity of geologic terranes that came and went over that enormous time span." [The only two pieces of "evidence" presented by Talkorigins in this article that there ever was an "enormous time span" are 1) we say so and 2) "thousands of geologists" did 'intensive field and laboratory investigations." If you believe that this misrepresents Talkorigins, we provided a direct link to this article which you may read for yourself and draw your own conclusions.]

Dr. Gentry's "claim that his samples represent 'primordial' basement rocks is patently incorrect." [Even if you believe this statement to be correct, this is not science. It is just a gratuitous assertion. Like *Wikipedia, Talkorigins* cites the flawed Wakefield report as evidence.]

"In Gentry's model..." "Gentry provides no explanation..." "Gentry's hypothesis would seem to suggest..." [This is classic straw man logical fallacy. A scientific theory begun in 1918 and modified by many scientists for nearly a century is assigned to just one person and they then proceed to assassinate his character. This classic form of character assassination is what creationists are falsely accused of. By this point in the Talkorigins article they invent the term "polonium halo hypothesis." Since radiohalos forms by the decay of polonium, leaving radiohalos, and this is an observed and proven concept, this is not a hypothesis.]

"... It is apparent that the association of concentric colored haloes with polonium is actually speculative." [This is just one more unsupported, gratuitous assertion. Probably the most serious error of this entire article is ignoring the work other creationists have done in this field for the past thirty years. There are many answers in many creationist journals to every single problem they raise. *ICR (the Institute for Creation Research),* and *AIG (Answers In Genesis), Creation Ministries International* are the most well-known, but there are many others. The article spends much time and effort pointing out that water transport is the most likely cause of polonium radiohalos. It seems odd that they are completely unaware that this is the creationist position. It is also the reason creation scientists have concluded that the evidence is in favor of a flood time period for the formation of radiohalos.]

Flood Legends Appendix

In this appendix we hope to point out and explain some things that are often not included in studies about the flood legends of other cultures. Some people are not aware that so many flood legends exist in cultures all over the world. Some don't realize how ancient some of these legends are.

It is important to point out that although there may be as many as 500 flood legends from around the world, many of them bear little similarity to the biblical narrative and likely only represent local floods or other isolated incidents. We have said before that many mythologies were created by rulers to consolidate their power in self-worship. Those would have made an effort to bury or discredit any truth of the Scriptures.

But there are cultures where some truth has remained buried in men's memories. The "common source" many anthropologists talk about is likely the post-flood preservation efforts and ministry of Noah and his descendants. This attempt to teach truth was disrupted by the building of the tower at Babel. That sin was judged by the confusion of languages at Babel. Small amounts of truth still followed man everywhere at the dividing and dispersing of people throughout the earth.

Anthropologists dismiss many of these similarities as "cultural corruption" by missionaries, but the missionaries themselves expressed amazement that these people already knew parts of what they were trying to teach them from the Bible. The knowledge was flawed and error-filled, but some of it was evidence of God's miraculous preservation of His truth through the ages.

TalkOrigins has a large, comprehensive list of these legends. http://www.talkorigins.org/faqs/flood-myths.html

The main purpose of this site, however, is to point out inconsistencies and discrepancies in the biblical account, to discredit scriptural truth, so its information must be taken with careful scrutiny. It does have many accounts which can be studied, compared with other sources, and analyzed for whatever value they have.

Variations of the chart included here appear on many creationist sites. It tries to list key elements of the Genesis account of the flood, along with 20+ representative flood legends of cultures around the world, and to show where these accounts have similarities and differences. Most sites that reproduce a chart similar to this one give as a source the following work:

B.C. Nelson, *The Deluge Story in Stone*, Appendix 11, Flood Traditions, Figure 38, Augsburg, Minneapolis, 1931.

It also has a later edition:

The Deluge Story in Stone, B. C. Nelson, 1968, 2nd ed., Bethany Fellowship, Minneapolis, Minnesota, pp. 165-176.

Our chart is adapted from several sources, including

http://nwcreation.net/noahlegends.html

http://www.answersingenesis.org/articles/am/v2/n2/flood-legends and

http://www.earthage.org/floodlegends/flood__legend
s.htm

It is not a perfect chart, a perfect list of points of
comparison, or, by any means, an exhaustive list of
flood legends. We include it as an example of how these
similarities can be studied more easily.

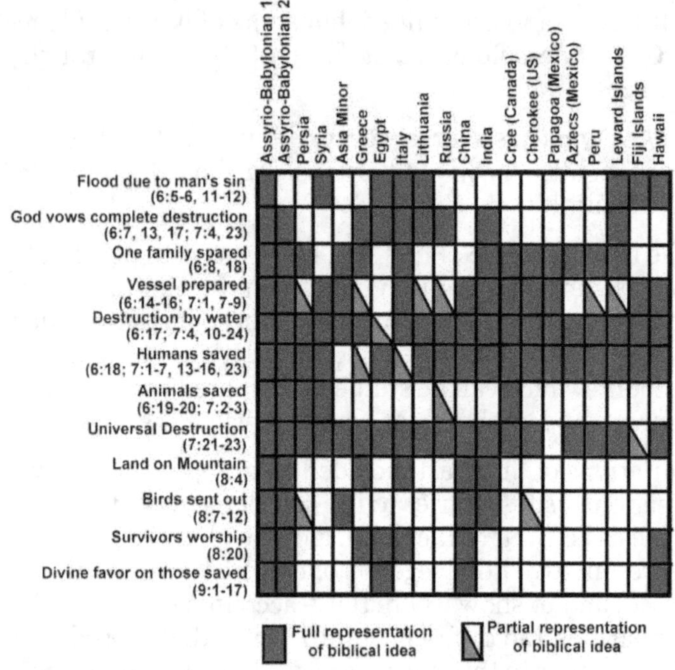

For each specific point in the Genesis account, the
chart shows whether a flood legend from another
culture includes the item ("Flood due to man's sin", for
example, occurs in eight of the charted legends), does
not include it (eleven of the accounts do not say that
God vowed complete destruction), or has a partial
similarity to the Scripture (six have some degree of
similarity to the statement that Noah was to build a
vessel).

"Full representation of biblical idea" means that the
creator of the chart believed the flood legend contains a
close approximation of the scriptural account, not that
it was exactly the same. Examples of these close
approximations show up in the Assyrian/Babylonian/

Akkadian/Sumerian legends. Many elements seem to be very similar to the scriptural truth, but it is not really correct to say all the items in the chart are "full representations".

For example, some variants of the Mesopotamian legends state that the gods were merely annoyed with human noise or that there were simply too many people, instead of being clear on the flood's purpose of destroying the evil men and their works. Some state that one god had to go behind the others' backs to warn his favorite, rather than saying that the man was righteous as opposed to the other people's evil.

The Persian (also middle-eastern roughly where modern-day Iran is located) legends describe it as a battle between good and evil and make no mention of saving any humans, merely of destroying and disposing of the evildoers. The Zoroastrian Persian flood legend includes this passage, however:

"[Ahura Mazda, the Creator, told] Yima [the earthly ruler] to build a vara, a large square enclosure, in which to keep specimens of small and large cattle, human beings, dogs, birds, red flaming fires, plants and foodstuffs, two of every kind. The men and cattle he brought in were to be the finest on earth."

It is similar to the biblical account but describes a shelter rather than a floating vessel.

When speaking about a particular culture's flood legend, it is wise to remember that it may not be one simple version. The *Epic of Gilgamesh* is one of the oldest and most well-known ancient written documents, yet multiple versions of the story exist in thousands of fragments of clay tablets throughout the ancient archaeological sites of the middle east. It includes a flood legend that has many similarities to the biblical account.

An Aboriginal (Australian) Flood Legend is the subject of a Creation Magazine article by Howard Coates from October 1, 1981.

"This is an old time story told by the earliest,

profoundly knowledgeable elders," said Mickie Bungunie [an old man from the Wunambal Aborigine tribe, Western Australia].

http://www.answersingenesis.org/articles/cm/v4/n3/aboriginal-flood-legend

This statement by the Aborigine tribe's representative is similar to the message of many of these native people. Their response to the question about whether the story is "real" or simply something they were told by white men is that it is ancient. The *Epic of Gilgamesh* is considered older than the seventh century B.C.

Legends of a flood in China's texts are found as early as 1000 B.C., in the *Book of Odes* and in the *Book of Documents*. The *Book of Documents* has some of the earliest writings of the Chinese, even older than bone oracle inscriptions of China. This book contains a flood story that runs as follows: "The flood waters were everywhere, destroying everything as they rose above the hills and swelled up to Heaven."

A Chinese flood story with the exact detail that eight people were saved is found in a document called the Huai-nan-tzu, dated from the 2nd century B.C.

The *Red Record* or "Wallam Olum" includes a flood story and is a pictographic record made by the Lenni Lenape (Delaware) Indians of their ancient history. In 1820 a doctor in Indiana tended a sick Lenni Lenape record keeper and received this pictoral history from him.

An account from the Masai tribe in Africa has so many similarities to the biblical flood record it is often dismissed as contamination but the people insist it is their own record, older than their contact with white men.

A Spanish historian, Herrera, recorded flood stories of the Incas in Peru. He said, "The ancient Indians reported, they had received it by tradition from their ancestors, [and that the flood took place] many years before the Incas ... "

http://www.ecreationscience.com/Flood_Legends.htm
l

The Cowichan people of the Salish, Native Americans of Montana and the Northwest Coast insist that their flood legend comes from a time "long before the missionaries ever arrived … " This account also says that many wise men had the same dream of rain or floods and came together to build a great raft, which scoffers ignored and ridiculed. This parallels ancient Jewish traditional accounts recorded by Josephus, stating that Adam, Enoch, and Methuselah all had warnings about the flood, though theirs were less clear and specific than Noah's.

The Salish legend also says that after the survivors of the flood began to resettle and multiply, the began to quarrel again as they had before, and ended up dividing into separate tribes and moving away.

http://www.firstpeople.us/FP-Html-
Legends/TheGreatFlood-Salish.html

A large number of flood legends have the survivors climb a high mountain rather than get in a ship. Some commentators say that may be a result of confusion with the beginning and ending of the biblical flood account, but another explanation seems more likely. We have talked in this volume about the probability that Noah built the ark on the highest point of land in existence at that time, and the reasons why that may have been the case. If these scattered people recalled that fact but lost the truth about the ark, perhaps they recounted the idea that going to the highest ground meant safety because that was all they remembered.

This topic is something we will cover again when we study World Literature in module 5 of this series. The legends are a part of the literature of these people, even if they are oral traditions.

While we do not endorse everything taught by the following sites, we include the list below as reference. They are some links that can be used for further study of the flood legends:

From the *Institute for Creation Research*

A fairly short article for this organization, non-technical, that does a good job of distilling the importance of this topic.

http://www.icr.org/article/why-does-nearly-every-culture-have-tradition-globa/

From Creation.com

A simple list with little commentary and some quotes from the original sources, and a bibliography of sources covering this topic.

http://creation.com/many-flood-legends

From Talkorigins.org

(Remember that this is a secular site, but it is a very well-researched and comprehensive list)

http://www.talkorigins.org/faqs/flood-myths.html

From *Apologetics Press*

Brief discussion of major legends and their importance, and a bibliography

http://www.apologeticspress.org/apcontent.aspx?category=9&article=64

From Northwest Creation Network

Includes different charts of legends compared with the biblical account, plus a number of legend summaries, and many links to other related articles.

http://www.nwcreation.net/noahlegends.html

From *Conservapedia*

http://www.conservapedia.com/Great_Flood

Answers in Genesis

Good, brief summary of the importance of studying this topic and a few comparative stories

http://www.answersingenesis.org/articles/am/v2/n2/flood-legends

Jewish History

This is a really great perspective on scriptural authority and personal choice. Well worth a read -through for a modern cultural perspective, but caution is advised when it comes to the account of Noah's "post-traumatic stress syndrome". The admonition that "there is something to be afraid of" is a little obscure, making it sound as if they believe there could be another worldwide cataclysm, but taking it to mean that we have an all-powerful God Who punishes sin is good.

http://www.jewishhistory.org/the-great-flood/

Cumorah.com

This is a Latter Day Saints site but has large, clear images and handwritten copies of ancient cuneiform tablets, with somewhat technical, critical analysis of flood legend studies.

http://www.cumorah.com/index.php?target=view_oth er_articles&story_id=59&cat_id=7

6. Material common to all 3 modules

Articles From Elk Jerky For The Soul

1. The Problem with Dates in History: Hammurabi's Law Code
http://elkjerkyforthesoul.wordpress.com/?s=law+c ode

In 1901-1902 AD a French team excavating in Susa, one of the ancient Capitals of Elam, then Persia, now modern Iran, discovered pieces of a basalt stele. It was completely reconstructed and now sits in the Louve, in Paris. The head of the French team, M. de Morgan used the surroundings where it was found to date the stele, the now famous Law Code of Hammurabi around 1100-1200 BC.

An American/German team headed by the German born American Hermann Hilprecht was excavating in Nippur at the same time. Nippur is in ancient

Mesopotamian, an area ruled over by the Assyrians, Babylonians, Persians, Greeks, Ottoman Turks and is now modern Iraq. They found a kings list with the name Hammurabi on it. This list made Hammurabi a ruler in the 24th century, BC. Hermann Hilprecht immediately (January 1903) proclaimed the Hammurabi stele as the oldest law code ever found in a lecture at the University of Pennsylvania.

A book entitled *The Oldest Code of Laws in the World, by Hammurabi, King of Babylon* was immediately published in early 1903 and is available as an ebook through Project Gutenberg. It proclaims that Hammurabi ruled from 2285-2242 B.C. The forward is by C.H.W. Johns, M.A. of Cambridge. The book was printed in Edinburgh.

Since 1903, several other Sumerian kings lists were discovered. A rather brief but thorough article in the Roman Catholic online encyclopedia New Advent describes the major positions mainstream archaeologists take on the time Hammurabi actually ruled. Most 21st century archaeologists hold to some type of a "middle" position, that Hammurabi ruled around 1700 B.C.

It is very important to Liberals and Secular Humanists that the law code of Hammurabi be older than the Law Code of Moses. They insist that the Mosaic Code "evolved" from the lower Hammurabi Code, and that our laws today have "evolved" beyond the Mosaic Code. Since the Law was divinely given by God, it makes no difference if Hammurabi wrote his Law Code before God gave Moses the Law on Sinai. Since God revealed His Law to Noah, Hammurabi's Law code is still a corruption of God's revealed Law. God saw that man had corrupted His Law and needed to reveal it once more in writing to Moses.

If the 1700 date for Hammurabi is correct, then Hammurabi ruled while the Children of Israel were slaves in Egypt. They would remain slaves for another 250+ years before Moses would lead them out.

However, if the original date of M. de Morgan is correct, then Hammurabi's Law Code was written about 250 years after God revealed His Law to Moses on Sinai. While this seems to make very little difference, it is anathema to Evolutionists.

The important point is how can the uncertain date of Hammurabi's Law Code be a "backbone" on which to base history? "Human history has become too much a matter of dogma taught by professionals in ivory towers as though it's all fact. Actually, much of human history is up for grabs. The further back you go, the more that the history that is taught in the schools and universities begins to look like some kind of faerie story." (Graham Hancock *Fingerprints of the Gods*

2. A Very Simple Overview Of Relativity

http://elkjerkyforthesoul.wordpress.com/2012/09/19/the-big-bang-or-the-big-crunch-pick-your-religion/

"The Big Bang or the Big Crunch? Pick Your Religion."

Certain types of relativity can be traced to the ancient Greeks, but an adequate study really begins with the classical or mechanical relativity of Sir Isaac Newton. He used the concept of inertia (an object at rest remains at rest or an object in motion remains in motion until an outside force acts upon it) to explain the universe as we find it.

To visualize Newton's mechanical relativity, imagine you are standing on a platform. A vehicle with a window is traveling past. You can see a ball bouncing up and down on a table inside the vehicle. To a person inside the vehicle the bouncing ball appears to bounce straight up and down. To those standing on the platform and looking in the window, the ball is taking a zigzag path as it both bounces up and down and moves past you. The path the ball takes is *relative* to your point of view. Except for the path of the ball, everything else is the same to both those in the vehicle and those on the platform. Most important, time is the same to those on the platform and those in the vehicle. Albert

Einstein called this *absolute time*, time which is same for everyone.

Albert Einstein first developed what we call *special relativity*. To use Einstein's own illustration, imagine that you are in an idealized elevator that is forever falling to the earth. You are in perpetual free fall. You release a steel ball and a handkerchief at the same time. Because you, the ball, the handkerchief and the elevator are all falling at the same rate, you, the ball and the handkerchief seem to "float." You are all part of what Albert Einstein calls "the same co-ordinate system (CS)." At this point you realize that you are falling and every part of your CS is in fact moving. Inertia is only apparent within your CS and time is another dimension which is also moving with your CS and is also relative. Today we would understand this illustration better if we replaced the elevator image with a space station orbiting the earth.

The last stage is the well-known theory of *general relativity*. You are now an observer outside of the elevator, watching someone inside it. You have a different CS. Time is different to you and to the man in the elevator. While he sees stationary objects, you see that everything is falling. There is no true inertia. Everything is always moving and this movement is *relative* to your CS, to your point of view.

Einstein found flaws in Newton's mechanical theory. Newton taught that time was absolute. Einstein's theory of Special Relativity, based on his discovery of the space-time continuum, taught that time is a dimension, like length width and height. Einstein thought at first that the universe was static. In 1917, fifteen years after developing his theory of Special Relativity, Einstein included what he called a Universal Constant to make formulas work in General Relativity. This was based on an assumption that the universe was static. Stars would move within the universe but the universe itself was a static force.

The theory that developed as a result of this conclusion taught that the universe will simply run out of energy and will cease expanding. Gravitational forces are not strong enough to cause contraction or collapse, but the universe will die a "heat death." Everything will arrive at a uniform temperature, near absolute zero. There will be a uniformity of elemental composition. Everything will be dead and motionless.

Years later Einstein retracted his universal constant statement as the greatest mistake of his career, when the astronomer Hubble pointed out to him that stars have a Doppler Red Shift, proving that the universe is in motion. We know the universe is in motion because of the Doppler effect, the shift to the infrared spectrum, visible in stars, indicating they are moving away from us. That may indicate that the universe is either expanding or contracting.

A common illustration of the Doppler effect uses trains and a train station. When a train is approaching, passing, and going away, the changes in the sound of the whistle and the engine noises are an example of the Doppler effect. In the case of light and more distant objects such as stars, the Doppler effect will appear as a shift in the light spectrums. A star approaching us will have a shift toward the ultraviolet spectrum. For stars receding or going away, the shift will be toward the infrared spectrum.

The second theory is that the big bang is true and the universe is infinite. Gravitational forces are too weak to hold it together and it will expand for eternity. This is the current position of mainstream Physics and Astronomy today, and the one you must hold to if you expect to be published in academic circles. This is Stephen Hawking's position.

The third possibility is that the universe will run out of the expansion force from the big bang. Gravitational force will pull it back together in what is sometimes called the Big Crunch, collapsing it back into a Black Hole. Some "mainstream" physicists hold this view, but believe that it does not matter since we are still in the expansion stage and the Big Crunch is billions of years into the future. But the appearance of the Doppler effect, that of distance increasing between Earth and other bodies, might actually be the universe collapsing. The Doppler red shift might mean we are pulling away from all other stars because we are in the lead, rushing toward a Black Hole and we are the closest to the event horizon.

The same Doppler effect is achieved whether you are at the station listening to a passing train's whistle, or riding past in a train, listening to a whistle on a train sitting at the station. This is a minority position among physicists and implies that we are rapidly approaching the "Big Crunch," the end of the universe as we know it, where we return to the original singularity.

These are the major positions postulated by Physics. Though there are many, many other positions and many, many variations on these positions, the important fact is that they are all religious beliefs which can never be proved. Physics uses mathematical formulas to arrive at their conclusions, but mathematics is a language. Like all languages, we must start with certain assumptions. We can observe and measure the universe and some observations fit some models better than others. There is no scientific data on origins

Albert Einstein, *The Evolution of Physics*, Touchstone (an Imprint of Simon and Schuster) New York, NY, 1967.

Stephen Hawking, *A Brief History of Time and The Universe In a Nutshell*. Bantam Books for Young Readers, New York, NY, 1996. return to text

3. A Not So Simple Look At Relativity

http://elkjerkyforthesoul.wordpress.com/2014/01/23/a-not-so-simple-look-at-relativity-post-by-michael-j-findley/

The importance of the theory of relativity is the religious conclusions rammed down our throats by religious bigots. This strong language is necessary to understand the unyielding priesthood these men have erected. These people have convinced themselves and many others that they are open minded, kind and gentle. In their world, however, disagreements are only tolerated within their general framework of their view of the universe.

The first tenet of their religion is that the current universe and the way it operates can be examined to discover all truths. The second tenet of their religion is that the universe is at least billions of years old, if not eternal. The third tenet is the necessary and important conclusion of the first two. The entire human race is an infinitesimally small and insignificant part of an eternal, or nearly eternal cosmos. The only significance anyone can ever have is the decisions we choose to call significant. At one time the concept of God creating the universe was permitted, but even that kind of a God is now intolerable. Everything is relative and the guardians (as they were to do in Plato's *Republic*) tell us what is good and how to live in order to best serve society.

Though it took longer than predicted, *1984* has arrived. The uniforms are blue jeans. Newspeak is a combination of psychobabble and pseudoscience jargon. All their conclusions claim a basis in relativity. In reality, Einstein's theory of general relativity has no relationship with moral relativism. The principles of general relativity are only observable on the cosmic level. Personal relationships, physical as well as personal, do not use relativity. We are all in the same co-ordinate system.

The concept of a space/time continuum is essential to understand general relativity. Time is just as much a dimension as space. The universal constant is the speed of light. Time can be altered in two ways. The first is the well-known Twins Paradox. If you are not familiar with the Twins Paradox, the 1956 juvenile story *Time for the Stars* by Robert Heinlein is an interesting introduction. A pair of twins have telepathic abilities which are not limited by distance. Because of this ability, one twin is placed on a spacecraft with near light speed and heads for the stars while the other twin remains on earth to receive and relay messages As the mass of the starship approaches the speed of light, the relative time on the starship slows down. Both twins experience a "normal" life with what they perceive to be a normal timeframe. As the twin on the spaceship travels and the twin on earth ages and the telepathic responsibilities are transferred first to his twin's daughter on earth, then his granddaughter and finally his great granddaughter. By the end of the book, the traveling twin has aged only a few years while time on earth has gone through decades. If you are not familiar with the book, there is a somewhat cute ending. This Twins Paradox concept is a frequent topic in space travel discussions, because people and spaceships have mass.

According to the theory of general relativity, an object with mass will have its perception of time altered as it approaches the speed of light. Since the amount of energy needed to propel a spacecraft at the actual speed of light is infinite, actual light speed is impossible. But as mass approaches the speed of light, time will seem to slow down those in other co-ordinate systems. A spacecraft near the speed of light will have normal time to those on board the spacecraft. Those on the spacecraft would view those on earth as racing around furiously as time raced by. Those on earth will view those on the spacecraft as moving in extreme slow motion.

Since we are unaware of any actual starships, our real, daily experience is actually reversed. On page 43 of Stephen Hawking's book *A Brief History of Time* there is a picture of a tower with two clocks, one in the base and one in the top. The clock at the top runs faster than the one in the base. "Another prediction of general relativity is that time should appear to run slower near a massive body like the earth." He takes several pages to explain this, but the important point is that satellite navigation systems which fail to account for this time difference caused by general relativity can be off by miles. Massless particles, such as light photons, traveling completely outside of gravitational fields, such as between galaxies, could easily travel at the speed of light yet travel for millions or even billions of years while only brief periods of time, perhaps only seconds, transpire on earth. The same principles apply to any electromagnetic energy. This important aspect of general relativity is rarely, if ever mentioned.

The reason for this sin of omission is explained by Dr. Russell Humphries in his work, *Starlight and Time.* The idea that the universe is billions of light years across and therefore the earth is millions or billions of years old is the single greatest deception in the secular humanist's arsenal. They frequently say that a look at distant galaxies is a look at the beginning of the universe because the light we see left those galaxies just after the big bang. Relativity is ignored when it is convenient.

Robert A. Heinlein, *Time for the Stars,* Tor Books, New York, NY, 1956.

Dr. Russell Humphreys, *Starlight and Time: Solving the Puzzle of Distant Starlight in a Young Universe,* Master Books, Green Forest, AR, 1996.
return to text

4. The Training Place of Mankind; God's Creation Explained For Normal Folk by David Bergsland

A Book Review by Michael J. Findley

I have read several books by this author and enjoy both his writing style and the content of his works. But I must admit that I am not part of the target audience; Normal Folk. No one has ever accused me of being "normal."

On my Android 7" ebook reader, type set to 100%, this is an eighty page book. According the author and the title, our brief life on earth is a training place. The table of contents and all links work. While a table of contents and working links is something you might just expect, sadly many ebooks fail in these simple basics. Our daughter, an elementary school teacher, believes this is one of the best book covers she has ever seen.

This is an overview of mankind on earth, from the original creation to the New Heavens and the New Earth. It does not cover every topic I would like, but in such a brief work that is simply not possible.

If you have never looked at an overview of God's Word, or you know someone like this, this book is a must read. If you know someone who is curious about the Bible but has never read it, then this book is a must read for them.

It is both an easy, enjoyable read and introduces most major topics of the Word of God in a single book. Not to mislead anyone; this is neither a theology book nor a Bible Doctrines overview. More than half of this brief book is devoted to the book of Genesis, creation, the flood, the birth of civilization and the beginning of the Jewish nation.

The three-plus pages titled, *So what happened to science?* and *My point is this: Creationism is basic to Christianity* are very important points that are both brief and thorough. *The Creation Week: 4000 B.C.* might just be the best nine-page overview of the Creation Week available.

This book looks at the Bible from a very Gentile perspective. The central chapter, *The pivot of history: Jesus* assumes that the reader is not even familiar with the most basic information about the Messiah. Sadly, that is probably a valid assumption and makes it so necessary. Many pastors I talk to would likely find the basic information in this book a real eye opener. That is so sad.

The book concludes with *Israel is Transformed* and *The End of Creation*. He explains prophecy with science to examine what the earth's future will be like.

Once again, it does not answer everything. But it is a great eye opener for anyone not familiar with the Word of God.

5. A Pocket Guide To The Global Flood
A Book Review by Michael J. Findley

There is a larger book with a similar title, *The Global Flood,* by Dr. John D. Morris on the same theme, providing essential information on the flood. While both books cover the same information from the same point of view, the larger book is more detailed and more technical.

The book *A Pocket Guide To The Global Flood* was written by four authors, according to the various chapters. Ken Ham and Tim Lovett collaborated on the first chapter, "Was There Really a World-wide Flood?" John Whitmore wrote the last chapter with another author: "Should Fragile Shell Fossils be Common?" The rest of the book is by Andrew A. Snelling. Andrew A. Snelling updated and rewrote the Whitcomb and Morris 1961 classic, *The Genesis Flood.*

The first chapter "Was There Really a World-wide Flood?" uses the same techniques we use in our series *The Conflict of Ages.* It provides a brief overview with the basic questions and answers based on the Word of God, but no details.

The first chapter by Andrew A. Snelling provides an overview of his topics. Each of the next chapters examine one point in more detail; "High and Dry Sea Creatures", "The World's Graveyard", "Transcontinental Rock Layers", "Sand Transported Cross-Country", "No Slow and Gradual Erosion", "Rock Layers Folded Not Fractured", and finally "A Scientific Look at Catastrophic Plate Tectonics: A Catastrophic Breakup and The Origin of Oil".

"Many creationist geologists now believe the catastrophic plate tectonics concept is very useful as the best explanation for how the Flood event occurred within the biblical framework for earth's history." This is historic science. We retain the biblical framework for earth's history and use the best explanation with the most current scientific information available. This is the correct attitude. More information might cause us to re-evaluate plate tectonics. But the biblical framework does not change.

"A catastrophic model of plate tectonics (as proposed by creation scientists) easily overcomes the problems of the slow and gradual model (as proposed by most evolutionist scientists)."

John Whitmore's final chapter in the technical section is somewhat puzzling to me. Uniformitarians do believe in catastrophes, just as creationists do. "Near the end of the Devonian, a mass extinction event occurred." http://www.ucmp.berkeley.edu/devonian/devonian.php They simply believe the catastrophes occurred millions of years ago. So John Whitmore's statement just before his conclusion is puzzling. "One explanation that they did not consider, that would readily explain their results, is the catastrophic formation of much of the fossil record." Uniformitarians actually believe there were five mass extinction events, as they call them. http://skepticalscience.com/Earths-five-mass-extinction-events.html

This is not a new or recent change in their position. The 1940s Disney movie *Fantasia* has a sequence depicting evolution set to Stravinski's *Rite of Spring*. During this sequence, they show the dinosaurs being killed by a catastrophe something like the Flood at the end of the Jurassic Period. The issue is not *how*, but *when*.

The Flood timeline near the end of *A Pocket Guide To The Global Flood* is helpful, but requires some thoughtful examination. The final chapter "The Flood and the Gospel", is something many works on the Flood lack. Many Christians fail to understand exactly why this material is so important. The personal application is very good.

Noah's Ark: A Feasibility Study by John Woodmorappe Chapter 6

6. Appendix on the Appearance of the Ark

What Did The Ark Of Noah Look Like? published 9 16 2011

An Egyptian sarcophagus cover coated with pitch
discovered in the Valley of Kings in 1905

"The Holy Scripture cannot err, ... the decrees therein
contained are absolutely true and inviolable. But I
should have in your place added that, though Scripture
cannot err, its expounders and interpreters are liable to
err in many ways," Galileo said in a 1613 letter to
Benedetto Castelli.

Anyone who dismisses the possibility of the scientific
accuracy of the Scriptures is ignorant of the facts of
science, which can lead anyone to the same
conclusions. Many people have repeatedly said that the
Bible does not say what the ark looked like. While it is
true that we have no detailed floorplan, many specifics
are available to us.

Before we examine these specifics, we must understand
the tools we are using. For the book of Genesis, the
Masoretic Hebrew is the authoritative source for study,
representing the original inspired Scriptures. The
Greek LXX is inspired when quoted in the original
Greek New Testament. The LXX and the Syriac
Peshitta, ancient and accurate translations, are very
useful for helping us understand the exact meaning of
words and phrases. This is especially useful when the
Hebrew has more than one possible meaning.

The final source is the vast treasure trove of ancient
literature unearthed in the last hundred and fifty years.
The *Epic of Gilgamesh* and other flood legends have
cuneiform tablets which date back to at least the eighth

century BC. Religious zealots who call themselves "mainstream" wonder if the Bible originated or derived from these fragmentary documents. The scientific evidence demands that even though these cuneiform tablets might date older than the oldest biblical manuscripts we have, their stories are not the original source of the information.

The information in the Bible is accurate. These cuneiform tablets are missing important pieces, plus, picking the factual from the fanciful from these tablets is difficult at best. Thankfully, we are only looking to The *Epic of Gilgamesh* and other ancient flood legends as support documents, as helps in understanding words and phrases.

"Make thee an ark of gopher wood; rooms shalt thou make in the ark, and shalt pitch it within and without with pitch. And this is the fashion which thou shalt make it of: The length of the ark shall be three hundred cubits, and the breadth of it fifty cubits, and the height of it thirty cubits. A window shalt thou make to the ark, and in a cubit shalt thou finish it above; and the door of the ark shalt thou set in the side thereof; with lower, second, and third stories shalt thou make it." Genesis 6:14-16 KJV

This is all the information we have about the appearance of the ark. The NASB and the NIV give the same information. So what does this say? First, the ark was made of wood. The exact type of wood varies from translation to translation, but it is always wood. Next, a cubit varied in size from about 18" to around 24". So the ark at the smallest possible size was 45'h x 75'w x 450'l and at the largest possible size 60'h x 100'w x 600'l. Except for someone who claims to know the exact size of Noah's cubit, there is little room for debate here. The next point with little debate is that it had a window. The phrase "in a cubit shalt thou finish it above" is usually understood as an opening one cubit wide all the way around the outside of the ark just below the roof (deck).

Though there are many versions of the *Epic of Gilgamesh,*newer translations have the ark built as a cube, length, width and height equal. The 1929 translation of Wallis Budge has the height and width equal, but the next line is "I covered (?) it six times." followed by the lines "I divided into seven, Its interior I divided into nine," If this actually refers to the length, then the ratio of 6 to 1 for width to length is the same ratio as we find in the Bible.

Most drawings have some sort of deck structure, but this is not mentioned. A deck structure would have required more work and was not necessary. A flat or slightly pitched deck that functioned like roof would fit the information given. The *Epic of Gilgamesh* says, "roof it over like the Apsu." Scholars say this means that Utnapishtim was familiar with "apsu boats," vessels for water transport, and he was to make his roof like theirs. The pitch-covered door would blend into the hull and was probably hinged above the waterline. In any case, the door would have little or no effect on the overall appearance.

The word pitch (referring to the coating on the Ark) can have several different meaning, but
the *LXX* translation "asphalt" has only one meaning. The English word asphalt is simply a transliteration of the Greek letters. So the ark before the Flood was soaked with and covered in black asphalt.

The most important word is translated in the KJV "rooms." In the *LXX*, a literal translation of the two words translated by the single English word "rooms" is "foursquare nested compartments." Most translators of the *LXX* find that this does not make much sense, so they translate the phrase with their own opinion, like "square timber." (Sir Lancelot C.L. Brenton, 1851) "Foursquare nested compartments" which are "rooms" make perfect sense if you understand the ark to be a barge. This is a perfectly sensible description of an ancient shipbuilding technique still used to make river barges today. There is no keel and the internal compartments provide the structural support. It seems that this is the type of shipbuilding described in the

Epic of Gilgamesh as well. Line 60 translated by R. Campbell Thompson (1928), *"Did I lay down, and did I fashion; aye, six times cross-pinn'd her, Sevenfold did I divide her ..., divided her inwards Ninefold: hammer'd the caulking within her, (and) found me a quant-pole."*

Noah's Ark, if this information is correct, was a black, asphalt covered wooden barge with a roof but no deck. The door was either invisible from the outside or difficult to detect because it blended in with the overall asphalt. It was rectangular and had no keel. Perhaps the bow and aft were slanted in or perhaps they were perpendicular. There was a one-cubit opening just under the overhang of the roof, which went up and down the length and perhaps all the way around.

One final thought. "Fifteen cubits upward did the waters prevail; and the mountains were covered" (Genesis 7:20). The Lord may have miraculously revealed this to Noah, who passed this information down to Moses. Moses may have communicated this information directly by God's inspiration. Noah and Moses may not have had any way of knowing how high the water would rise above the mountains apart from God telling them.

Or, there is a third possibility. Noah may have built the ark on top of the highest mountain, and fifteen cubits is the draft of the ark. Noah then knew that the mountains were covered because the ark floated off the highest one.

Excerpts From Antidisestablishmentarianism

1. Preface

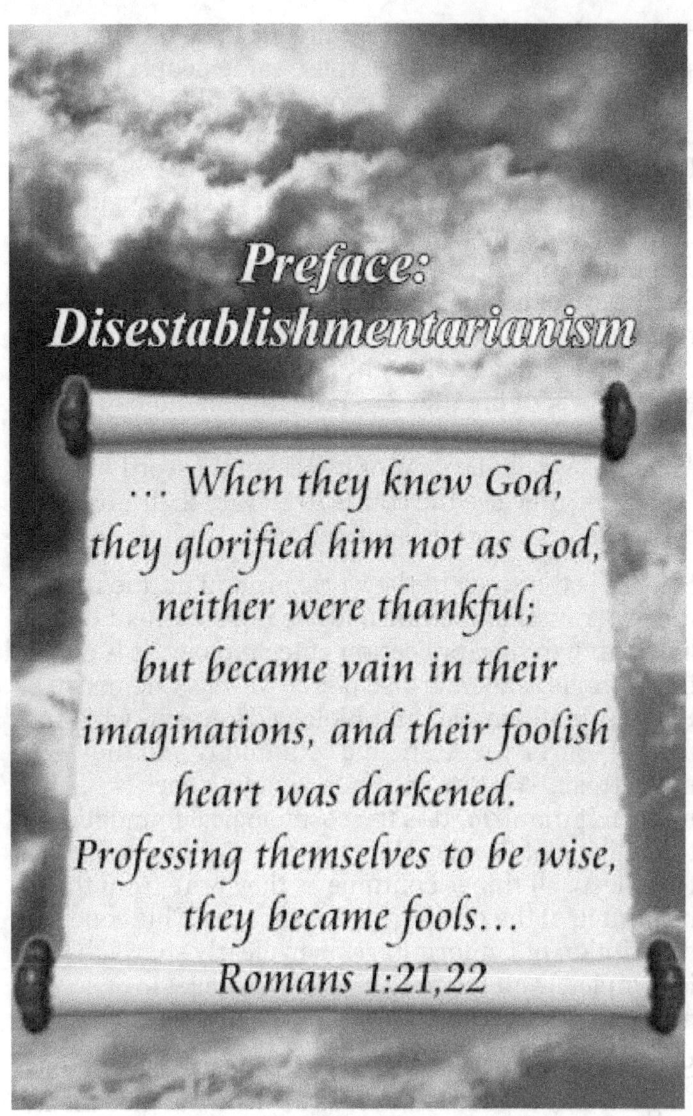

Preface: Disestablishmentarianism

... When they knew God, they glorified him not as God, neither were thankful; but became vain in their imaginations, and their foolish heart was darkened. Professing themselves to be wise, they became fools...
Romans 1:21,22

The most religious people on earth are those who claim not to have any religion. Dogmatic, intolerant, and bigoted, they refuse to allow anyone to so much as speak their opposition. Yet these same people demand political power and tax support. The mildest opposition, such as the mere mention of Intelligent Design (not God), has blacklisted tenured professors. Just two parents in a middle school in Texas made the national news by objecting to Gideon Bibles placed, without comment, on a table outside the school office.[1] Such people dishonestly claim that they are not religious and "religion" is a group of mythologies. The truth is that they are the ones promoting mythology. In every aspect of life they promote this mythology with unproven dogmatic assertions under the guise of "Science" vocabulary. After hijacking the word "Science," they use the courts to elevate their misuse of the term to an established religion.

Science is the study of the world around us, the use of the experimental method and the improvement of our lives through the application of technology. It is divided into various academic disciplines such as Chemistry, Physics, Mathematics and Biology. However, what the federal courts, the Academic community and the mainstream Western media mean by science is uniformitarianism. It is the cosmological foundation of the religion of Secular Humanism. "Since the fathers fell asleep, all things continue as they were from the beginning of the creation" (II Peter 3:4). This concise description of Uniformitarianism clearly shows that it is completely and entirely a religious belief in antiscientific myths.

Secular Humanists use words which have been in the English language for hundreds of years but give them "new" meanings. However, "there is no new thing under the sun" (Ecclesiastes 1:9, KJV). The words believe, faith and trust are all historic judicial terms and they also form the foundation of the true scientific method. What Secular Humanists promote as their version of the scientific method consists of preconceptions, presuppositions and assumptions. It is the opposite of an open mind.

A true open mind is founded in belief, faith and trust. The historic meaning of believe is to perceive or understand with the mind and then make an informed decision.[2] The most basic use of the word believe which the average American would understand is that of a juror in court. Which witness do you believe? Which piece of evidence is believable? A synonym would be the word credible. When we believe something or someone and then act on that belief, that is faith. The active part of belief is faith. The passive part of belief is trust. Suppose your brother says that he will drive you to the doctor. If you believe him, then you understand what he says and you make a decision to get ready. If you get in the vehicle with him, that is faith. You act on your belief. When you sit in the vehicle as he drives, that is trust, a passive reliance on what you have proven true. You trust in his driving skills. You trust in the vehicle. You trust the roads, etc. Everything we do is a combination of belief, faith or trust. By restoring their historic definitions, belief, faith and trust re-emerge as the clear language of true experimental science. These terms were deliberately segregated from science to deceive people into believing Secular Humanism.

Liberals, Secular Humanists and materialists, however, use the word "belief" as a synonym for a philosophical position, just an opinion. Faith and trust to them are metaphysical words which mean different things to different people. And this is just the tip of an enormous iceberg. Secular Humanists have redefined hundreds of words to support their religion, such as sin, judgment and anthropology. A conversation with them can be very difficult since they use historical English words but mean something entirely different.

The traditional role of religion is to place priesthood as intermediary between God and man. The traditional role of an establishment of religion places the government in that intermediary role between God and man. In the Middle Ages the Roman Catholic Church put itself between man and God, as other religions have in the past. Johann Tetzel, a "professional pardoner," sold indulgences representing forgiveness for sins in Germany. Indulgences were based on the "storehouse" of good works believed to exist because of the sacrifice of Christ and the good deeds and prayers of past saints. Tetzel was said to promise that, "As soon as a coin in the coffer rings, a soul from purgatory springs."[3]

Selling indulgences was the final act of many which brought on the Reformation. People wouldn't have bought them if they hadn't believed the Catholic Church alone could placate God on their behalf. Martin Luther convinced the princes of Germany that they did not need to send their money to Rome because they could go to God directly. Rome sent armies to collect the money. Even Modern Roman Catholics who do not believe that their church today claims to stand between them and God have to admit that the medieval Roman Catholic Church did.

The combined power of Church and State restricted personal worship, scientific study and access to historical truth. Today Secular Humanism has done the same by removing foundational truths from education. It excludes study and discovery that contradicts uniformitarianism. It rewrites history to undermine morality and freedom of expression.

The union between the medieval Romanist church and the state came to an end in two ways. In Southern Europe during the Renaissance, art, architecture, literature, and learning opened up to all men, not just those who were part of the church and state system. The Renaissance left the power intact, however. In Northern Europe, the Reformation abolished the need for a church like Rome through the great affirmations of the Reformation: The Scriptures are the absolute authority; Justification is by faith alone apart from works; and every believer is his own priest with direct access to God. The Reformation made a special priesthood class unnecessary because men could pray directly to God and read His Word on their own.

The medieval Roman Catholic Church kept the Scriptures almost exclusively in Latin to prevent ordinary people from studying them, forcing people to come to the priest. The priest would not only tell them what the Scriptures said, but he also mingled that with the church's interpretation. In order for ordinary people who did not know Latin to read the Bible for themselves, the Scriptures had to be translated into the language of the ordinary people. Translation work by Reformers was essential to enable ordinary men to read the Scriptures for themselves, even though it was punishable by death under the Church-State system. The Renaissance and the Reformation worked together in the development of moveable type to make printing and distribution of translations of the Scriptures easier. Renaissance scholars revived interest in studying forgotten manuscripts and making translations into the vernacular. Erasmus's Greek New Testament provided a basis for more accurate translations of the Scriptures.

The Medieval Romanist Church-State system took away freedom by forcing man to rely on and accept its teachings. The Renaissance and the Reformation restored freedom by returning art, science, and all forms of learning to ordinary people. In particular the people were able to worship God as the Scriptures taught, without Church-State control. Modern western culture, and American culture in particular, was founded on this religious freedom. American culture is more Christian than European cultures, but neither of these cultures can survive if the foundation of religious freedom is destroyed.

It is this Christian foundation of religious freedom which is the real target of Secular Humanists. These Secular Humanists have taken outrageous liberties in their unrelenting quest to replace religious freedom with their established religion of Secular Humanism, which they incorrectly call science or Natural Law. Their major tool is the US court system. Sympathetic US courts have consistently supported Secular Humanism by using every possible opportunity to replace the word religion with the ancient concept of Natural Law. However, since Natural Law has been used so many different ways, the courts had to standardize the term Natural Law. Their version of Natural Law goes back to Plato's *Republic*. Though Plato never used the phrase "natural law" in his *Republic*, translator Benjamin Jowett's notes state that, "Plato among the Greeks, like Bacon among the moderns, was the first who conceived a method of knowledge... "[4] Plato's *Republic* is at least the foundation of modern Natural Law, if not the detailed finished product. Together with Aristotle, Plato is supposed by secularists to have laid the foundation for learning and development of the Sciences. This really is the essence of Natural Law.

Jowett goes on to say that Plato provided for a means to spread his method of acquiring knowledge. "In the ideal State which is constructed by Socrates, the first care of the rulers is to be education."[4] Jowett makes it clear that Socrates meant to impart much more than mere academic knowledge, just as Natural Law means to teach more than mere Science. Socrates promoted "the conception of a higher State, in which 'no man calls anything his own,' and in which there is neither 'marrying nor giving in marriage,' and 'kings are philosophers' and 'philosophers are kings;' and there is another and higher education, intellectual as well as moral and religious, of science as well as of art, and not of youth only but of the whole of life."[4]

Many know that Plato in his *Republic* based his state on a philosopher/king. Few, however, are aware that he believed in communism and free love and that these two "natural" principles were to be foundational principles of the state.

Though the preceding condensation by Benjamin Jowett is an excellent job, as you can read for yourself, the actual words of Socrates, as quoted by Plato, are much longer and more difficult to understand. "None of them will have anything specially his or her own." "... Their legislator, having selected the men, will now select the women and give them to them [the legislator gives selected women to selected men]... they must live in common houses and meet at common meals ... they will be together ... And so they will be drawn by a necessity of their natures to have intercourse with each other… " "… Until philosophers are kings, or the kings and princes … have the spirit and power of philosophy, and political greatness and wisdom meet in one … cities will never have rest from their evils."5

The philosopher/king, according to Socrates, was to lay these foundational ideas through education. Though he did not use the phrase "establishment of religion," Plato clearly advocated an established religion. It was to be put in place by a philosopher/king through education based on a state where "no man calls anything his own" and where there is neither "marrying nor giving in marriage." Though this education would begin with children, it would continue throughout a person's entire life. This is the Natural Law which the US Court system has imposed.

The US needs to disestablish its Establishment of Religion and reestablish religious freedom. In the 1800's churches which tried to break away from the Church of England were called disestablishmentarians. The people who fought against the disestablishment of those churches within the Church of England in the 1800s were called Antidisestablishmentarians. Today, the mainstream media, liberal politicians, the academic community, the liberal courts and all others who file lawsuits, blacklist, fire, refuse to hire, tax, legislate against, libel, slander and do whatever is necessary to maintain their positions of privilege and power are modern Antidisestablishmentarians.

------

1 (No author) "Parents Fuming as Texas Schools Let Gideons Provide Bibles to Students," Tuesday, May 19, 2009, *Fox News.com.* "A spokeswoman for the school district said that a number of materials are made available to students this way, including newspapers, camp brochures and tutoring pamphlets. College and military recruitment information is available all year long. The Gideon Bibles were made available for just one day. 'We have to handle this request in the same manner as other requests to distribute non-school

literature: in a view-point neutral manner,' Shana Wortham, director of communications for the district, wrote in an e-mail to *FoxNews.com.*

2 Alexander Hamilton, in an 1802 letter to James Bayard. "I have carefully examined the evidences of the Christian religion, and if I was sitting as a juror upon its authenticity I would un-hesitatingly give my verdict in its favor. I can prove its truth as clearly as any proposition ever submitted to the mind of man."

3 Philip Schaff, *History of the Christian Church,* Volume 7, "The Reformation," Charles Scribner's Sons, 1910.

4 Plato, *The Republic* (c. 360 B.C.), translated by Benjamin Jowett over a period of 30 years until his death in 1893, completed posthumously by Lewis Campbell. (Introductory material (in double quotes) and paraphrases of Plato's ideas (in single quotes) were written by Jowett.)

5 Plato, *The Republic*, Book Five Dialogue excerpts among Socrates, Adeimantus, Glaucon and Thrasymachus have been placed in parentheses within Jowett's introductory material. return to text

2. Introduction

Introduction

"Facts are stubborn things;
and whatever
may be our wishes,
our inclinations,
or the dictates of our passion,
they cannot alter
the state of facts and evidence."
John Adams

Introduction

Facts are stubborn things; and whatever may be our wishes, our inclinations, or the dictates of our passion, they cannot alter the state of facts and evidence.[1]
John Adams

Sometime in the early twentieth century, Secular Humanist indoctrination convinced almost everyone in the United States that "an establishment of religion" in the first phrase of the first amendment of the United States Constitution is vague and can mean just about anything. "The state of the facts and evidence," as John Adams so eloquently put it, is the exact opposite.

Section One of this work documents what the founders meant by the phrase "an establishment of religion. " The Founding Fathers made as clear a statement as the English language permitted. The Constitution of the United States is founded on English law and to a lesser extent, various European laws, especially German and Dutch. In each of these countries, an Establishment of Religion was the collection of taxes to support education, welfare and public worship. The various governments appointed the teachers, welfare workers and pastors and expected these people to support the government in turn.

The original state constitutions not only permitted, but openly encouraged establishments of religion, especially in the areas of welfare and education. The foundation of the US Constitution is the fact that federal government was to have no control whatsoever in these areas. Their concept of a separation of Church and State was the exact opposite of what the courts have rammed down our throats for the past hundred years. The church should have the right to pray and teach without any federal intervention whatsoever. Judges should have the right to post any Scriptures they want. The courts should have no authority whatsoever to comment. Removing a state judge from office for posting the Ten Commandments is not merely an Establishment of Religion. It is the Inquisition.

Section Two documents the foundations of Secular
Humanism and how it grew to become America's
Establishment of Religion. The words "Secular
Humanism "come from various groups in the 1950's.
The phrase "Secular Humanist " is found in court
documents to describe this set of beliefs. Secular
Humanism is as old as civilization, but the primary
foundation of twenty first century Secular Humanism
is Plato's *Republic.* In America, Secular Humanism can
be said to have originated with Thomas Paine. Secular
Humanism has specific beliefs which are written down
in various manifestos. Like Christianity, Islam and
Judaism, Secular Humanism has many variations.
Though Secular Humanists do not like the term, the
most accurate words to describe these variants are
"sects " or "denominations. " Like Christians, Muslims
and Jews, many Secular Humanist denominations do
not get along with one another. Therefore, we have
attempted to point out the beliefs which have the
greatest agreement.

Section Three defines science, since Secular Humanists
claim that science separates them from all other
religions. Since true science is founded in the belief,
faith and trust of the Bible, all of these words are
defined carefully and in detail. In the Bible, belief, faith
and trust are legal terms. Believe means to examine the
evidence and come to a reasoned conclusion. Action
taken on that belief is faith. Trust is the passive version
of faith.

The Scientific Method is the biblical version of belief,
faith and trust applied to the material world which God
created for us. In the Bible, the Scientific Method
recognizes that God is the creator, that we are required
to be responsible managers of the material world God
has given us and that there is a final judgment after
death which will include how well we managed the gifts
God allowed us to use.

Our book concludes with Section Four, the results of
having Secular Humanism as an Establishment of
Religion. With the exception of America's founding
documents and the ancient documents such as Plato,

Plutarch and Genesis, hundreds of other quotes could easily be substituted for the quotes that appear here. There is nothing new or unique in this book. It is a combination of what used to be common knowledge in America before Secular Humanism took over and destroyed the education system and current events. If we were to start over today, we would pull different stories from the daily news. Though the individual stories would be different, the points would be the same. "There is nothing new under the sun " (Ecclesiastes 1:9). Or to state the same thing another way, the more things change, the more they stay the same.

America's Established Religion is Secular Humanism. This work is dedicated to exposing, defining and disestablishing it.

---

1 John Adams, "Argument in defence of the [English] soldiers in the Boston Massacre trial," December 1770.

2 "Alabama's Judicial Ethics Panel removed Chief Justice Roy Moore from office Thursday for defying a Federal judge's order to move a ten commandments monument from the State Supreme Court building. " Friday, November 14, 2003. Posted 6:56 AM Eastern time. *CNN.com* Return to text

3. "What Is Secular Humanism?"

Excerpt from Chapter Six: "What Is Secular Humanism?" This excerpt discusses the oral versus written tradition in literature.

Since the opposite is drilled into everyone through western culture and western education, we need to think the following example through slowly and carefully. The Exodus of the children of Israel from Egypt is told in the Bible as a straightforward, factual, historic event. Charlton Heston, in his narration of the picturesque Bible video series, presents the Bible as part of the "oral tradition in storytelling " as if teachings passed on orally were understood to be less accurate or reliable and therefore merely legends and myths. Socrates, in Plato's Dialogue *Phaedrus,* addresses the subject of oral versus written history.

"[Writing] will make
the Egyptians wiser
and give them better
memories." said [Thoth].

[Amun] replied:
"You attribute to them a quality they
cannot have; this will create forget-
fulness in the learners' souls, they will
trust to the written characters.

An aid only [to] the
semblance of truth; they
will be hearers and will
have learned nothing; they
will appear omniscient
and will know nothing; the show of
wisdom without reality."

> *Theuth [Thoth] ... was the inventor of many
> arts, ... but his great discovery was the use of
> letters. ... Thammus [the god Amun] was the
> king of ... Egypt; ...To him came Theuth ...
> desiring that the other Egyptians might be
> allowed to have the benefit of [his
> inventions]; ... when they came to letters,
> "This," said Theuth, "will make the Egyptians
> wiser and give them better memories; " ...
> Thamus replied: ... "You ... attribute to them a
> quality which they cannot have; for this ...
> will create forgetfulness in the learners' souls,
> ... they will trust to the external written
> characters ... This is an aid not to memory,
> but to reminiscence, ... not truth, but only the
> semblance of truth; they will be hearers of
> many things and will have learned nothing;
> they will appear to be omniscient and will
> generally know nothing; they will be
> tiresome company, having the show of
> wisdom without the reality. "[4]*

Plutarch, in his discourse on the life of Lycurgus and his rule in ancient Greece, expresses the belief that oral tradition is a way of making the law more firmly fixed in the mind.

> *None of his laws were put into writing by
> Lycurgus, indeed, one of the so-called
> "rhetras " forbids it. For he thought that if the
> most important and binding principles which
> conduce to the prosperity and virtue of a city
> were implanted in the habits and training of
> its citizens, they would remain unchanged
> and secure, having a stronger bond than
> compulsion in the fixed purposes imparted to
> the young by education, which performs the
> office of a law-giver for every one of them.*[5]

There is considerable disagreement about whether the Scriptures were in some part orally communicated before being written down. The point is that even if they were it does not make them less authoritative or reliable. Socrates may not be entirely justified in discounting the value of written records but he reinforces the point that oral communication of history does not make it unreliable or inaccurate. Memorizing and passing on history demands great discipline and does not result in a form of the child's game "gossip. "

Gossip, sometimes called Telephone or other names, consists of a group made to stand in a line. The first person in line is given a piece of paper on which is written a phrase to whisper into the ear of the second person. Frequently there is only one opportunity to whisper the message. The second person whispers what he heard to the third, and so on down the line. The last person is to write down or speak aloud what he heard the person before him say. When the final form of the "gossip " message is made public, frequently it bears little resemblance to the original phrase. The distortion of the oral message in the game gossip is simply due to the indifference of the people playing the game. In fact, one simple change in the rules of the game of gossip produces correct transmission of the message even by children. Simply offer everyone who is playing a large enough reward, or punishment, if the final message is correct.

Modern prisoners of war, inmates in prison, gang members, spies and others today pass on important information without writing it down and without changing the message. Most American Indian tribes had no written language and saw no need for one, until Europeans demonstrated the ability to talk to people far away. In the popular TV series *Mission: Impossible*, the leader of the team received his orders on a recording that self-destructed after he had heard it one time. He was forced to memorize the mission immediately or he would be unable to complete it. return to text

from Antidisestablishmentarianism Chapter Six: What Is Secular Humanism?

But the predominant form of unbelief in the world today is Secular Humanism. We use the term "Secular Humanist" or "Secular Humanism" because that is what they called themselves. *The Humanist Manifesto I* is a religious document, written by a Unitarian Minister, Raymond B. Bragg, in 1933. Thirty men who believed themselves to be representative of a vast multitude "forging a new philosophy " signed it. "… There is no new thing under the sun. " (Ecclesiastes 1:9, KJV)

The Humanist Manifestos I, II and *III* can be viewed on the website *americanhumanist.org*. They cannot be reprinted here because of the following notice on the site:

> *Copyright renewed 1973 by the American Humanist Association. Permission to reproduce this material, complete and unmodified, in electronic or printout form is hereby granted free of charge by the copyright holder to nonprofit humanist and freethought publications. All other uses, and uses by all others, requires that requests for permission be made through the American Humanist Association.*[15]

These men quickly learned that using the word "religion" actually hampered their cause. If they could deceive people into believing that secular humanism was not a religion and that religion was bad, then they could get state funding (follow the money trail) and political power while putting ungodly restrictions on those who actually dared to call themselves religious. Humanist Manifestos II and III call traditional religions "traditional theism " and describe them as "obstacles to human progress. " Many have also dropped the word "secular " and simply call themselves "humanists."

This is an effective propaganda technique, since they are now denying that they are a religion. The 1973 *Humanist Manifesto II* is lengthy and filled with doublespeak. It is exactly what George Orwell in 1984 and Aldous Huxley in *Brave New World* warned us about. It is important because it was signed by more than one hundred influential people, including doctors, university professors, and others like Isaac Asimov, scientist and writer, B. F. Skinner, Prof. of Psychology, Harvard University, Betty Friedan, Founder of *N.O.W*, and Sir Julian Huxley, former head, *UNESCO,* Great Britain. All the manifesto texts can be viewed online. *Humanist Manifesto III* is the most seductive. True intentions are cleverly obscured and it sounds very good. As commentator Bill O'Reilly points out, the term Secular Humanist is not very accurate. It is, however, the oldest and most accurate of the labels they have chosen for themselves.

It is also the term used in court documents, including the US Supreme Court, so we will continue to use it. "Among religions in this country which do not teach what would generally be considered a belief in the existence of God are Buddhism, Taoism, Ethical Culture, Secular Humanism, and others."[16] Justice Black based his comments on the 1957 case of *Fellowship of Humanity v. County of Alameda.* In this case an organization of humanists sought a tax exemption on the ground that they used their property "solely and exclusively for religious worship. " The court ruled that the activities of *Fellowship of Humanity* entitled it to an exemption. These activities included weekly Sunday meetings. The *Fellowship of Humanity* case used the word humanism, not secular humanism.[16]

Secular Humanism also made a separate manifesto, first published in 1980 as *A Secular Humanist Declaration* by *CODESH (Council for Democratic Secular Humanism)* co-authored by Paul Kurtz and Edwin H. Wilson, both editors of *The Humanist* magazine. Its principle purpose was to declare its compatibility with democracy and how enlightened man should view traditional religions as inferior to secular humanism.

Still," ...There is nothing new under the sun. " (Ecclesiastes 1:9, NIV). Plato praised many of these same follies in his dialogue *The Republic*. Since Plato is so verbose, few study him in detail today, which is good. Where Aldous Huxley in *Brave New World* and George Orwell in 1984 viewed the following principles as deplorable, Plato praised them as necessary. His philosopher king would use thugs he called guardians to enforce the will of the legislators on a hapless society divided into classes. Plato's philosopher/king together with legislators and guardians would determine what the classes would be and who would belong to which class. The class you belonged to would determine every aspect of your life.

But Secular Humanism is older than Plato. It is older than anything written which is still in existence. "What has been will be again, what has been done will be done again; there is nothing new under the sun. " (Ecclesiastes 1:9, NIV). Contrary to scientific facts, the modern version of the religion of Secular Humanism believes that a simple, chaotic universe evolved into a complex, ordered universe. To oversimplify, everything came from nothing. Secular Humanists deny that they are a religion for the express purpose of attacking all other religions, collecting tax money and obtaining political power. They also deny that same political power to anyone who disagrees with them. As no two Christians, Jews, Taoists, etc. believe exactly the same way, so no two Secular Humanists believe the same thing. Despite their differences, Secular Humanists hold many beliefs in common.

People who hold beliefs in common can be labeled by those common beliefs. For example, the *Niagara Bible Conference* is where the term Fundamentalism first began to be used. The term was also used to describe "The Fundamentals," a collection of twelve books funded by Milton and Lyman Stewart. These men collected as many addresses of Christian teachers, preachers and other leaders as they could find. They published the books and sent them to these addresses over a period of time ending around 1910. This group of beliefs became known as Fundamentalism.

Fundamentalists defined their beliefs so clearly that anyone willing to be called a Fundamentalist told others something about what they believe.[17] The term Fundamentalist, however, applies to every aspect of life. A football coach who emphasizes the basics of blocking and tackling as opposed to trick plays or a wide open offence like the West Coast offence is known as a Fundamentalist. An architect who designs simple, inexpensive buildings using the basics of engineering is a Fundamentalist. And a believer in the following list of fundamentals for Secular Humanism makes a person a Fundamentalist in Secular Humanism.

The Fundamentals of Secular Humanism

1. Secular Humanism is a religion based on feelings and emotion, not reason.

2. Secular Humanism denies anything non-material. Anything spiritual is redefined as "energy." Various humanists use terms such as "Life Energy," "Life-Force," "Interdimensional Energy," etc. The source of the energy is always material or natural, not supernatural.

3. Secular Humanism denies the existence of a supreme being including Intelligent Design.

4. While acknowledging the existence of evil it denies the concept of original sin. It believes in the perfectibility of man.

5. Though Secular Humanism is open to things not yet discovered, at this time there is no scientific evidence for life after death.

6. Man's existence on the Earth, like everything else in the universe, is a result of chance and not a plan. The most likely explanation for this chance is evolution, which is based on uniformitarianism.

7. Secular Humanism demands that science include only what is within the scope of "natural law " but does not allow for any explanation for the origin of natural law, and therefore the origins of matter or energy; nor

is there any reliable information on a possible end to the universe.

8. Only secular humanist beliefs are reasonable; all other religions raise false hopes, restrict personal fulfillment, or both.

9. The purpose of life is to make you a better person. This is accomplished by service to others and seeking fulfillment in this life. Though each person might have a different concept of fulfillment, no one has the right to tell another person that what he is doing is wrong, unless it harms someone else. This is especially true with sexual gratification.

10. The accumulated improvements of many individuals will drive the evolution of the human race.

11. The best way for society to survive and thrive is to allow enlightened leaders complete freedom to guide all institutions and organizations that serve all people from the beginning to the end of life.

12. Man exists only as a member of the world community. The world community is responsible to provide for the protection and guidance of the enlightened society from the earliest age. Children must not be separated from the world community. Any persons of majority age who oppose the ideals of the world community must be forced into conformity through employment sanctions or reeducation. Opposition must be suppressed by any necessary means.

13. Improvement of society is the essential duty of the enlightened guardians and includes guidance to prevent nonproductive, undesirable or inferior types.

14. Enlightened leaders guide others to fulfillment in this life. The community chooses the values of these enlightened leaders. The enlightened leaders help to guide the community in developing their values system.

15. Compulsory education indoctrinates the citizen of the world community. It is the catechism of the new society.

16. Personal property is evil. This includes any type of marriage since marriage is a property arrangement. Since Secular Humanists recognize evil, it is the responsibility of the guardians to supervise the distribution of material possessions, including social contracts. Individuals corrupt material possessions by unnecessarily hoarding them.

17. National sovereignty is the cause of war, poverty, overpopulation, and waste or destruction of resources. A unified world government is essential to stable economics and freedom in the areas of communication, travel, arts, sciences and education.

18. Unity means eradication of opposition. Secular Humanists characterize anyone who differs from them on these fundamentals as opponents. Opponents are characterized as being oppressive, divisive, fearful of change, bigoted or guilty of hatred.

Some of these items may seem extreme, even to those who claim to be humanists. Some will protest, "I don't believe that!" As was said before, not all humanists believe all these points exactly in these words. The position of the Secular Humanists has been evolving over millennia, not just centuries, and in the next chapters some surprising adherents will come to light. Prepare to hear from people who lived in times when they could see and touch the gods the state demanded they worship, yet their words produced the echoes secularists proclaim today as "new ideas for new times. " Look for parallels of these "modern " beliefs in the words of ancient writers who were required by law to believe in the gods of Sumeria, Babylonia, Egypt, India, Meso-America, Greece and Rome. They still spoke clearly about how they had already forged their own beliefs with man as his own prophet, priest and object of worship. Moving closer to modern times, hundreds of well-known humanists will make it clear that those who are influencing every aspect of our culture have believed these concepts for centuries and do, in fact, believe them and work for their realization today.
return to text

3. Comments on *Segraves vs. State of California,*
   1981

from *Antidisestablishmentarianism,* Chapter 9, How
Was Secular Humanism Established?

Segraves vs. State of California, 1981, took up the case
of a man who sued because he said his children's free
exercise rights were being violated by the teaching of
evolution in the schools. California had a provision of
accommodation that included the following:

> *The anti-dogmatism policy provided that
> class discussions of origins should emphasize
> that scientific explanations focus on "how,"
> not "ultimate cause," and that any speculative
> statements concerning origins, both in texts
> and in classes, should be presented
> conditionally, not dogmatically.*

> *Now, when you begin to think of textbooks
> that talk about belief, now to me belief is not a
> scientific word. One knows, one accumulates
> data, one has a comprehension of, one
> understands, one does a lot of things, but to
> me belief always, in my situation, has been
> something I associate with my theology. I
> would not like to see my theology and my
> science get mixed. I have never dealt with a
> scientific process where somebody says, 'I
> believe.' I have dealt with theological
> processes where one believes. In short, I think
> at that point you begin to mix epistemologies,
> and that's confusing.*

The judge seems to have forgotten his historic
jurisprudence, because belief is a legal term. It's like a
jury examining evidence on a case and reaching a
verdict. It's not even primarily a religious term, and it
applies to Science as well as law when properly defined.
There's no question that Evolution is a belief by the
judge's definition, dealing in more presuppositions and
theories than facts. And it certainly can become
confusing when it gets mixed up with Science.

Court case source: *Segraves v. California* (1981) Sacramento Superior Court #278978) excerpts from the personal website built by Frank Fire.

5. Evidences of a Young Earth

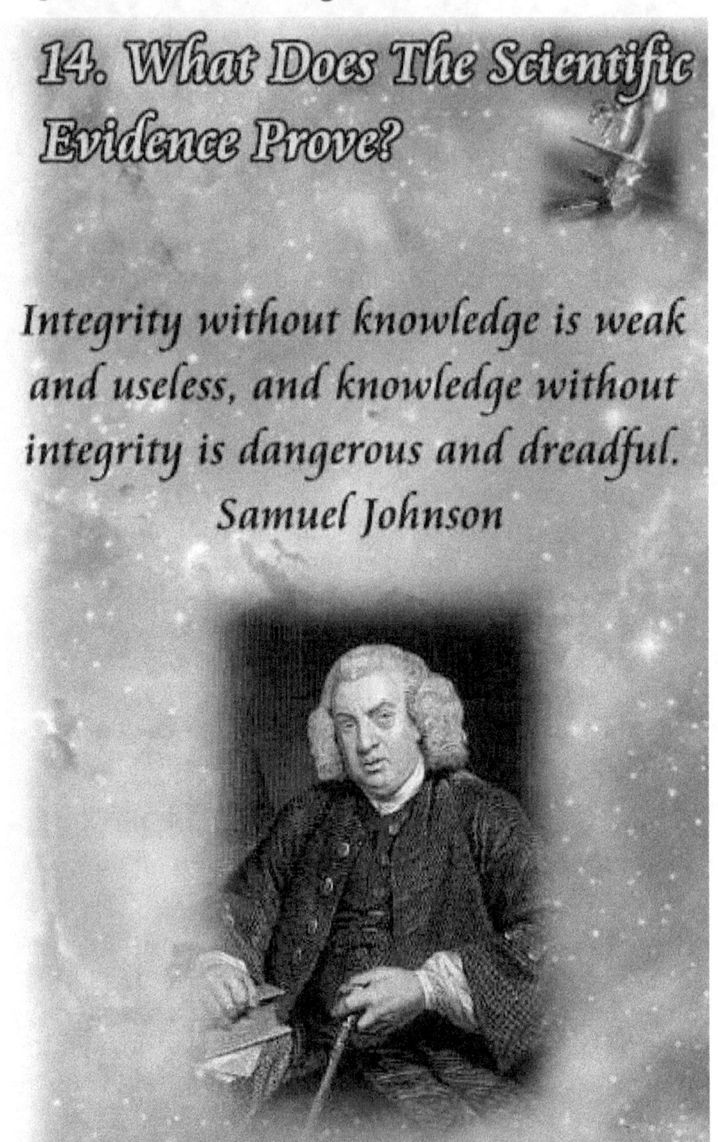

14. What Does The Scientific Evidence Prove?

"I am quite conscious that my speculations run quite beyond the bounds of true science."
Charles Darwin[1]

"Facts are stubborn things; and whatever may be our wishes, our inclinations, or the dictates of our passion, they cannot alter the state of facts and evidence."
John Adams[2]

"In the space of one hundred and seventy-six years the Mississippi has shortened itself two hundred and forty-two miles. Therefore ... in the Old Silurian Period the Mississippi River was upward of one million three hundred thousand miles long ... seven hundred and forty-two years from now the Mississippi will be only a mile and three-quarters long. ... There is something fascinating about science. One gets such wholesale returns of conjecture out of such a trifling investment of fact."
Mark Twain[3]

Samuel Johnson said, "Integrity without knowledge is weak and useless, and knowledge without integrity is dangerous and dreadful."[4] Christians often believe that science is an enemy. They think this way because most who use the word "science" have completely abandoned Johnson's demand that integrity go hand-in-hand with knowledge. Uniformitarians replace truth with selective evidence which supports preconceived conclusions. Christians should neither develop an antagonism toward true science, nor should they ignore the very real contributions of true science. True scientists should not ignore the very real foundation of science in Christianity. Dennis Prager, author, columnist, radio show host and historian, laments the unthinking reliance on pseudo-science in today's society.

"In much of the West, the well-educated have been taught to believe they can know nothing and they can draw no independent conclusions about truth, unless they cite a study and 'experts' have affirmed it. 'Studies show' is to the modern secular college graduate what 'Scripture says' is to the religious fundamentalist."[5]

"I am quite conscious that my speculations run beyond the bounds of true science."
Charles Darwin

"Facts are stubborn things; and whatever may be our wishes, our inclinations, or the dictates of our passion, they cannot alter the state of facts and evidence."
John Adams

"In the space of one hundred and seventy-six years the Mississippi has shortened two hundred and forty-two miles. In the Old Silurian Period [it] was one million three hundred thousand miles long. [In]Seven hundred and forty- two years [it] will be only 1 and 3/4 miles long. There is something fascinating about science. One gets such wholesale returns of conjecture out of such a trifling investment of fact.
Mark Twain

In everyday life, probably the greatest area of conflict between Christianity and those who misuse the word science is moral relativism. This came about because of the dishonest use of the word relativity. The theories of relativity (special and general) neither support nor have any reference to moral relativism. The similarity in the sound of the words is simply a propaganda technique. Neither do the moral absolutes of the Word of God belittle true science. However, since the established religion of Secular Humanism teaches just the opposite, the following list of scientific facts can help us understand that true science can only be explained by the world as described in the Bible. None of these scientific facts prove the Bible. Each does prove the religious belief in deep time to be a scientific impossibility.

Sun Energy Source

Until shortly after WWII, the majority of scientists believed the sun shrank by an average of .01 percent per year. They concluded, based on 400 years' worth of scientific observations, that this was proof that the sun was powered by gravitational collapse. In the late 1800s the Kelvin-Helmholtz Contraction Theory was developed to explain both the observed contraction and how the sun was powered.[6]

In the 1930s religious Secular Humanists, understanding the consequences of this theory, proposed nuclear fusion as the energy source for the sun. In 1928 George Gamow published a paper proposing a theory. The Gamow theory included what came to be known as the Gamow factor.[7] This was the first serious step toward the idea that stars are powered by nuclear fusion. General acceptance was slow. Gamow's ideas were further explored in the 1930s. This exploration grew into Hans Bethe's theory of Stellar Nucleosynthesis.[8] Bethe won a Nobel Prize for this work in 1967. The detonation of the atomic bombs actually did more to convince people than the theoretical papers. According to the Kelvin-Helmoltz

Contraction Theory, with gravitational collapse powering the sun, the sun would have been so large and hot around 50,000 years ago that it would have boiled all the water out of all the oceans on the earth. A mere million years ago the orbit of the earth would have been inside the sun.[9]

These are not just creationist rantings. While we might disagree about the exact numbers, there is no questioning the basic principle. Here are the words of very committed uniformitarians.

"But Kelvin-Helmholtz contraction cannot be the major source of the Sun's energy today. If it were, the Sun would have had to be much larger in the relatively recent past. Helmholtz's own calculations showed that the Sun could have started its initial collapse from the solar nebula no more than about 2.5 million years ago. But the geological and fossil record shows that the earth is far older than that, and so the Sun must be as well. Hence, this model of a Sun that shines because it shrinks cannot be correct."[10]

Why is the Kelvin-Helmholtz contraction incorrect? Because they *believe* "that the earth is far older than that."

Secularists' religious belief that life on earth has existed for billions of years required the sun to be billions of years old. So they eagerly accepted that the sun was powered by nuclear fusion. It is also true that the sun's surface is not static, as is the case with water, rock, or ice on a planet's surface, so a consistent measurement of the sun's diameter is not possible. Two different measurements on the same day might yield different diameters because of massive fluctuations on the sun.

The sun's life cycle in this theory would be 9.2 billion years. At 4.6 billion years the sun would be roughly half way through its life cycle. The problem with this theory is that the sun would have been too cool; forty percent of its present brightness, 4.6 billion years ago, and the earth would have been a frozen wasteland. This is also known as the early faint sun paradox.

"*While the early faint Sun paradox does not tell us that the Solar System is only thousands of years old, it does seem to rule out the age being billions of years.*"
Dr. Danny R. Faulkner

Project *SOHO*, launched in 1995, has provided us with more information about the sun. Unwilling to change their belief about the age of the sun and life on earth, some Secular Humanists now believe that the sun is powered by a perfect balance of different types of nuclear fusion combined with gravitational collapse, which has produced a uniform temperature for life on earth for the last 4.6 billion years. The best way to describe this kind of balance is "miraculous."[11]

NASA's Solar Dynamics Observatory Satellite, or SDO, was launched in February 2010 and chief scientist Dean Pesnell said it has already reshaped our theories of how the star works.[12]

ScienceBlogs.com contributor Ethan Siegal, PhD in theoretical astrophysics at the University of Florida, writes a blog called "Starts with a Bang." In a post titled, "How the Sun works, from the inside out", originally written August 12, 2011 he has included crossed out and updated information, indicating how rapidly information changes. Theories about the sun must be changed, updated, and corrected to match the most up-to-date information.[13]

Many who insist on billions of years agree that 4.6 billion years is just a rough estimate. They explain that the 9.2 billion year figure is correct, but that they simply are not certain how far our sun is into its 9.2 billion year lifecycle. With such rapid changes in information, how is it possible to state dogmatically that the sun has a lifespan of 9.2 billion years?

Radiohalos and Radiometric Dating

The 4.6 billion year figure comes from radiometric dating. The most common radiohalos are found in zircons. Zircons are found all over the earth and range in size from microscopic to the size of rocks. Zircons are crystals of zirconium silicate. Zircons can be of gemstone quality and large zircons are often used as substitutes for diamonds (cubic zirconia is a close man-made synthetic). Most zircons, however, are around the size of very small grains of sand. Though the wide range of impurities creates an enormous variety of zircons, the most important geological use for zircons is radiometric dating. Zircons contain trace amounts of uranium and thorium. Tiny zircons are sliced open to examine fission tracks produced by decaying uranium. These fission tracks and the U→Pb (Uranium to lead) methods of radiometric dating have dated zircons as old as 4.404 billion years.[14] This means, according to uniformitarian assumptions, that the original crystal formation of these tested zircon samples occurred

4.404 billion years ago. As with all radiometric samples, there is no scientific way of knowing the original condition of the sample tested.

The same zircons also contain helium, which provides another dating method. Helium retention rates in these zircons have a date range beginning as young as 4000 years.[14] While there are a tremendous number of articles attacking this date as too young, most of these articles read like tabloids reporting on British royalty, not honest science. A true scientist would look for an explanation that accounted for both the uranium radiohalos and helium retention. It is far easier to come up with an explanation for the radiohalos' presence if the rocks have a young age. It is nearly impossible to explain the retained helium if the rocks are ancient. One possible explanation for young radiohalos is that they were created at the same time the earth was created.

Zircons are sliced open to examine fission tracks produced by decaying Uranium. These methods have dated zircons as old as 4.404 billion years. Helium diffusion dating of the same samples returns a date of 6,000 years ± 2,000 years.

Background images are from NASA zircon studies done in Australia including chart of presumed age.

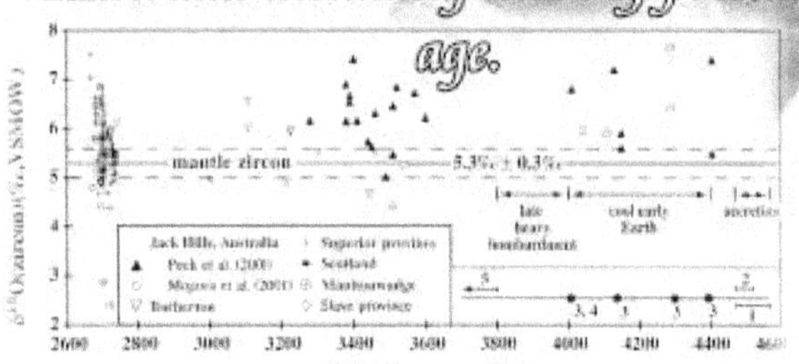

Another possible answer is that a massive thermonuclear event such as the sun exploding and losing an outer layer sent thermonuclear radiation through the entire planet. Since such an event would have destroyed all non-aquatic life on earth, this would have happened around 2350 BC, at the time of the flood.

Whatever the trigger, the most likely scenario is accelerated nuclear decay during the flood. The accelerated nuclear decay during the flood is the only explanation we are aware of which properly balances all the existing evidence.

Dating Rock Formations

Travel anywhere and you will see signs proclaiming various rocks or layers of rocks to be millions or even billions of years old. "The Little Willow Formation consists primarily of contorted quartz schist and gneiss; at 1.7 billion years old, it is the oldest rock in the Salt Lake City area."[15] This religious belief in the myth of great ages is proclaimed in textbooks, school classrooms, museums, and, most importantly, by employers, who will either refuse to hire or actually fire anyone who refuses to openly support this religious myth. Though many supposed scientific facts are used to support these dates, radiometric dating is the foundation for all dating methods.[16]

Since fossils have no direct methods of dating, such as radiometric dating, how is the age of a particular fossil determined? It is compared to other fossils of a "known" age or it is dated according to strata where it was found. How is the age of the other fossils or the strata determined? The usual answer is more fossils of a "known" age or strata of a "known" age. This circular reasoning is standard textbook content. Radiometric dating is the only dating method that does not rely on a comparison with something else already dated. Radiometric dating is not valid on fossils. Radiometric dating must be used on the rocks in the surrounding strata.

Every form of radiometric dating always depends on an unstable radioactive isotope deteriorating (decaying) to a stable isotope at a known, stable rate. K→Ar (Potassium to Argon) and U→Pb (^{235}U to Lead) are just two examples of isotopes used as radiometric clocks. All radioactive isotopes used as radiometric clocks work the same way. A sample is taken and analyzed. The result is always a ratio of radioactive isotope to the stable final element. The ratio can be found on a chart because the rate of decay is stable, that is, unaffected by any known outside influence.

Everyone who uses radioactive isotopes as clocks must, however, rely on three invalid religious assumptions. The first is the unscientific religious leap of faith that the sample being tested had no daughter material when it was formed. For radiometric clocks to work, it is an absolutely essential scientific necessity to know the original condition of the sample. If the original condition of the sample is less than one hundred percent radioactive, then the date is less than the published date. These widely publicized dates, however, assume that the tested sample began its existence (at the time it was formed) one hundred per cent radioactive with no daughter element present. In reality, the only scientific information we learn from these radiometric tests is the current ratio of radioactive material to nonradioactive material. The published dates are always the upper possible date of a range of possible dates.

The second assumption is that nothing contaminated the sample during its existence. It is impossible to know the conditions of the sample during its existence. Simply to assume that contamination never occurred is not science. It is especially bad science when the very people claiming the accuracy of radiometric dating also claim that the earth underwent a series of what they call extinction events which catastrophically changed the surface of the earth.

The third assumption is that nothing changed the decay rate. While the second assumption is something changed the individual sample or the immediate environment of the sample, this assumption is worldwide or throughout the universe. In other words, is the present really the key to the past? How can we know that?

If there was a sample with a known date, other samples could be calibrated against it. Not only do such calibration samples not exist, without a time machine to go back in time and obtain a calibration sample, it is not possible to have a calibration sample. With very few exceptions, the published dates of tens of thousands to billions of years are based purely on mythological religious assumptions.

There are a few exceptions, however. Thermoluminescence is used to date pottery. Thermoluminescence is based on the time the pottery was fired, a known event. ^{14}C is another one of these exceptions. The radioactive isotope ^{14}C is integrated into the tissue of living organisms throughout the lifetime of that organism. At the time of death that amount of ^{14}C becomes a fixed amount and begins to radioactively decay into ^{14}N. That amount of ^{14}C at the time of death is equal to the amount of ^{14}C in the atmosphere at the time of death. The ratio of ^{14}C in the sample tested at the time of death compared to the assumed amount of ^{14}C in the atmosphere at the time of death should be an almost perfect radiometric clock. However, certain conditions can alter that ratio. If the ratio is in some way tampered with, that tampering is normally leaching. That particular sample will then test to be older than it really is. ^{14}C dates older than 1000 B.C. also assume atmospheric amounts of ^{14}C and absorption rates of ^{14}C similar to current absorption rates. That is almost certainly an invalid assumption, making many, if not all ^{14}C dates for items dated older than 1000 B.C. older than they actually are.

Finally, radiometric dating never gives an absolute date. It only tells us the upper limit of a range of possible dates. One of the most important but rarely published conclusions by secularists about ^{14}C dating is that even they admit that after approximately 60,000 years, the remaining ^{14}C is such a small amount that it is difficult to test for it. They have also concluded that ^{14}C disappears entirely after a little more than 100,000 years. Though fossils which are pronounced older than 100,000 years are rarely tested for ^{14}C, those few which have been tested usually have some trace of ^{14}C.

"Carbon-14 (^{14}C) dating of multiple samples of bone from 8 dinosaurs from Texas, Alaska, Colorado, and

Montana revealed that they are only 22,000 to 39,000 years old."

"After the AOGS-AGU conference in Singapore, the abstract was removed from the conference website by two chairmen because they could not accept the findings. Unwilling to challenge the data openly, they erased the report from public view without a word to the authors or even to the AOGS officers, until after an investigation. It won't be restored.

The researchers presented their findings at the 2012 Western Pacific Geophysics Meeting in Singapore, August 13-17, a conference of the American Geophysical Union (AGU) and the Asia Oceania Geosciences Society (AOGS)."[17]

Lunar Recession

"Scotty, I need power now!" pleads a desperate Captain Kirk, on *Star Trek* the original series, only to hear his Chief Engineer reply, "He's turned the engines off. Completely cold. Thirty minutes to startup. I canna change the laws of physics, Captain!" The only hope of pulling out of a decaying orbit and saving the *Enterprise* is a restart of her engines.

Why? The Earth is surrounded by nonpowered satellites. Why does the *Enterprise* need power? The *Enterprise* needs to remain in a slow orbit as near the planet as possible while maintaining a fixed point over it. The only way to accomplish that is to keep the engines powered up to constantly change the orbit and counter the pull of gravity. The closer a satellite is to the object it is orbiting, the faster it has to travel to maintain a stable orbit without engine power. Mercury is the fastest-traveling planet orbiting the sun. Venus, Earth and Mars are all progressively slower at their greater distances.

For a given velocity there is only one stable orbit around (distance from) a planet (or sun). The closer the satellite (or starship) is to the object it is orbiting, the faster it needs to travel (without power or thrust). Otherwise it needs power (thrust) to maintain the orbit.

All orbiting objects have one of three types of orbits.

1) The orbit is a decaying orbit (being pulled into the planet),

2) A stable orbit (no change in orbit over time) or

3) A receding orbit (moving away from the planet).

The closer the satellite (or starship) is to the object it is orbiting, the faster it must travel or the more power (thrust) it must use to counteract the attraction of gravity.

The laser reflectors left by the Apollo missions on the lunar surface have been hit with lasers from earth many times. It proves the moon is moving away from the earth at a rate of about 1.5 inches per year.[18] Assuming the Moon has not changed mass, velocity or direction of orbit, sometime in the past it would have possessed a stable orbit closer to the Earth. Even closer to the earth, inside that stable orbit, the moon's orbit with no change in mass, velocity, or orbital direction, would have decayed.

The important point is the stable or equilibrium orbit.

At the current rate of recession, the moon is receding from the earth at a rate of approximately one mile every 42,240 years. If the Moon were to remain unchanged in mass, velocity and rate of recession, just over 42 million years ago, the moon would be more than one thousand miles closer to the earth. With no change in its mass and velocity, in far less than 42 million years the moon's orbit would be a decaying orbit, not a receding orbit. The moon would be drawing closer to the Earth and not moving away from the earth as it is now. Just like the *Enterprise*, the moon would have a decaying orbit.

The moon is receding, that is, moving away from the earth at a rate of 1.5 inches per year. This seemingly insignificant movement is measured with instruments invented within the last fifty years.

Since the lunar orbit is receding, not decaying, it means that the existing lunar orbit is, geologically speaking, very young. If you reject the conclusion that this indicates a recent creation, you are left with only two choices:

1) The Moon is a very recent addition to the Earth or

2) Some sort of catastrophe has relatively recently altered the Moon's orbit. This catastrophe would have required far more energy than what could be produced by the simultaneous detonation of all the nuclear weapons on Earth.

That catastrophic event would have occurred quite recently, even according to uniformitarians. Any catastrophe powerful enough to alter the moon's orbit would also have catastrophically affected the Earth as well.

Geomagnetic Field Decay

The earth's magnetic field seems to have a half-life of around 1400 years. Assuming that to be correct, just 11,200 years ago the earth's magnetic field would have been 256 times stronger than it is now. 14,000 years ago the earth's magnetic field would have been 1024 times stronger than it is now. That would make animal life impossible.[19]

Dr. Russell Humphreys has continued to work in this field. He believes that a strict linear half-life is unlikely and concludes his article with the following: "These ideas weigh heavily against the idea that there is currently a "dynamo" process at work in the core that would ultimately restore the lost energy back to the field. Without such a restoration mechanism, the field can only have a limited lifetime, in the thousands of years. So the clarity of this new fit, especially the exponential part, is further evidence that the earth's magnetic field is young."[20]

The *dynamo process* Dr. Humphreys references is the theory that instead of continually decaying, earth's magnetic field is continually rebuilding or restoring itself. Its existence would make the entire life cycle of the earth's magnetic field much more stable and therefore much, much older.

Many articles purport to "debunk" these observations. They usually begin with personal attacks on the original authors. Even if the "debunkers" are correct that the half-life of the earth's magnetic field is longer than 1,400 years, for life to exist hundreds of millions years ago, the half-life must be hundreds of times larger. Instead of making personal attacks, detractors should present data supporting a much longer half-life. Instead, they use data based on the presupposition that the earth is millions of years old to insist that the earth's magnetic field must have a large half-life.

An excellent response to these uniformitarian proposals is Jonathan Sarfati's article, *The Earth's Magnetic Field: Evidence That the Earth Is Young*. After including many detailed examples, it concludes, "The clear decay pattern shows the earth could not be older than about 10,000 years."[21]

A key element of the decay of the earth's magnetic field is the evidence of magnetic field reversals found in cooled lava flows. "Lava flows in Nevada's Sheep Creek Range may have preserved evidence that the planet's magnetic field rapidly changed direction." Other evidence in the paleomagnetic lava flow at Steens Mountain in Oregon shows that the earth's magnetic field reversed its polarity in just over two weeks. This is in line with a magnetic field half-life of 1,400 years, but entirely unexplainable with a magnetic field hundreds of millions or billions of years old. Also, the sun reverses the polarity of its magnetic field every eleven years. [22]

The earth's magnetic field has a half-life of 1,400 years. Just 14,000 years ago the earth's magnetic field would have been ten times stronger than it is now. 1.4 million years ago the earth's magnetic field would have been 1,000 times stronger than it is now. That would make animal life impossible.

Mount Saint Helens Canyon Formation

Though the eruption of this volcano was observed by millions via television, internet and print media, few are aware of the significance. It carved another "Little Grand Canyon" similar to the Grand Canyon in Arizona in days or perhaps only hours. Millions witnessed this event. We saw it happening live or on video in real time. To those who understand, the evidence is so overwhelming that even some evolutionists are admitting it, though quite grudgingly. They still believe, without any evidence, that the catastrophe creating most other prominent geologic sites happened millions of years ago. But the evidence has forced them to admit that the Grand Canyon's formation was rapid, created with massive amounts of water.[23]

Varves

Paint brush shows scale.

Photo Information/Credit[24]

Mount Saint Helens produced more scientifically observable evidence, in the form of something remarkably like varves. According to most dictionaries, a varve is a layer of alternating fine and course (light and dark) silt at the bottom of a pond or lake. Counting varves used to be considered a very important method of dating. Each layer has two parts, one lighter and the other darker. One part is the time of year when water moves quickly and brings many deposits. The other part is the time of year when water is stationary, perhaps even stagnant, such as the winter when the lake is covered in ice. All honest scientists admit that there might be more than one varve per year. A core sample, which counts varves to determine the age of a lake, might give a date older than the actual date. The assumption that conditions in the past were similar to the present is an assumption that the difference in dates is slight. Though the varve count might be slightly older than the actual date, it is still assumed to be reliable.

The eruption of Mt. St. Helens discredited the use of varves as a dating method (based on the assumption that one mud/silt layer equals one year). Ash and mud sandwiched together in thin light and dark layers, just like varves, accumulated up to twenty-five feet thick with thousands of layers and within hours, perhaps only minutes.

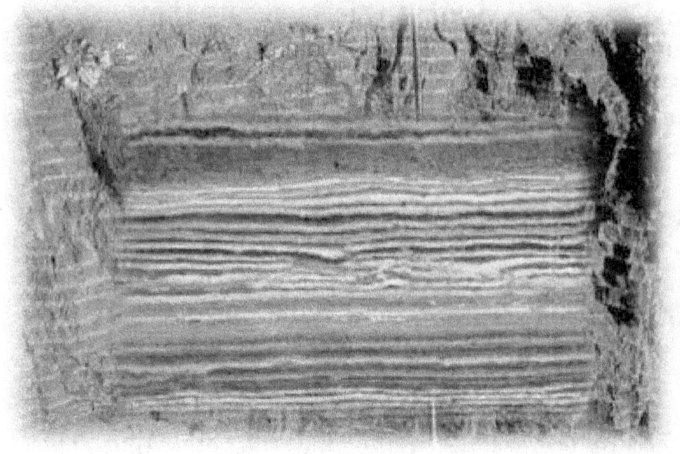

The eruption of Mount St. Helens on May 18, 1980 scientifically proved that assumption to be in error. Ash and mud up to twenty-five feet thick with thousands of layers filled the region. Though these layers are never called varves, they display the same characteristics as varves, a thin light and dark layer sandwiched together. These thousands of layers, put down in a matter of hours, perhaps minutes, completely discredit the concept of using layers for dating. People who use varves for dating never acknowledge or even mention this.[25]

Lake Titicaca

Catastrophes change the shape of the land where they occur forever. Few places have been changed more dramatically than Lake Titicaca. It rises 12,500 feet (3,800 meters) above sea level in South America between Bolivia and Peru. Fresh water rivers and streams feed the lake now, but the salt content is about five-and-a-half parts per thousand, classifying the lake as brackish. No current conditions explain the salt content of the lake. The most likely explanation is that Lake Titicaca was once at or below sea level and that a catastrophic uplift moved a lake full of seawater almost two and a half miles above sea level. Marine fossils are preserved around the lake. The current salt level of Lake Titicaca is about fifteen percent of the Pacific Ocean off Peru, where the Pacific Ocean varies from 34 to 37 parts per thousand.

"In the heart of the Andes ... is Lake Titicaca." [Its saltiness and the present fauna (It contains sea horses)] strongly suggested that the present fauna of Lake Titicaca has survived from a time when the lake communicated directly with [was connected to] the ocean."[26]

Theories other than uplift have been postulated. These theories, however, require completely speculative processes that have never been observed. That is not a scientific process. Some evolutionists believe the uplift theory because the scientific evidence is so overwhelming, but say that the catastrophe occurred millions of years ago. A past waterline is slanted in relation to the current waterline.

At one time Lake Titicaca had more water than it does now, and this waterline is much higher at one end of the lake, proving that a catastrophe tipped the lake in the past.

"The strandline [near Lake Titicaca] was carefully surveyed for a length of about 375 miles [603 km]. And then it was established that it is not 'straight.' ... Its level showed a slant of a most peculiar character in relation to the present ocean-level, or, which amounts to the same, relative to the present level of Lake Titicaca."[27]

Past irrigation and buildings in and around the lake prove an ancient civilization built the port city of Tiahuanaco. It is approximately 800 feet higher than the current lake surface. Tiahuanaco was a harbor, but is now twelve miles south of the lake, and the ship berths are of a size most likely built for ocean-going vessels. The lake "is large, 3,261 square miles. It contains sea horses, suggesting that this region or its water were once below sea level. On the mountain sides ... are terraces of ancient corn fields going up to 17,000 feet. Yet corn will not germinate [sprout] above 11,500 feet!"[20] There is also a building beneath the lake, about 660 feet long, with a road running to it and roads and steps leading down into deeper water. It is twice the size of a modern soccer field and modern archaeologists believe it to be a temple.[28]

Himalayan Yellow Band Ammonites

Geological features suddenly and catastrophically created by water can be found all over the world. Near the top of the Himalayan Mountains, reaching up to 29,029 feet (8,848 m) above sea level, is a layer of rock known as the yellow band. This yellow band is filled with marine fossils called ammonites. "Marine fossils are also found high in the Himalayas, the world's tallest mountain range, reaching up to 29,029 feet (8,848 m) above sea level. For example, fossil ammonites (coiled marine cephalopods) are found in limestone beds in the Himalayas of Nepal. All geologists agree that ocean waters must have buried these marine fossils in these limestone beds. "[29] Ammonites are common fossils found all over the earth and are similar to a modern marine creature known as the Nautilus. These fossilized marine creatures lived in oceans, not a freshwater lake. All of the Himalayan mountain chain had to have been under seawater. This many fossilized ammonites were not transported somehow after the mountains were formed. Sometime in the past either the entire Himalayan Mountain chain was five miles lower than it is now or the entire planet had more than twice the water volume than it has now.

Ammonite fossils

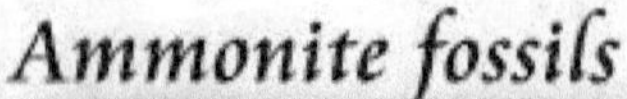

Modern Nautilus

Near the top of many Himalayan Mountains, including Mount Everest, is a layer of rock known as the yellow band. This yellow band is filled with marine fossils called ammonites.

Also, these ammonite fossils are not crushed. They were moved by a catastrophic (sudden) event while the entire layer was plastic (mud). The ammonites had to be protected to keep them from being crushed. The only scientific answer is that the surrounding mud protected them. A slow uplift over a long period of time would have dried out the surrounding mud. Instead of protecting the ammonites, the hardened rock would have ground the ammonites to powder. Since water weighs approximately eight pounds per gallon, the energy necessary to create the Himalayan Mountains was thousands of times greater than all the nuclear weapons in all the nuclear arsenals in every country on earth detonating at the same time.

On a much smaller scale, highway engineers have carved into mountains all over the earth. Thousands of mountains at every possible elevation all over the earth show bent, folded and twisted layers intact without cracks. These layers had to be plastic [mud] when they were put in place. This is the only way these mountains could have formed.

Catastrophic Fossil Formation

Fossils like the ammonites of the yellow band were formed in a catastrophic event. Even evolutionists have to admit that. Insects, microbes and weathering combine to destroy everything except bones in less than one hundred years, often in less than a week. Tissue deteriorates too rapidly for fossilization without a catastrophe. The question is: When did this catastrophe occur? Once again, the only available scientific evidence indicates a more recent event. Since fossils were bones, they once contained ¹⁴C. If a standard test for ¹⁴C discovered any ¹⁴C, the tested sample would scientifically prove a date less than 60,000 years old.

Since the religion of Secular Humanism demands that these fossils are millions of years old, and they control both the fossils to be tested and the testing procedures, ¹⁴C testing is never done on fossils. There is only the dogmatic assertion that fossils are now stone and there is no carbon to test.

There have been carbon tests on mollusks that indicate a much younger date on certain samples. Without ¹⁴C testing, however, there is no scientific dating of fossils, only religious pronouncements.[30]

Secular Humanists
must admit that fossils
were formed in a
catastrophic event.

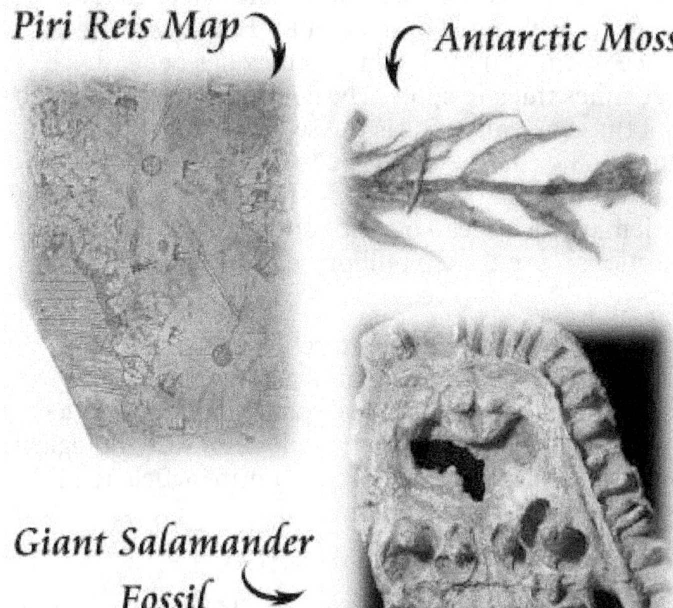

There is abundant evidence that Antarctica was once warm. Warm climate animal and plant fossils abound.

Ice core samples have revealed that many of these fossils are below sea level.

There is abundant evidence that Antarctica was once warm. Warm climate animal and plant fossils abound. Antarctica also has a coal bed. Formation of a coal bed requires a massive number of warm climate plants. The ice core samples have discovered that many of these fossils are below sea level.[31] The question is, why? Possible explanations include that Antarctica was once in a warmer latitude and moved, or that the magnetic poles have shifted (as mentioned earlier), or that the oceans have changed dramatically. The facts are clear. A once warm-climate land mass now lies beneath ice three miles thick in spots. The common thread through all of these explanations is the scientific fact of a catastrophic change. Sadly, instead of completely scientific explanations, supposed scientific and academic articles lead off with dogmatic mythological assertions: "around 40 million years ago," "millions of years ago," "40,000 year cycles."

A catastrophe could turn Antarctica from a warm climate into a frozen wasteland very quickly. The articles describing Antarctica's past might have much correct scientific data, but these dogmatic mythological foundational assertions make the entire article read like something from a tabloid.

Ice Core Samples and *Glacier Girl*

Researchers annually take core samples of glaciers and massive ice caps such as those covering Antarctica. They count each layer as a single year and publish a date. As with radiometric dating, it is not possible to know the original condition of the ice cap or glacier. However, unlike radiometric dating, starting with a zero condition (no ice, bare ground) is reasonable. Assuming that the earth is older than the glacier or ice cap is also reasonable. So the speed with which a glacier or ice cap forms is critical to an accurate date.

The layers (of annual ice core samples) are counted as if each layer was a single year and a date is published. The speed with which a glacier forms is critical to an accurate date.

A squadron of P-38s made an emergency landing on a glacier in Greenland on July 15, 1942. For 50 years the squadron of planes had flowed with the glacier, being covered with more ice. One plane was buried in 268 feet of ice. The recovered plane was restored and renamed Glacier Girl.

A squadron of P-38s made an emergency landing on a glacier in Greenland on July 15, 1942. The pilots were rescued and the planes abandoned. On July 15, 1992, the final piece of one P-38 was dug out of the glacier. For 50 years the squadron of planes had flowed with the glacier while being covered with more ice. One plane was pulled out of the glacier more than two miles from the landing point, buried in 268 feet of ice. The recovered plane was restored and renamed *Glacier Girl*.[32]

If the same techniques which boldly pronounce with absolute certainty that core samples are tens of thousands of years old were applied to the ice which covered *Glacier Girl*, then that ice would have to be thousands of years old. Yet the scientific fact is that *Glacier Girl* was covered by 268 feet of ice. It is also a scientific fact that this ice was fifty years old. This particular glacier grew at a rate of almost 5.5 feet per year. At this rate, the thickest ice sheet in the world, Terre Adelie in Antarctica, could be formed in just over 2,500 years. Secular Humanists would insist that different conditions in the past required a much longer formation time. Any change in the conditions could just as easily have resulted in a shorter time for formation.

Besides counting the layers in core samples, methods of dating a glacier include testing the oxygen content of the water, studying the presence of CO_2, finding evidence of radioactive decay, and examining pieces of volcanic material. Fred Hall wrote a brief article, "Ice Cores Not All That Simple,"[33] showing how complicated glaciers really are. None of these methods are entirely reliable. While there have been hundreds, perhaps thousands, of computer and theoretical models developed to explain glacier formation, the only scientific observations are in line with the glacier which covered *Glacier Girl*.

Water Scale

Formations like the Grand Canyon were carved by water action. No one disputes this, but water action is a topic on which scientists can still find points of disagreement.

Bridges built in powerful rivers, especially rivers prone to flood, are often washed away. Engineers building a new bridge over the Mississippi River at Alton, IL, between 1990 and 1994, built a scale model to help prevent that from happening. The scale model they built used real water to examine the direction and amount of force the Mississippi River would exert on the new bridge.

Anyone who has watched a movie from the 1950s or earlier has seen the common, at that time, technique of filming a scale model ship in a tank of water. Even with rather large ships, such as the ones used in Ben Hur, the water never looks quite real. The explanation is that water does not scale, that is, large amounts of water look and behave differently than smaller amounts of water. For realistic water, producers and directors had to either build full sized models or wait decades for 3-D animation.

Since water does not scale visually, scale models using water were believed to be inaccurate also. For example, water can cut channels through layers of mud. The resulting canyons look something like a scale model of the Grand Canyon. These models have been dismissed as unrealistic simply because water does not scale. This idea that water does not scale, however, is not always true. Bridges built in powerful rivers, especially rivers prone to flooding, are often washed away. Engineers building a new bridge over the Mississippi River at Alton, IL, between 1990 and 1994, built a scale model to help prevent that from happening. The scale model they built used real water to examine the direction and amount of force the Mississippi River would exert on the new bridge.[34]

Though the water did not "look" to scale, the water flow and pressure information was accurate enough to allow the engineers to see what forces they had to contend with. Because of the model, modifications were made in the bridge's design. These modifications are likely the reason the bridge is still standing today.

Water Salinity

The study of water and its properties gives scientists many ways to learn about the earth. It is also a very much-abused study when it comes to dating the earth. One of the most unusual methods of dating is measuring the salt content of the sea. This method assumes a constant and steady addition of salt to the sea by freshwater rivers and a constant and steady evaporation rate.[35]

*One of the most unusual methods
of dating is measuring the salt
content of the sea. This method
assumes a constant and steady
addition of salt to the sea by
freshwater rivers and a constant and
steady evaporation rate.*

(Pictured are Computer models of
ocean salinity)

While this method is often cited in textbooks as one of many dating methods "proving" an ancient earth, it is fraught with so many difficulties that it has few educated defenders. It is usually referred to as an "additional" or "support" method of dating.

The first major scientific problem with using the salt content of the sea as a dating method is the wide disparity in salt content among the world's bodies of water. The Mediterranean Sea has a much higher salt content than the Atlantic, which has a higher salt content than the Antarctic. Is the Mediterranean older than the rest of the oceans of the world? Are the rivers that flow into the Mediterranean saltier than the rest of the rivers of the world? The scientific answer to both of these questions is either "no" or "we do not know".

People have attempted to date the seas using salt content since at least Sir Isaac Newton's time. Simply measuring the contact of salt requires a date no more than 100 million years old. Drs. "Austin and Humphreys calculated that the ocean must be less than 62 million years old. It's important to stress that this is not the actual age, but a maximum age. That is, this evidence is consistent with any age up to 62 million years, including the biblical age of about 6000 years."[36]

Providence Canyon

Water's power to shape the landscape provides us with another amazing creation in southwest Georgia. Providence Canyon, sometimes called "Georgia's Little Grand Canyon" is 1100 acres of canyons carved out by erosion since the early 1800s.[37] Though much smaller than the Grand Canyon, it is still one of the largest canyons in America. As the model of the Alton, Illinois bridge helped engineers understand the Mississippi River; Providence Canyon helps us understand the Grand Canyon in Arizona. While neither the Alton Bridge nor the Providence Canyon are perfect models, on a small scale they both accurately model the effects of far greater amounts of water.

Providence Canyon in southwest Georgia, sometimes called "Georgia's Little Grand Canyon" is 1100 acres of canyons carved out by erosion since the early 1800s.

Though Providence Canyon is smaller than the Grand Canyon, it has many similar features. The formation of Providence is a scientific fact. Since Providence Canyon is less than two hundred years old, there is no scientific reason to believe the Grand Canyon, or any other canyon, must be millions of years old. All that is needed to make a canyon larger than Providence Canyon is more water, not more time.

Arches National Park

Just a few hundred miles north of the Grand Canyon is Arches National Park in Southeast Utah. When the National Park Service took over management of the park in 1971 there were over 2000 natural sandstone arches. Since then many arches have collapsed, the most famous being the collapse of Wall Arch on August 4-5, 2008. Though the exact number of collapsed arches is not documented, if only one arch were to collapse every three years, in less than 675 years there would not be any arches left. There is no evidence that there were ever hundreds of thousands or millions of arches. The evidence indicates that there were never many more arches than we see now. And there is evidence that many arches have fallen since 1971.

The scientific conclusion, based on the scientifically observed collapse of arches, is that either conditions in the recent past were drastically different to preserve the arches or that the arches are much younger than Secular Humanism proclaims them to be. If conditions were similar to the conditions we know now, the arches could be not older than about 4000 years old. They could easily be younger.[38]

Landscape Arch, collapsed 1991

Just a few hundred miles north
of the Grand Canyon is Arches
National Park in Southeast Utah.
When the National Park Service
took over management of the park
in 1971 there were over 2000
natural sandstone arches.

Wall Arch, collapsed 2008

The picture was taken in late 1987 at level 5 workings in the lead-zinc mine at Mt Isa, in north-western Queensland, Australia.

Photo taken beneath the Lincoln Memorial in the 1960s

Photo Credits[40]

Stalactites and stalagmites are another geologic feature formed by water. The Lincoln Memorial was built between 1914 and 1922 over land formerly at the bottom of the Potomac River. Stalactites and stalagmites have formed beneath the stairs in the period since the construction was completed (less than 100 years at the time of this writing) as described below.

"... Supports were driven down almost 100 feet to bedrock. This cavernous foundation provides an ideal location for cave-like formations to actively grow. Water on the surface slowly makes its way down through cement stairs into the empty space below. Cement is 'glued' together by calcium carbonate. As the water passes through the cement, it dissolves some calcium carbonate and carries it downward. When the water reaches the open space, it leaves behind the calcium carbonate, creating stalactites and stalagmites. This is the same way cave stalactites and stalagmites form, only instead of passing through cement stairs, natural cave features usually form when ground water passes through limestone. Since the cave formations at the Lincoln Memorial aren't in an actual cave, maybe we should call them 'under-the-stair-ites'."[40]

Dave E. Matson attempts to claim that all the stalactites and stalagmites in existence could not have formed in less than 5000 years.

"The Bulletin of the National Speleological Society (37: p.21, 1975) gives a stalactite/stalagmite growth rate of ... 0.1 to 10 centimeters per thousand years. An exceptional spurt of growth might exceed ... 10 centimeters or 2.5 inches per thousand years. ...Thus, a 60 foot giant, as might be found in Carlsbad Caverns, would have a minimum estimated age of about 180,000 years."[41]

Timpanogos Cave National Monument, in American Fork, Utah, is described in park literature as being roughly 65 million years old. Although the claim that the stalactites and stalagmites are millions of years old is no longer being made, secularists still demand thousands of years for the formation of these cave features, usually tens or hundreds of thousands, not the less than a hundred necessary in the Lincoln Memorial.

"Water trickling through the limestone overlying the caves dissolved calcite and other minerals from the rock. ...The water deposited its mineral load as tiny crystals on a cave ceiling, wall, or floor. Over thousands of years, as countless crystals were deposited, a variety of cave formations took shape--stalactites, stalagmites, flowstone, helictites, and others." [42]

Julia E. Cole, University of Tucson professor of Geosciences, studied a limestone cave in southern AZ. The article described the cave formations as "natural climate archives" and said, "The stalagmite yielded an almost continuous century-by-century climate record spanning 55,000 to 11,000 years ago. ... Each climate regime lasted from a few hundred years to more than one thousand years."[43] The article's photo shows Sarah Truebe, a geosciences doctoral student, with a cave formation less than 2 feet tall. The cave itself appears to be less than ten feet in height. The use of these cave features as "natural climate archives" is based on utter conjecture and uniformitarian presupposition.

Each of these claims is nothing more than a gratuitous assertion. The evidence shows the formation of these features, especially of stalactites, take only decades.[44]

Diamonds

Diamonds are reported by Secular Humanists to be at least 45 million years old, formed 75 miles or deeper beneath the earth. Yet laboratory-produced diamonds are made commercially. In 1953 the first industrial grade laboratory-produced diamonds were made. These tiny laboratory-produced diamonds were and still are manufactured for industrial applications such as cutting tools and electrical coatings. More advanced processes coat lenses with laboratory-produced diamond. The laboratory produced diamond industry gradually increased the size and quality of laboratory-produced diamonds. In early 2010 a 2-carat laboratory-produced gemstone-quality diamond was produced in about three days.

Russian Diamond Mine

Laboratory-produced diamonds were commercially made in 1953.

The first laboratory-produced diamonds were industrial grade.

H. Tracy Hall

The FTC (Federal Trade Commission) requires the label of laboratory-produced, laboratory-manufactured, or for the product to be identified by the name of the manufacturer along with the specific type of gem rather than using the term synthetic when referring to the type of gem. A laboratory-produced diamond is identical to a geologically-produced diamond is every way; chemically, structurally, and appearance, even on the microscopic level.

A synthetic diamond is still a technically correct term when applied to a laboratory-produced diamond, but some vendors use the term "synthetic" diamond to refer to cubic zirconia, cut glass or any other manmade substitute for a diamond. So the FTC wants to distinguish between real diamonds, both geologic and laboratory-produced, and other crystals which are not diamonds. These other crystals which are not diamonds are often marketed as synthetic diamonds, which they are not.

The existence of laboratory-produced diamonds is a scientific fact. They are produced and reproduced under controlled conditions. Depending on color desired, other chemicals can be added to the crystal-growing process and the resulting gemstone can be pink, green, blue, yellow, and colorless (white). The diamond mining industry is concerned about the number of laboratory-produced diamonds being manufactured. Proclaiming the youngest naturally-occurring diamond to be 45 million years old is a dogmatic religious pronouncement contrary to science. The most reasonable scientific theory is that diamonds were formed suddenly under the correct conditions.[45]

The RATE (Radioisotopes and the Age of The Earth) research project at the Institute for Creation Research found Carbon 14 in both natural diamonds and ten US coal beds. The upper range of the possible dates for the diamonds was 55,000 years.[46]

"R.E. Taylor of the Department of Anthropology at the University of California-Riverside and of the Cotsen Institute of Archaeology at the University of California-Los Angeles teamed with J. Southon at the Keck Accelerator Mass Spectrometry Laboratory of the Department of Earth System Science at the University of California-Irvine to analyze nine natural diamonds from Brazil. All nine diamonds are conventionally regarded as being at least of early Paleozoic age, that is, at least several hundred million years old. So if they really are that old they should not have any intrinsic ^{14}C in them. Eight of the diamonds yielded radiocarbon 'ages' of 64,900 years to 80,000 years."[46]

Coal and Oil

Carbon can be turned into diamonds, coal and oil. Most of the world uses coal and oil to heat homes and run electric generators. Coal and oil are abundant. Coal was made from plant material that was covered with water and neither coal nor oil is being formed geologically today. There is, however, one possible exception.

When Mount St. Helens erupted in 1980, the explosion filled Spirit Lake with logs. The bottom of the lake was filled with plant material covered in mud from the eruption. This was under the lake water. Examination of this material showed the early stages of the formation of coal. This, however, is a very tiny deposit compared to the massive coal deposits worldwide.[47]

Crude petroleum is also produced on a small scale in laboratories from garbage. Like diamonds and petrified wood, the processes that formed coal beds and oil deposits are not going on today. Something is dramatically different about conditions today. Like diamond formation and petrified wood formation, the only possible scientific example of oil and coal formation shows coal and oil being formed rapidly in a catastrophic event.[48]

Spirit Lake Log Mat

Coal was made from plant material which was covered with water and is not being made today. There is, however, one possible exception. When Mount St. Helens erupted in 1980, the explosion filled Spirit Lake with plant material covered in mud from the eruption. Examination of this material showed the early stages of the formation of coal.

Petrified Wood

Wood today is not becoming petrified except synthetically. Though modern wood can be synthetically turned into petrified wood, the process only works under highly controlled conditions.

Electron Microscopic image of laboratory-petrified wood.

Just off of Interstate 40 in the Navajo Indian reservation in northeast Arizona is the Petrified Forest. While the Petrified Forest in Arizona is the most well-known of the Petrified Forests, petrified wood can be found all over the world, though it is abundant in dry regions of the western United States. Petrified wood is wood that has turned to stone. The authors have seen petrified tree stumps in South Dakota more than twenty feet in diameter. Perhaps there is a rare exception somewhere, but wood today is not becoming petrified except synthetically. Though modern wood can be synthetically turned into petrified wood, the process only works under highly-controlled conditions.

The existence of synthetic diamonds and manmade petrified wood both scientifically prove that these substances require not immense periods of time but proper conditions to form them. They can be made in days, weeks or months. The religious belief that wood petrified over a great period of time and that the process took place thousands or millions of years ago is without scientific evidence. Even people who insist that wood petrified thousands or millions of years ago must admit wood is not naturally petrifying today. Therefore, something has dramatically changed. Though the most reasonable scientific explanation is a catastrophe, religious dogmas refuse to allow for these scientific explanations.[49]

Japanese scientists fastened pieces of wood in a hot acid lake. They observed that "after only 7 years the wood had turned into stone, petrified with silica."[50]

Preservation in Ice, Tar, and Peat

There is an entire class of creatures entombed in tar, peat bogs, muck and sand; organic remains clearly younger than fossils. Some of the more well-known of these creatures are woolly mammoths, mastodons, saber-toothed tigers, woolly rhinos, and giant ground sloths. These creatures are not fossilized, that is, turned to stone, but frozen. Though some were preserved in warmer areas by tar, most specimens are frozen and decay quickly when thawed.

Undigested plant remains in their stomachs prove that the animals were frozen quickly. Though pop culture places these animals in the Ice Age, the types of undigested plants found in their stomachs suggest that at the time the animals were frozen they and the plants lived in a warm climate. This indicates that tropical, subtropical or at least temperate conditions existed even in Siberia, Alaska, and northern Canada. Though these creatures obviously died in a catastrophe, this catastrophe was far more recent than the catastrophe which fossilized billions of other creatures worldwide.[51]

Soft Tissue in Dinosaur Bones

Creatures found in tar and ice are said by evolutionists to have come from a later time period than those fossilized, thus minimizing the troublesome issues of their real age. It is harder to dismiss one discovery, soft tissue from the bone of a dinosaur. There is no question that soft tissue deteriorates very rapidly. There is no question as to what such a discovery must mean. Dinosaurs, at least the ones leaving remains with soft tissue, had to have been living at the same time humans lived. The question is, has such a discovery actually been made? Paleontologist Mary Higby Schweitzer of North Carolina University has published her discovery of the remains of blood cells in dinosaur fossils and soft tissue remains in a T. Rex. John Asara of Harvard Medical School and researchers at Palo Alto have verified it.

Blood for transfusions can only be stored for about six weeks. Cryopreservation is only good for about ten years. These facts should help put this discovery into perspective. Not only did Dr. Schweitzer's team find bone cells, blood cells, and proteins, they also found dinosaur DNA.[52]

We should also compare this to the soft tissue discovered in a female wooly mammoth carcass. Even uniformitarians only date this to be 10,000 years old. We know that this is more than twice the actual age of the wooly mammoth. The conditions for preservation of the tissue were much better. It was preserved in permafrost at -10° C. Physiologist Kevin Campbell of the University of Manitoba wrote in an email to Kate Wong in a May 30, 2013 article that, "ancient DNA is highly fragmented and by no means "ready to go" into the next mammoth embryo." He also said "how were these samples preserved in this state for so long?"[53]

So the soft tissue of Ice Age woolly mammoths preserved in very favorable conditions is puzzling. The preservation of dinosaur soft tissue for millions of years is, by comparison, impossible.[54]

The evidence is overwhelming. The conclusions, however, are even more astounding. Rather than admit the obvious, that the bones with the remains of soft tissue were young, the published reports maintain that the bones are millions of years old, but some process not now understood preserved the soft tissue. There is no evidence of such an unknown process. This is a classic attempt to make the evidence fit the preconception.[54] It is also a glaring example of professional bigotry. This kind of article can never be published without a claim that the bones are millions of years old.

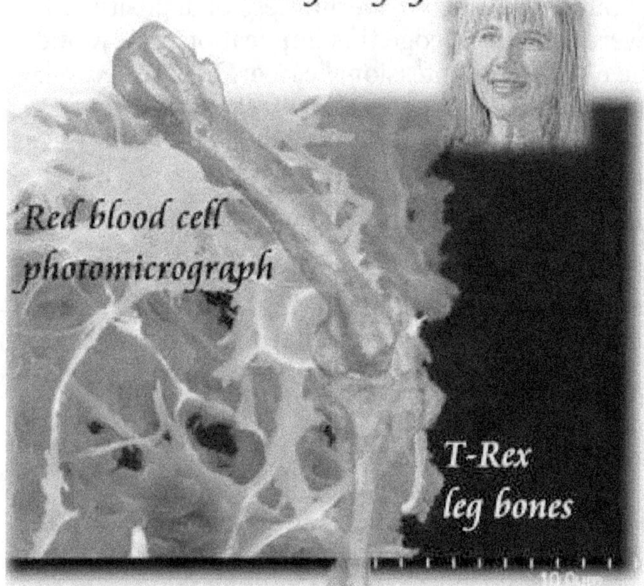

One highly controversial discovery is soft tissue from the bone of a dinosaur. There is no question that soft tissue deteriorates very rapidly and can be at most a few thousand years old.

Mary Schweitzer is firmly committed to ignoring the implications of her work, that these bones are very, very young. That secures her professional position. If she were to acknowledge this implication, that would be the end of her professional career. Eventually well-orchestrated condemnation would cost the author her job, as documented repeatedly in Ben Stein's movie *Expelled*.[55]

No Great Ape Fossils

"No fossils of any of the great apes: gorillas, chimpanzees or orangutans; have ever been found. As far as the fossil record is concerned, they never existed; and yet we know from the evidence of our own eyes that they did, and do."[56]

Though hundreds, perhaps thousands, of news releases, newspaper articles, magazine articles, radio, video, and internet announcements have proclaimed the discovery of a fossil of a great ape, none has ever been verified. Such discoveries have either proven to not be fossilized, and therefore much younger, or not to be a great ape. Some who carefully examine the evidence come to the reasoned conclusion that evolution is not scientifically valid. They do not find reproductive links in the evolutionary chain. Creationists are frequently charged with ignoring the evidence. Richard Dawkins claims to refute the fossil gap arguments in his numerous books, although he doesn't really refute them at all. He just dismisses the arguments with a bald, unsupported statement that large numbers of intermediates exist.

"Creationists are deeply enamored of the fossil record ...[They] repeat, over and over, the mantra that it is full of 'gaps': 'Show me your "intermediates!"' ...We [have]...massive numbers ... to document evolutionary history ... beautiful 'intermediates.' ... The fossil evidence for evolution in many major animal groups is wonderfully strong. Nevertheless there are, of course, gaps, and creationists love them obsessively."[57]

The truth is that there is nothing for mankind to link to. Neanderthals interbred with modern man. A skull found in *Pestera cu Oase,* "The Cave of Bones" in Romania, has characteristics of both so-called "species."

"The skull bearing both older and modern characteristics is discussed in a paper by Erik Trinkaus of Washington University in St. Louis. The report appears in today's [January 15, 2007] issue of *Proceedings of the National Academy of Sciences.*

"...The researchers said the skull had the same proportions as a modern human head and lacked the large brow ridge commonly associated with Neanderthals. However, there were also features that are unusual in modern humans, such as frontal flattening, a fairly large bone behind the ear and exceptionally large upper molars, which are seen among Neanderthals and other early hominids.

"Such differences raise important questions about the evolutionary history of modern humans," said co-author João Zilhão of the University of Bristol, England.[58]

Therefore, Neanderthals are men. Without any fossil evidence of creatures for man to evolve from, evolution of humans is a religious leap of faith. There is no evidence of any link and no fossil evidence of anything to link to.

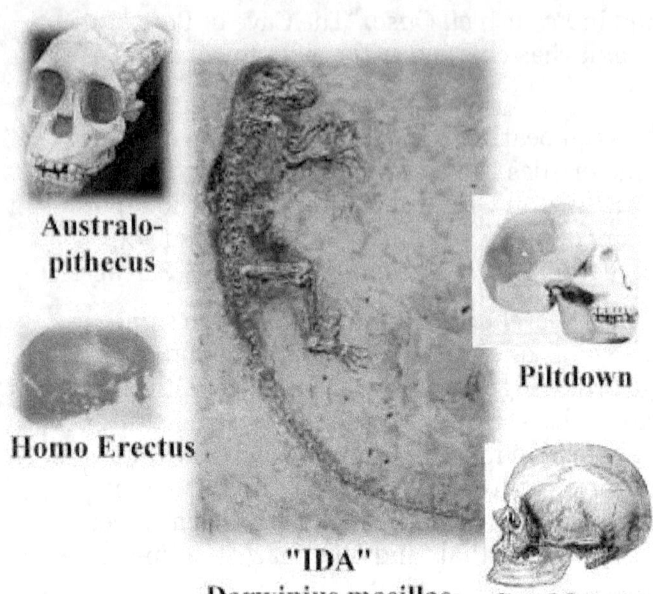

"No fossils of any of the great apes - gorillas, chimpanzees or orangutans - have ever been found. As far as the fossil record is concerned, they never existed; and yet we know from the evidence of our own eyes that they did, and do."

Mitochondrial DNA

Any link would be controlled by DNA. The most important aspect of the soft tissue discovery in the dinosaur is the DNA. DNA is in all cells of all living organisms. The tiniest cell in the human body contains the same DNA in the nucleus as the largest cell. This genetic coding determines hair color, shape of our nostrils, and every other detail of our body. As every student of high school biology knows, this DNA inside the nucleus contains genetic material from both our mother and our father. But many people are unaware of another type of DNA known as mitochondrial DNA. Mitochondrial DNA exists within the cell's mitochondria outside of the nucleus and contains only genetic material from our mothers. Since there is no mixing of genetic material, a child's mitochondrial DNA should be an exact duplicate of the mother's mitochondrial DNA.

Mitochondrial DNA controls individual cell functions, not genetically encoded information. Infinite generations with genetically different fathers can have identical mitochondrial DNA but radically different physical characteristics. This should allow for a trace of mitochondrial DNA back to the beginning the human race. We could perform this trace, except for the problem of genetic mutations. Since a child's normal mitochondrial DNA is identical to his mother's, any mutation starts a new line. Minor mutations are difficult to detect and major mutations, such as those caused by massive radiation exposure, produce children who are unable to survive. But a few extremely rare mutations have produced traceable lines.

In 1997, *Nature Genetics* published an article with the innocuous title "A high observed substitution rate in the human mitochondrial DNA control rate." An abstract is available online for free. Though the technical language is absolutely necessary for accuracy, it distracts the average reader. Even with nothing but the abstract, the force of this study is overwhelming.

"...We report a direct measurement of the intergenerational substitution rate in the human CR [Control Region – a section of the DNA that controls other sections of DNA]. We compared DNA sequences of two CR hypervariable segments from close maternal relatives, from 134 independent mtDNA lineages spanning 327 generational events. Ten substitutions were observed, resulting in an empirical rate of 1/33 generations, or 2.5/site/Myr. This is roughly twenty-fold higher than estimates derived from phylogenetic analyses. This disparity cannot be accounted for simply by substitutions at mutational hot spots, suggesting additional factors that produce the discrepancy between very near-term and long-term apparent rates of sequence divergence. The data also indicate that extremely rapid segregation of CR sequence variants between generations is common in humans, with a very small mtDNA bottleneck."[59]

What this study did was take mitochondrial DNA samples from living volunteers and compared it to mitochondrial DNA from their ancestors. The test subjects had to have accurate records of their ancestors for hundreds of years, so all test subjects had to be European. Corpses had to be available with accurate records and preserved well enough that mitochondrial DNA could be obtained. The study went back approximately 550 years.

The test results proved that mutations happen at a significantly higher rate than geneticists thought possible. The resulting statistical analysis came to two stunning conclusions.

First, applying this data to other studies gives an approximate date of 6000-6,500 BP (Before Present) for Mitochondrial Eve.[60]

The most important aspect of the soft tissue discovery in this dinosaur is the DNA. Many people are unaware of another type of DNA known as mitochondrial DNA. Mitochondrial DNA exists within the cell's mitochondria outside of the nucleus and contains only genetic material from our mothers.

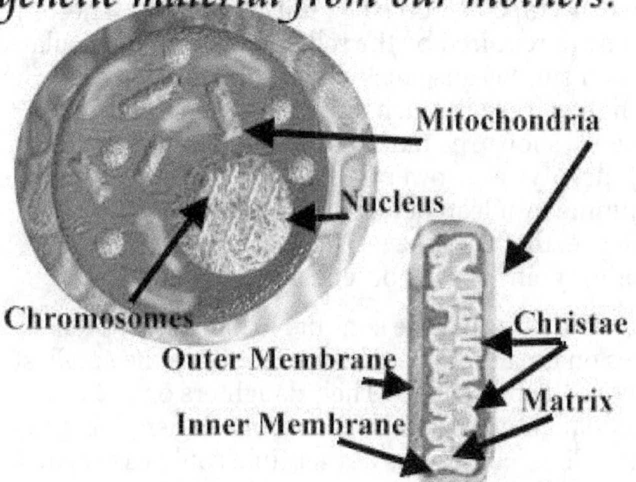

Mitochondrial DNA is not contained in the Nucleus but is in the cytoplasm of the Cell.

Catastrophes powerful enough to move marine ammonites to the top of Mount Everest, and tilt Lake Titicaca, could easily, temporarily and dramatically, increase the mutation rate, making even the 6000-year-old date too old.

Second is the "very small mtDNA bottleneck." This means that at some point in the history of the human race there were very few women. Bryan Sykes, author of *The Seven Daughters of Eve* believes that all Europeans currently alive can be traced back to one of seven women. Though Sykes is a well-respected English geneticist, as a committed Secular Humanist he makes two common though critical errors. These two errors have become the "standard" which any geneticist who expects to be published must adhere to. These errors are required by the religious dogma of Secular Humanism. Because his religious dogma demands that the human race is much older than the scientific evidence shows, he makes the leap of faith that the 2.5/site/Myr was lower in the past. His second error is assuming by a leap of faith, without any scientific evidence, that these seven women represent the smallest point of the bottleneck.

The Bible says that the sons of Noah brought their wives on the ark. These three women are the smallest point of the bottleneck. Their daughters or granddaughters might be the seven women of Bryan Sykes. Since conditions at that time could easily cause increased genetic mutations, their daughters, granddaughters or great granddaughters could easily be the seven women isolated by Bryan Sykes. When you read *The Seven Daughters of Eve,* understand that the last part of the book is devoted to fictional indoctrination. He novelizes each of these women and places each of them in a "cavewoman" setting. This is as antiscientific an approach as possible. Nevertheless the book was published. The scientific evidence of Mitochondrial DNA concludes that the human race is much younger than the published dates, less than 10,000 years, and that at one time in the very recent past the entire human race had no more than seven women. Bryan Sykes added the cavewoman fictions to assure publication. Such fabrications are the essence of the academic requirements for upholding the secularist dogma.[56]

He also claims that this genetic bottleneck of seven women is only for women of European descent, not the entire human race.

A much better study, without the approval of the academic community, therefore without the publicity, is Dr. Robert W. Carter's *Adam, Eve and Noah vs Modern Genetics*. This article also explores why the Y chromosome supports a recent genetic bottleneck. Dr. Carter states, "There are three main mitochondrial DNA lineages found across the world. The evolutionists have labeled these lines "M", "N", and "R"…"[61]

Thermodynamics

Engineers can earn a PhD in many subcategories of the massive field of thermodynamics. The dynamics of heat affects all other aspects of engineering. The first two laws of thermodynamics are well-tested and well-proved. While the implications are massive, the first two laws are simple. The first law of thermodynamics: The conservation of energy. Energy can be changed from one form to another, but it cannot be created or destroyed. The total amount of energy and matter in the universe remains constant, merely changing from one form to another.

Albert Einstein popularized the first law of thermodynamics with his famous proposition "If a body at rest emits a total energy of E while remaining at rest, then the mass of that body decreases by E/c^2."

This is oversimplified into $E=mc^2$. Though technically this only applies to a body at rest, it is a workable understanding of the concept that matter and energy are interchangeable. In this formula, "c" represents the speed of light, in a vacuum, 299, 792, 458 meters per second or 186,300 miles per second.

Here is a link to a blog which works through the Lorentz transformation to explain how Albert Einstein arrived at his final formula. [62]

According to the first law of thermodynamics the universe is either 1) eternal, 2) created out of nothing, or 3) came into existence through some process that we know nothing about.

The Second Law of Thermodynamics states "in all energy exchanges, if no energy enters or leaves the system, the potential energy of the state will always be less than that of the initial state." This is also commonly referred to as entropy. Another way of stating entropy is that all energy changes are in a downward direction.[63] Without a belief in the religious dogma that the universe is infinite and can therefore obtain energy from "outside" the system (which is scientifically unprovable), entropy will eventually lead to a "heat death" for the entire universe. Everything in the universe will be motionless, at a uniform temperature near absolute zero, broken down into subatomic particles.

*First Law: Energy changes form,
cannot be created or destroyed.
Amount of energy and matter
constant, only changes form.
The universe is either 1) eternal,
2) created out of nothing, or
3) came into existence through some
unknown process.*

*Second Law:
Potential energy always less
than initial state.
Entropy = "heat death" for the
entire universe. Motionless,
at a uniform temperature
near absolute zero, broken down into
subatomic particles.*

Each one of these examples of physical evidence has the same message. To repeat a quote from Dr. Danny R. Faulkner at the beginning of this chapter:

"While the early faint Sun paradox does not tell us that the Solar System is only thousands of years old, it does seem to rule out the age being billions of years."
Dr. Danny R. Faulkner

"While the early faint Sun paradox does not tell us that the Solar System is only thousands of years old, it does seem to rule out the age being billions of years."[64]

We can rephrase this statement to make it more inclusive. While none of these points in this chapter tell us that the earth is only thousands of years old, each one individually and all of them collectively seem to rule out the age being billions of years.

We close with the words of the committed Secular Humanist, Isaac Asimov, as he condemns not only his own belief system, but also the belief systems of everyone who reject the evidence for the Word of God.

"I believe in evidence. I believe in observation, measurement, and reasoning, confirmed by independent observers. I'll believe anything, no matter how wild and ridiculous, if there is evidence for it. The wilder and more ridiculous something is, however, the firmer and more solid the evidence will have to be."[65]

Isaac Asimov

"I believe in evidence. I believe in observation, measurement, and reasoning, confirmed by independent observers. I'll believe anything, no matter how wild and ridiculous, if there is evidence for it. The wilder and more ridiculous something is, however, the firmer and more solid the evidence will have to be."

Isaac Asimov

"We can make inspired guesses, but we don't know for certain what physical and chemical properties of the planet's crust, its ocean, and its atmosphere made it so conducive to such a sudden appearance of life..."

1 Charles Darwin, "Letter to Asa Gray," (Harvard Professor of Biology), 18 June, 1857.

2 John Adams, "Argument in defence of the [English] soldiers in the Boston Massacre trial," December 1770.

3 Mark Twain, *Life on the Mississippi,* first edition published by Osgood and Company, 1883.

4 Samuel Johnson, *The History of Rasselas, Prince of Abissinia,* 1759.

5 Dennis Prager, "Breastfeeding as a Religion," World Net Daily, http://wnd.com/, posted November 11, 2003 1:00 am Eastern.

6 Richard W. Pogge, Astronomy 162: Introduction to Stars, Galaxies, & the Universe, 2006, http://www.astronomy.ohio-state.edu/-pogge/Ast162/Unit2/sunshine.html

7 "Fusion", *Nobelprize.org* updated 9 Mar 2013 http://nobelprize.org/nobel_prizes/physics/articles/fusion/sun_4.html

8 Ian T Durham, "Hans Bethe" (Biographic article about Hans Bethe), Saint Anselm College, Goffstown, NH, http://www-history.mcs.st-and.ac.uk/Biographies/Bethe.html

9 Akridge, R. 1980. "The Sun Is Shrinking." *Acts & Facts.* 9 (4) and Faulkner, D. 1998. "The Young Faint Sun Paradox and the Age of the Solar System." *Acts & Facts.* 27 (6). [these two articles are quoted and paraphrased from throughout this section]

10 Roger Freedman, Robert Geller, William J. Kaufmann, *Universe: The Solar System,* Macmillan, New York, NY, 2010.

11 Two links to articles which examine the early faint sun paradox problem in more detail:

http://creation.com/our-steady-sun-a-problem-for-billions-of-years

http://creation.com/the-young-faint-sun-paradox-

and-the-age-of-the-solar-system

12 Daily Mail online, October 3, 2011 http://www.dailymail.co.uk/sciencetech/article-2044480/NASAs-SDO-satellite-shows-boiling-sun-stunning-detail.html#ixzz2MnMZZ5lS

13 Ethan Siegal PhD in theoretical astrophysics at the University of Florida *Starts with a Bang.* "How the Sun works, from the inside out", originally posted August 12, 2011.

14 D. Russell Humphreys, Steven A. Austin, John R. Baumgardner, and Andrew A. Snelling, "Helium Diffusion Age of 6000 Years Supports Accelerated Nuclear Decay," *Creation Research Society Quarterly Journal. (CRSQ)* Vol 41 No 1 June 2004, *Creation Research.org,* Copyright © 2004 by Creation Research Society. Also Dr. Don DeYoung, *Thousands, Not Billions: Challenging an Icon of Evolution Questioning the Age of the Earth,* Green Forest, AR: Master Books, Inc., 2005.

15 Utah Geological Survey, *Utah.gov.*

16 Radiometric Dating background from the position of those who believe it to be valid can be studied on *TalkOrigins.org.,* especially the article *Radiometric Dating and the Geological Time Scale: Circular Reasoning or Reliable Tools?* Andrew MacRae Copyright 1997-2004 [Text last updated: October 2, 1998] and also these two books: G. Brent Dalrymple, *The Age of the Earth.* Stanford University Press: Stanford, CA, 1991. G. Faure, *Principles of Isotope Geology,* 2nd. edition. John Wiley and Sons: New York, NY, 1986.

17 John Michael Fischer, *Dinosaur bones have been Carbon-14 dated to less than 40,000 years,* http://newgeology.us/presentation48.html, 2012-2014.

18 Press release, Public Information Office, Jet Propulsion Laboratory, California Institute of Technology, *NASA,* July 21, 1994.

19 Andrew A. Snelling, "The Earth's magnetic field and the age of the Earth," first published: *Creation (Creation Ministries International)*, 13(4):44-48 September 1991.

20 D. Russell Humphreys, *Earth's Magnetic Field is Decaying Steadily –with a Little Rhythm*, CRSQ (Creation Research Society Quarterly) July 1, 2010. http://www.creationresearch.org/crsq/articles/47/47_3/CRSQ%20Winter%202011%20Humphreys.pdf

21 Jonathan Sarfati, *The Earth's Magnetic Field: Evidence That the Earth Is Young* http://creation.com/the-earths-magnetic-field-evidence-that-the-earth-is-young

22 Alexandra Witze, "Geomagnetic Flip-Flops in a Flash," *Science News,* September 25, 210 Vol. 178, Number 7, and R.S. Coe, and M. Prevot, 1989. "Evidence suggesting extremely rapid field variation during a geomagnetic reversal," *Earth and Planetary Science Letters, Elsevier*, Amsterdam, Netherlands, vol. 92, pp. 296-297.

23 http://www.answersingenesis.org/home/area/cfol/ch3-grand-canyon.asp

24 Type/Process: Pyroclastic Flow
Volcanic Status: Historical
Image Number: 029-008
Photographer: Norm Banks, 1980 (U.S. Geological Survey)
Summit Elevation: 2549 meters
Latitude/Longitude: 46.20 N / 122.18 W
Timeframe: Last known eruption 1964 or later
Region: Canada and Western USA

25 G.R. Morton, (An old-earth supporter who calls himself a creationist apologist) "Young-Earth Arguments: A Second Look," 1998, *home.entouch.net.*

26 J.B. Delair and E.F. Oppe, "The Lost Sea of Andes," in Charles Hapgood's *The Path of the Pole,* Chilton Book Company, Philadelphia, PA, 1970.

27 Donald W. Patten and Samuel R. Windsor, "Catastrophic Theory of Mountain Uplifts (A Crustal Deformation Theory)," *Catastrophism and Ancient History* Vol. XIII Part 1 January 1991.

28 "Ancient temple found under Lake Titicaca," *BBC News, UK*, Wednesday, 23 August, 2000, 11:04 GMT 12:04.

29 J. P. Davidson, W. E. Reed, and P. M. Davis, "The Rise and Fall of Mountain Ranges," in *Exploring Earth: An Introduction to Physical Geology,* Upper Saddle River, New Jersey, Prentice Hall, 1997.

30 Erich A. Von Fange, "Time Upside Down," *Creation Research Quarterly,* June 1974.

31 *National Geographic,* July 26, 2008, "Tiny Fossils reveal Warm Antarctic Past," and *AntarcticConnection.com* reports on the Antarctic research stations.

32 Sean Pitman, M.D., in a PowerPoint presentation titled "Ancient Ice," created in Jan 2006, including testimony from a phone interview with Bob Cardin, project manager to recover one of the P38s lost on the glacier.

33 Fred Hall, "Ice Cores Not All That Simple," *AEON II:* 1, 1989:199.

34 "Superbridge," *NOVA*, PBS, November 12, 1997.

35 Dr. Nathan Green, online course overview for GEO.101, "Introduction to Geology," Spring 2006, University of Alabama.

36 Jonathan Sarfati, *Salty Seas: Evidence for a Young Earth, Creation* 21(1):16-17, December 1998, http://creation.com/salty-seas-evidence-for-a-young-earth

37 *GeorgiaEncyclopedia.org* gives background on the canyon but attributes its underlying geology to the "millions of years" formation theory. See also "Canyon Creation," by Rebecca Gibson, *Answers in Genesis,* September 2000.

38 National Park Service report on Wall Arch collapse with before and after photos, August 4-5, 2008.

39 Photo of recently-formed stalactites courtesy of Creation Ministries International (see footnote 44 for commentary on the Australian Mine photo). Lincoln Memorial Photo from National Parks services website.

40. National Park Services Website.

41 Dave E. Matson, "How Good Are Those Young-Earth Arguments?" on *Infidels.org.* copyright 1995.

42 *GORP.com* (Great Outdoor Recreation Page.)

43 "Cave Reveals Southwest's Abrupt Climate Swings During Ice Age," *Science Daily.com,* January 25, 2010.

44 http://creation.com/stalactites-do-not-take-millions-of-years

45 American Museum of Natural History website, "How Old are Kimberlites and Diamonds?" see also *Novori.com* for history and manufacture of laboratory produced diamonds.

46 Andrew Snelling (Dr.), "Radiocarbon in Diamonds Confirmed," *Answers in Genesis,* November 7, 2007. (This study was conducted during the *RATE (Radioisotopes and the Age of The Earth)* research project at the Institute for Creation Research.)

47 "Coal, Volcanism and Noah's Flood," *TJ (Technical Journal)* 1(1): *Creation Ministries International,* 11-29 April 1984.

48 A.A. Snelling, "The Recent Origin of Bass Strait Oil and Gas," Creation, 5 (2):43-46 March 1982.5

49 Phil McCafferty, "Instant petrified wood?" *Popular Science,* October 1992, pp. 56-57. also Hamilton Hicks, 'Mineralized sodium silicate solutions for artificial petrification of wood,' United States Patent Number 4,612,050, September 16,1986, pp. 1-3. As cited by: Steven Austin, *CatastroRef*—"Catastrophe Reference Database: Catastrophes in Earth History, Geologic Evidence, Speculation and Theory,*" Institute for Creation Research,* San Diego. Entry no. 267.

50 *Petrified Wood: Fast or Slow?*
http://creation.com/petrified-wood-fast-or-slow

51 Michael Oard, *Frozen in Time: The Wooly Mammoth, The Ice Age and the Bible,* Green Forest, AR: Master Books, Inc., 2004.

52 http://creation.com/dino-dna-bone-cells#endRef5

53 http://www.nature.com/news/can-a-mammoth-carcass-really-preserve-flowing-blood-and-possibly-live-cells-1.13103

54 Schweitzer, Mary H. and Jennifer L. Wittmeyer, North Carolina State University; John R. Horner, Montana State University; Jan B. Toporski, Carnegie Institution of Washington Geophysical Laboratory. "Soft-Tissue Vessels and Cellular Preservation in Tyrannosaurus Rex." *Science,* March 25, 2005. (NC State, the N.C. Museum of Natural Sciences and the National Science Foundation funded the research.)

55 Kevin Miller, Ben Stein, writers, Producers Logan Craft, Walt Ruloff and John Sullivan, Director Nathan Frankowski. Assoc. Prod. Mark Mathis. Ed. Simon Tondeur. *Expelled: No Intelligence Allowed.* © 2008 Premise Media Corporation, Rampart Films Production.

56 Bryan Sykes, *The Seven Daughters of Eve: The Science That Reveals Our Genetic Ancestry.* W.W. Norton, New York, N.Y., 2001.

57 Richard Dawkins, *The Greatest Show on Earth,* Free Press, Simon and Schuster, New York, NY, also by Bantam Press Transworld Publishers in Great Britain, 2009.

58 Randolph E. Schmid (Associated Press), "Skull Suggests Interbreeding of Neanderthal and Modern Man," *The Denver Post,* January 15, 2007.

59 Parsons, Thomas J., et. al. "A high observed substitution rate in the human mitochondrial DNA control region." Nature Genetics 15, 363 - 368 (1997).

60 http://creation.com/refuting-evolution-chapter-6-humans-images-of-god-or-advanced-apes#r25

61 http://creation.com/noah-and-genetics

62 http://terrytao.wordpress.com/2007/12/28/einsteins-derivation-of-emc2/

63 M.J. Farabee, *The Online Biology Book* (Farabee is a member of the Biology faculty at Estrella Mountain Community College, Avondale, Arizona. *emc.maricopa.edu*

64 Faulkner, D. 1998. "The Young Faint Sun Paradox and the Age of the Solar System. " Acts & Facts. 27 (6).

65 Isaac Asimov, *The Roving Mind.* Prometheus Books, 1997.

Christian Books in Multiple Genres, Join Christian Indie Author ~ Readers Group on Facebook. Opportunities for free books and giveaways. https://www.facebook.com/groups/291215317668431/

Other Books and Products from Findley Family Video Publications

Antidisestablishmentarianism by Michael and Mary Findley

(Also available in an illustrated version, with over 200 full-page illustrations throughout the book, and in four separate sections, both illustrated and unillustrated versions.)

The Bible is a Book of Science
Secular Humanism is a Religion of Mythology

Secularism in America has occurred in defiance of the the founding writings, which spelled out the dangers of Government-Church union. But Christianity wasn't a contradiction of the so-called "separation principle".

All the history,of the world echoes the message that man cloaks secularism, the worship of himself, in religion. He demands unlimited power for his religion, Secular Humanism. Secularists have hijacked words like belief, faith, and trust,. Secularists demand that Science depend on presupposition, assumptions, and "deep time. " The Scriptures themselves prove their scientific nature and worth.

From "Chapter 14 What Does the Scientific Evidence Prove?"

Integrity without knowledge is weak and useless, and knowledge
without integrity is dangerous and dreadful.
Samuel Johnson

Christians, unfortunately, believe that science is an enemy. There is good reason, since most who use the word "science" have completely abandoned Johnson's demand that integrity go hand in hand with knowledge, replacing truth with selective evidence which supports preconceived conclusions. Christians should not develop either an antagonism toward true science or ignore the very real contributions of true science. Neither should true scientists ignore the very real foundation of science in Christianity. Dennis Prager, anthropologist and historian, laments the unthinking reliance on pseudo-science in today's society.

> "In much of the West, the well-educated have been taught to believe they can know nothing and they can draw no independent conclusions about truth, unless they cite a study and 'experts' have affirmed it. 'Studies show' is to the modern secular college graduate what 'Scripture says' is to the religious fundamentalist."

Empire Saga by Michael J. Findley (Also available as six separate short stories and novellas, including the *Space Empire Trilogy*)

Look at the future of persecution. One day soon the only refuge for the faithful may be Space. Follow a desperate couple fighting isolation and equipment malfunction to pilot a gas-collecting balloon ship to the outer planets. Michael, crown prince of the Space Empire hopes to save his people from external attack with an internal rebellion and a battle cruiser like no other. His plans are shaken by a forbidden romance, political turmoil, and the discovery of Earth's Fourth Empire. Michael and his best friend Randolph might save or shatter the Space Empire's last hope for the future.

Michael's crystals had their fire change from red to blue to green and back to red again. With each change the fire grew weaker.
"Discovery to Earthpost Q."
"Earthpost Q."
"Your father's quit waiting on the Lord. The Occidental outpost has twelve SSTs assembling a particle beam gun. It's Imperial, Michael. Your father set us up. I don't have a chance."
"Is it operational?"
"Yes, but it's not fully charged yet."
"Destroy it."
"I'm by myself. The only way I can fly and fire at the same time is to route the fire control through the forward directional sensors."
"Do it."
"I'll kill everyone down there. There's over a thousand people there, mostly women and children."

Nehemiah, LLC (This book takes place between *Sojourner* and *Empire One: Humiliation* in the Space Empire Universe.)

Why doesn't Tony know what a paper cup is? What is it about a "Glop Drop" that kids can't resist? How can Joan keep the goats where they belong? And, most important of all, can Tony and Joan make the launch window to see the Sojourner on its way to the outer planets?

No light sabres. No warp drive. It's more like the real thing: an Apollo mission plus floating farms plus Martian underground parks. "It won't fail because of me" takes on a whole new meaning.

from *Chapter Nine: The Task*

"So we can move people in three or four days?" asked Anthony.
"Well, after we finish sandblasting..." said Joan.
"So this is sandblasting?" asked Anthony.
"Well, he can say something besides 'How long will this take?'" said Joan. "You spend your entire life dreaming up ways to give other people work. Stick around and do some of the work yourself. Let me give you a list. We could do more sandblasting. There are at least a hundred projects that need enlargement. If that's not to your taste, we could fill with foam insulation, finish rooms, weld, install furniture, work on making the roof of the production area open to the surface, enlarge the life support systems to cover the new area, synthesize more air and water, transport materials ... "
"I really like one thing you said," interrupted Anthony. "That's

the 'we could' part."

The Baron's Ring by Mary C. Findley

Prince Tristan tumbles a hundred miles downriver and a world away from his kingdom. How does cloak bartering get him a place in impoverished Larcondale? Why does his best student suddenly disappear from the tiny school?

Disaster might blot out his last hope for love and a future. Will he survive his confrontation with a Witch Queen in the King's Hole?

For wickedness burneth as the fire: it shall devour the briers and thorns, and shall kindle in the thickets of the forest, and they shall mount up like the lifting up of smoke.
Isaiah 9:18

"Do you mind if I continue on a little way?" Tristan asked casually. "I thought I heard voices up ahead, and there's that cursed smell of smoke again."
"All the more reason you should come back with us," Alex said firmly. "None of your men are out here at this time of day. I can't pretend to hear what you're talking about, or smell it either, but if there is someone out there I don't want you here alone."
Tristan drew the sword he always carried when he left the estate, again, in spite of Mayra's protests. "Alex, men are coming this way. I have no idea how many, but it sounds like at least twenty. They're still a mile or two off. As you say, they aren't ours, but I do hear sounds like armor and swords clashing. I need you to take the Lady Mayra back to the house and bring some of our men as quickly as you can."
"I can't leave you here!" Alex cried.
"I can't run," Tristan said desperately. "I can try to hide, and I will, but I have to know that you're taking Mayra to safety."

Benny and the Bank Robber by Mary C. Findley

Benny Richardson and his widowed mother have to move to his uncle's Missouri farm. John Clancy saves them from a sinking barge and when his mother is injured agrees to get Benny to Missouri. But a bag of disguises, a long, sharp knife, and too many secrets to make him anything but a safe traveling companion.

A fleeing bank robber, a savage black stallion, and a "cougar evangelist" all play a part in Benny's journey to accept of God's will when it isn't at all humanly sensible or safe. Benny faces an implacable bully and finds a long-lost treasure from his dead father.
from *Chapter Three: "He'll Go Far!"*

"How come you stopped the barge if you already had a good horse? And why were you hiding that black bag under your saddle?" Benny kept talking, so fast that Mr. Clancy couldn't have answered his questions if he had wanted to. And he certainly didn't seem to want to.
"It looked just like the bag Mr. Carlisle put on the train, and the one that man in the black suit was carrying. What was in all those bags?

Or was that you pretending to be somebody else again? Were you the one that killed that man at the bank and stole the money?" Mr. Clancy had been staring at him all this time without moving. Suddenly he jumped forward and grabbed Benny. He covered Benny's mouth with one hand and with the other pulled out a big, long knife. Holding Benny so tight it hurt, he laid the knife up against his throat and whispered in his ear.

"I guess you do get to go along with me, after all, Benny my boy," he hissed. "But somehow I don't think we'll make it to Uncle Tom's. The chickens'll be so disappointed."

Benny and the Bank Robber 2: Doctor Dad

A new marriage for Benny's mother should be a time of rejoicing. But why is Uncle Tom so angry? While substitute teaching for his mother Benny meets twin girls who turn his world upside down.

A terrifying mystery at a private boys' school in Detroit includes gambling, extortion and attempted murder. Benny makes the mistake of trying to impress members of a secret society, discovers he may have a double, and hopes to survive a meeting with someone who may already have murdered to enforce his will.
from *Chapter Fifteen: "An Ultimatum"*

That night Benny took one more look through his footlocker. Suddenly he noticed a slip of paper tucked into his winter boots. He pulled it out and opened it.
"The box is the key. Use it to unlock the door to the cat." At the end was a symbol Benny recognized as the Greek letter Omega. Like lightning, Jason leaped across the room and slammed Joseph down on the floor.
"You're the one who stole it!" Jason snarled. "I knew it all the time. We want it back right now!"
"Make him get off of me, or you'll be sorry!" Joseph squealed to Benny.
"Let him up, Jason," Benny ordered. "Joseph, I guess you don't want to be expelled, do you? I just want my cougar skin back. I don't want any trouble."
"You can't prove I had anything to do with that note or your cougar skin," Joseph said with an oath. "You can tell me now what's in the box. Then they'll let you know what they want next."

Benny and the Bank Robber 3: The Oregon Sentinel

Ben Carlisle's longtime dream has been to travel west with his family. When he is offered a newspaper job in Detroit, he is forced to question whether moving west is really God's will for him. Can he leave behind his grandfather, the girl he thought he loved, and an opportunity few writers could even dream about? Can he risk the life of one of his best friends, or face an old enemy head-on? What price will he have to pay just to make his writing live?

from Chapter Two: A New Partner and an Old Enemy

A giant man on a huge buckskin gelding suddenly clambered up out of the gully behind the bush. He pulled up sharply and scooped Sarah up with his long, powerfully-muscled arm. Ben's mother gratefully took Sarah from the newcomer. Sarah giggled delightedly and reached up as if she wanted to ride up into the air again.

"Thanks, Mister," Jeremy said as the man lifted his wide-brimmed tan hat. "I'm Jeremy Carlisle, and this is ..."

He broke off sharply and Ben came up beside him as Caleb Sutter looked slowly around at them.

"I guess I know who you are." His blond hair trailed long as an Indian's down his broad back. His shirt hung open and an intricate beaded choker clung to his corded neck. Caleb turned his head slightly and Ben saw a jagged scar running from where his left earlobe should have been halfway down his massive chest.

"I saw your names on the roster, so this wasn't exactly a surprise for me," Caleb went on as the family remained speechless. "Bet it was for you, though. Let me try to make this trip easier for all of us. I'll do my job, and you'll take care of your family, Doc. I don't want to dig up any stuff that's been buried. I sure don't want any trouble. Boss Tibbs relies on me, and what was between Ben an' me ... well ... Just do me the favor of keeping out of my way as much as is humanly possible so I can keep out of yours."

Hope and the Knight of the Black Lion by Mary C. Findley

(Also available in the "Illuminated Version," echoing the style of a medieval manuscript. "Home to My Father: A Knight's Tale," is a stand-alone excerpt from this novel.)

Seventeen-year-old-Hope rebels against arranged marriage in medieval England. The earl's handsome son Robert tempts her to defiance. A mysterious knight appears to help Hope find her missing family. Does Hugo Brun de March truly travel on a Holy Quest?

What is the a strange diary the Arab Sadaquah gives Hope? When her protector is captured she discovers a plot to subvert English law and justice.

from *Chapter Eleven*

"Sir Knight. I hear that thou wilt not say thy name nor thy true business to anyone. "

"It is a vow I have made, that Baron Cloyes must be the first in England to know of these things. "

"Man, thy story might turn my heart completely to thy cause," Lord Godwin said.

"It matters little now, my lord. " Sir Chris coughed several times. "The earl has said I am to be made to confess to the burning of the manor house. To that I cannot confess, and so ... Lady Hope?"

"Yes, Sir Chris?"

"I am sorry I could not help you," he said in a voice I could scarcely hear. "I am sorry, too, that you were not persuaded to know Christ."

Chasing the Texas Wind by Mary C. Findley

Hamilton Jessup agrees a sham marriage with socialite singer Maeve Collinswood. This beautiful spinster needs a handsome wounded war hero husband to show off at Texas fundraisers. Ham has no choice, but they both have secrets to keep from each other.

Ham was supposed to ignore her frequent disappearances. Falling in love with her changed all that. His discovery that their secrets are connected plunges both of them into a race to outwit whoever is supplying arms to Mexico as the countdown ticks away toward the Battle of Monterrey.
from *Part One, between June, 1844 and March, 1845*

  "Hamilton?" Maeve said suddenly.
"Yes, Ma'am?" Ham asked.
"The story you told about Goliad," Maeve said, looking pained, "Was it some sort of alcoholic raving or did you tell a true tale?"
Ham looked away. "A true tale, Ma'am," he said. "I could never be intoxicated enough to show so much disrespect to the memory of that event as to fabricate a tale about it."
  "Thank you," Maeve said.

Send a White Rose by Mary C. Findley

Leah Masters came to the New Mexico Territory hoping to make a "mail order match" with handsome Judge Bartholomew Durant. She fainted at his feet and when she woke up discovered she had stepped into an assassination plot with her hot-tempered brother as the prime suspect.

Who does Bart Durant trust when facing revolution theology and a still-unknown assassin? How can he ignore the sudden realization that his heart might already belong to someone else besides the woman he still thinks is a stuck-up weakling?
from *Chapter Two*

  Bartholomew caught sight of a half-wild rose climber in the chapel garden. *White roses.*
"You -- you know *la Señorita* Alethia at the Orphanage? I am sure ... she would give you a sweet ... if you ... pick the prettiest white rose on that bush over there and take it to her."
"It is a good thing I have my *burro,* or I would not go. It is a long way. I will be back later, but I will not have any more time to waste on you, dead man. I hope you will be quiet, like the other one is. "
  Bartholomew did not answer, and the footsteps shuffled away.

Carrie's Hired Hand by Mary C. Findley (Novella)

Carrie Wilkes is the Northern widow of a Southern soldier in the middle of the Civil War. Robert Salinger,may be handsome but his promise to take care of Ben's family rings hollow as she struggles alone with the farm work. She is grateful to give a deaf and dumb stranger work for food and a place to stay. Southern soldiers come with accusations of spying. Robbie's "secret code" might spell terror for Carrie and her children.

"God bless you ... for all you've done, Rob," Ben whispered, half-opening his eyes and gripping Robert's shoulder. The handsome young man continued his work, but he stared at Ben with the same look of intensity he had given Carrie. "You're ...that friend that ... sticketh closer than a brother ... the Scriptures ...talk about."

Robert produced a canteen and Carrie gave Ben a drink. He choked and groaned. "Carrie, I don't ... want to leave you ... alone like this," Ben said when he could speak again. "All alone."
"I'll look after them, Ben," Robert said suddenly, gripping the dying man's shoulder. "As God is my witness. This was my doing, and I will take care of your family."
"The work's got to get done ... " Ben said faintly.
"It will," Robert promised. Carrie couldn't help wondering how this slight young man, dapper in spite of the filth around them, was going to help get the farm work done.
"You give me the Lord, Rob," Ben said. "Try to give Him to my Carrie, an' my babies too."
Carrie strained to hear. What Ben had just said didn't make any sense. Robert nodded.
"I will try," he said softly.

Biblical Studies Curriculum by Michael J. and Mary C. Findley

(Student and Teacher Editions) Bible Study aids for children, homeschoolers, and adults. Commentary, Review Questions, Free Videos on YouTube. Bible Doctrines, children's whole book studies of Jonah and Ruth with 3D puppet commentary, Proverbs, Adult studies in the New Testament and Major Prophets background, featuring more than 30 videos in the Revelation study alone, Old Testament and New Testament Manuscript History

The Conflict of the Ages Part One: The Scientific History of Origins by Michael J. and Mary C. Findley (Student and Teacher Editions)

Based on biblical, scientific, and ancient manuscript evidence, this book begins a series studying history, science and literature to correct misconceptions and outright lies about creation, chronology, and geological and cosmological truth.

The Conflict of the Ages Part Two: The origin of Evil in the World that Was by Michael J. and Mary C. Findley (Student and Teacher Editions)

Based on biblical, scientific, and ancient manuscript evidence, this book covers the period from the Fall of Man to the Worldwide Flood.

A Dodge, a Twist, and a Tobacconist, The Alexander Legacy Book One: by Sophronia Belle Lyon

The Alexander Legacy Company is on the track of a ruthless enslaver of souls. Prowl the foggy London streets. Encounter a nightmare from the Indian jungles.

Travel the Thames in Sluefoot Sue's Giant Catfish. Soar on a stealth glider with a Bohemian prince. When Oliver Twist unwraps the Algerian mummy at Charley Bates' funeral, will he discover his real enemy? Or is it all just another "dodge"?

"He's going to ram Twist's ship," Kera breathed. "They'll both crash into the house and Mrs. Rose just might have her bomb going off."
I ran along the edge of the roof as if I were looking for a shot. But I already knew my pistol was empty, useless, and the guard was trying to get around another gable to get a clear shot while staying behind cover. I had come to a conclusion a moment earlier that I dared not say out loud lest I be grabbed and thrown down on the roof by both women, but I knew what I had to do.

Just as the spy craft hove around the corner of the house, only a few feet away from the airship, I launched myself off the roof. The smaller ship disappeared and my heart leaped in panic at the thought of being sliced into quarters by the tail rotor. But my fingertips caught hold of a solid object. I found the fuselage of the spy ship and wrapped my legs around it. The thing slewed and spun and began to fall tail-first toward the green lawn.

The Alexander Legacy Book Two: The 'Pprentices, the Puppets, and the Pirates, by Sophronia Belle Lyon

Can Oliver Twist trust Spring-heeled Jack when he offers to "bodyguard the little'un"? Do costume balls conceal more than the faces of the wealthy and powerful? Trevor Newsome disappears just days before the election but the Legacy Company can't search for him from the London Lockup. When the trip to Switzerland finally becomes a reality, it's for a funeral, not for a wedding.

Quests for immortality meld with the worship of poweful men, with terrifying and tragic consequences. When Long John Silver arrives, Oliver has to think fast to protect more than just his own life from the pirate who says he only cares about rescuing his daughter.
"Twist! Look out!" I spun and swung wildly as the crack of a Colt revolver split the air. Sluefoot Sue had both her firearms out and was shooting at something below me. To my astonishment tentacles rose out of the Thames and wrapped themselves around the Catfish. Each time one of Sue's bullets struck them they disappeared under the water again, but when she paused to reload they re-emerged and began to reach for me, climbing the Catfish sub. I hastily winched myself over toward the dock but a tentacle grabbed hold of my leg just as I started to set myself down. It flung me down on the dock and started dragging me to the edge.

"Hey, boss lady!" Dobbs, Sue's assistant, hollered out from inside the workshop. I was just able to see a pump-action shotgun cartwheel through the air and land in Sue's gloved hands. Just before it began to blast me deaf, I realized that it was in fact no ordinary shotgun, rather had some sort of gattling action, and a bit more. I hoped I would get a better look at it rather than end up 20,000 leagues under in some sea monster's maw.

Write for the King of Glory

Share the fruits of my first five years of publishing. Learn about blogging, writing, cover design, editing, marketing, and find a bunch of great resources to help you in your publishing journey, many of them free. I'm not the be-all and end all of Christian publishing, but I'm here to help, and so are a bunch of other Christian writers and service providers.

I'm living proof that you can get your book published. It doesn't have to stay in those pre-publication versions, or be taken out of your hands and changed to the point where you hardly recognize it. God educated me through some amazing preparation and hard times to the point where I realized that it's up to me to make my books. Nobody's going to do it for me. At least not so that I can control it from start to finish, or within my mostly nonexistent budget, or on my timetable.
So, I have learned to be a cover designer, an editor, an ebook formatter, and everything else I need to create my own books. I have also learned some things about online marketing, to the point where we have regular monthly sales that continue to grow.
Sample our longer works with free excerpts of full-length titles. All our publications are linked on our blogs.
Elk Jerky for the Soul includes posts on current issues, excerpts from our fiction and nonfiction works, Bible teaching, travel and everyday observations, and more.
http://elkjerkyforthesoul.wordpress.com/

Visit our tiny but mighty website, which features basic information about Findley Family Video Publications and changing special features at http://findleyfamilyvideopublications.com
Visit our YouTube Channel
http://www.youtube.com/user/ffvp5657. Watch Jonah and Ruth as well as "Sojourner," part of the Space Empire Saga, in full 3D animation, book teasers, and upcoming projects related to biblical study and the Conflict of the Ages.
Science, History, Literature, and biblical worldview studies are the focus of our book and video projects.

www.ingramcontent.com/pod-product-compliance
Lightning Source LLC
Chambersburg PA
CBHW071917150726
47999CB00001B/17